Victory Harvest
Diary of a Canadian in the Women's Land Army, 1940–1944

Based on the diary Marion Kelsey kept while in the Women's Land Army during World War II, *Victory Harvest* is a personal remembrance of wartime Britain through the eyes of a young Canadian woman. Financed by a kind cousin (who gave Kelsey money for an airline ticket instead of making a donation to the Spitfire fund) she travelled to England to join her army husband. There she joined the Women's Land Army and spent the next four years planting crops, milking cows, and driving a tractor. Her tour of duty was cut short by tragedy when her husband was seriously wounded by shrapnel at Falaise in 1944. Kelsey's indomitable character and enthusiasm shine through in her writing and, as a woman and a Canadian, she provides a new perspective on the war.

Kelsey's observations range from descriptions of the Battle of Britain from the ground, bombing raids on civilian populations, and a meeting with a possible German spy to more personal accounts of the difficulties of obtaining a bath. She and her husband were reunited on his quarterly leaves and the journal records their travels through England, Ireland and Scotland amid air raids, bombings, and machine-gun fire. The reader discovers, as Kelsey came to realize, that agricultural work, which involved much struggle, labour, stress, and danger with little recognition, was an important part of the overall war effort in Britain.

MARION KELSEY lives in Hunts Point, Nova Scotia

Gyp and I

VICTORY HARVEST

Diary of a Canadian in the Women's Land Army, 1940–1944

Marion Kelsey

McGill-Queen's University Press
Montreal & Kingston · London · Buffalo

© McGill-Queen's University Press 1997
ISBN 0-7735-1663-8

Legal deposit fourth quarter 1997
Bibliothèque nationale du Québec

Printed in Canada on acid-free paper

McGill-Queen's University Press acknowledges the
support received for its publishing program from the
Canada Council's Block Grants program.

_____

Canadian Cataloguing in Publication Data

Kelsey, Marion, 1912-
    Victory harvest: diary of a Canadian in the Women's
    Land Army, 1940-1944
    ISBN 0-7735-1663-8
    1. Kelsey, Marion, 1912–   2. Women's Land Army (Great
    Britain). 3. World War, 1939–1945 – Personal narratives,
    Canadian. 4. World War, 1939–1945 – Women – Great
    Britain. 5. World War, 1939–1945 – War work – Great
    Britain. I. Title.
    D811.5.K44 1997   940.53'082'0941   C97-900758-5

_____

This book was typeset by Typo Litho Composition Inc. in
11/14 Adobe Caslon.

Endpaper map: Pat Walker

To Cousin Lilian

CONTENTS

ACKNOWLEDGMENTS

One day three or four years ago, Wendy Wickwire and Michael M'Gonigle brought their boys to see Charlie and me. They began to ask endless questions about "our war," 1939–44, and I was amazed to realize how totally unaware they were of any of our circumstances. "Wait a minute," I said, "my old scrapbook is up in the attic and there's a diary that goes with it. Read that."

And now, after much effort on their part, here it is.

I had no plans to be a writer, but talking to Wendy and Michael, now each PhD's but born after the war was all over, proved to me how many there are who could not know what should be remembered, should be shared. My memories are not cruel, nor as highly geared as those of many who were battlefield involved, but there can be no finer memories, no greater inspiration than England geared to endure, to achieve, than those days when I knew of work, of kindliness, and of love.

I am powerless to express what it has meant to me, incapable through inexperience and partly through personal tragedies, to have had Wendy and Michael take over. Since Charlie's death, my eighty-five years have taken their toll and this could not even have been envisaged without them.

While I wrote it, the publication of this book is wholly theirs.

It is with great pleasure that I take this opportunity to express my gratitude to all the folk who helped me so that they may be aware of the comfort and progress that their help has meant to me.

When I say progress, I refer to many moons ago when our lives centred on Ste-Anne-de-Bellevue Military Hospital in Quebec. It was about 1946 that I began to organize my notes and diaries and it was then that our friend George Whalley, condemned to lie for many months on his stomach, typed all my famously undecipherable pages with a typewriter on a table at the head of his bed, within his limited reach. I regret that George has been gone these twenty years, but I can now thank Flo, his wife, who did most of the deciphering and arranging and changing of positions in the short periods when George could work with his so limited movements. (George's wound was cervical and he was totally paralysed from the neck down, his arms miraculously spared, though impaired.) As well, my thanks go to Flo for her many trips to the P.O. for me as, since my stroke, I am forbidden to drive.

Sincere thanks go to Linda MacAdams, at Port Joli, who tidied and typed the original, now dog-eared, pages on proper paper, and to Pat Walker for her careful work on the map on the end papers. My thanks again to Blanca Chester who edited the material. And finally, my thanks go to all at McGill-Queen's University Press for their efforts in making this book a reality.

As this story goes back almost three generations, I wonder what it has meant to each of you who have read it at different stages – Flo and George, who of course lived through it all in England – Linda, just a teen-ager, perhaps learned a bit about "our war" – and Wendy and Michael and Blanca, adults who understand what it has meant to me.

I hope that it proves worthy of all your care and interest and that you accept my thanks with fifty years of compound interest.

INTRODUCTION

The memory of that hot afternoon in July 1991 is still vivid for us both. It was the day we first learned of Marion Kelsey's war diary, and it was the start of a shared journey that now, with the publication of *Victory Harvest*, comes to a close.

As she did every summer, Marion had invited us to tea. When we arrived, however, she was upset, having just returned from one of her many trips to Halifax to visit her husband, Charlie, who had been hospitalized yet again for complications stemming from his paraplegia. Nevertheless tea was graciously served and, in the ornately cluttered living room of their home, we talked about the adventures of the past year. Sitting next to Charlie's built-in bednook – his daybed – with its large picture window overlooking the sea, we found ourselves asking questions about Charlie that we would not normally have asked: Was he in much pain? How were his spirits? What was the latest prognosis? Almost inevitably, the questions turned to a topic that both of us had wondered about for many years, the source of Charlie's paraplegia.

It was, of course, an injury from "the war," but how it had happened was not something that Charlie talked about. In our discussions, it came out that not long after Charlie had gone overseas, Marion had followed him, a piece of information that only increased our curiosity. As our questions continued, Marion told us that if we really wanted to know the details of their war experience, we could read the account she had assembled in 1945 from her letters home and daily journal.

Surprised, we both said that we would love to read it, but we were soon heading back to BC. Could we take a copy with us? In a hesitant voice, she confessed that she had no copies, only an original which had been typed by a friend, George Whalley, recuperating alongside Charlie at the war vets' hospital in 1946. She had lent this out about a year ago, but could not immediately recall to whom. We were now doubly surprised – a wartime diary nearly a half a century old and in a single copy, floating about in someone's home. After some calls she located it down the lane at a neighbour's. Living in a nervous writer's world where multiple disks and hard copies are mandatory, we went off to retrieve it. We found all 250 legal-sized pages of typsescript and carried it, like a piece of fine china, to the local copy centre.

During the flight home, we devoured the photocopied manuscript. By the time we touched down in Vancouver, we were convinced that this was a story that had to be published. Written in a graceful style with a startling visual clarity that draws the reader into a world of real people and rich settings, the manuscript went well beyond answering our simple questions about the wartime experiences that were the source of Charlie's injury. Instead we found a unique historical chronicle of the daily lives of two young Canadians pulled from a comfortable Montreal existence into a perilous wartime existence in England. The result is a story of a part of the war about which, as Marion had sensed with us, few today have any knowledge, let alone appreciation.

In the wake of the First War, where so many of the "boys" who left did not live to return, Marion was determined not to be among those left behind. Once in England, with the prospect of an invasion looming, Marion felt compelled to do something. As she later explained to us: "I'd been in England about a week and decided that I had to find a niche to enable me to remain. I was eating English food, using English transportation, and anyway I was there to help, wasn't I? We discussed the women's services – ATS, WAAF, WRENS ... but Charlie knew that my rebel nature was not geared to regimentation. Then I saw this small clipping. We investigated immediately." What she had seen was a notice for the "Women's Land Army."

The Women's Land Army (WLA) was established on June 1, 1939 to recruit a force to replace the many male workers who had joined the services and to bolster the labour force necessary for wartime farm-work. Modelled after a similar initiative in the First World War in which thousands of women were employed as milkers, tractor drivers, fieldworkers, carters, ploughmen, thatchers, and shepherds, the WLA had a critical task – to bring in the harvest. As offshore foodstuffs were quickly becoming inaccessible, and the number of mouths to feed was growing every day with the arrival of troops from overseas, a push had been undertaken to plough and seed two million extra acres of grassland. By the spring of 1940, 6,000 "Land Girls" had helped the nation to reach that target, but still more workers were needed to tend the crop and harvest it.

Marion arrived in England on May 10, 1940 at the height of a recruitment frenzy. By May 28, a week after making a WLA applica-tion, she received her official acceptance. Shortly thereafter, she was notified that she was to be posted at Nunningham in Sussex to be trained in farmwork. For the next four and one-half years, she partic-ipated in a force which, at its height, included 80,000 women. Her Land Girl duties included everything from pitching and threshing hay to shovelling manure, feeding and milking cows, and running farm machinery.

This was, it might seem, a far stretch from anything Marion had experienced in her upbringing, first in the French Canadian village of Longueuil, Quebec, where she had attended a convent, and later in Montreal, where she finished high school and graduated from McGill University. But Marion quickly adapted to long hours of farm life which allowed her to channel her tremendous energy and even reminded her of her endless summers and winter weekends of physical exertion in the Laurentians and a job at a Labrador Grenfell Mission hospital: "Many of my camping experiences stood me in good stead and my stay in a Labrador Grenfell Mission hospital with neither power nor water made me grateful that I was not a totally helpless city gal. My life has always been more outdoors than in. My Dad said that it was only an accident that I was not born on his boat. And then skating, skiing, and swimming had absorbed all my spare hours."

Though busier in England than she had ever been before, Marion kept a careful record of her day-to-day activities as a Land Girl, her travels with Charlie, her impressions of English relatives and acquaintances, and her concerns regarding the state of the war. Like many women of her day, she saved every scrap of memorabilia that came her way – invitations to tea, postcards, train tickets, special cards and letters, photographs, newspaper stories, special flowers – and assembled a scrapbook that is as intriguing as the diary. (This, at least, she stored in her attic!) As we read Marion's diary and studied the scrapbook, small fragments of which are reproduced in this book, we became aware of a layer of wartime history which is largely unknown today. After all, most war stories originate with men. Glamorous stories of battles won and lost, spine-tingling accounts of espionage behind enemy lines – this is the stuff of the best-seller and movies. Meanwhile, the stories of the people beneath the bombs, or the men and women in the fields and factories, remain largely unexplored.

Nicola Tyrer, the author of *They Fought in the Fields*, a new book on the Women's Land Army, notes that, even in England, a whole generation of women has grown up knowing nothing about the Women's Land Army. Marion's *Victory Harvest*, like Tyrer's book and a small handful of other studies, helps to fill this critical gap. This account of an important chapter of British history in which large numbers of British women did work traditionally associated with men is replete with insights not only about everyday life during the war but about farming practices, many of which are no longer followed, and about many segments of English society. It is, as well, the enthusiastic chronicle of a Canadian couple working in England, enthralled with the country and actually "fighting" in the war together.

During the first part of his stay in England, Charlie, like most of the Canadian forces, spent much of his time waiting to be sent into battle. Luckily he was posted close to the farms where Marion was working and was able to visit her on many weekends. On such occasions, when needed, he would join in the farmwork. English by birth, Charlie organized many visits with relatives – a grandmother, aunt, uncle, and cousins. During lulls in farmwork in winter, early spring, and late fall, the couple used Charlie's week-long leaves (like everyone in the forces, he had four of these per year) to travel further afield – to Canterbury, London, Oxford, Devon, Cornwall, Scotland, and Ireland.

While Marion's life was literally an open book, Charlie never confided in her about the nature of his work. He stuck dutifully to the military prescription that "if you've private information, keep it dark." Marion knew little about his war work other than that he was with the Royal Montreal Regiment in the first Canadian Division to go overseas in December 1939. But the couple made a secret pact that if Marion received a postcard of any sort from him, she would know that he had left England. The postcard arrived on July 6, 1944. Only after his return did she learn that he had been in charge of a staghound, a small armoured car which carried six men including himself.

The rich and romantic adventure told in the diary ends shortly after August 17, 1944 when Marion received a wire notifying her that Charlie had been wounded. When she arrived at Basingstoke Neurological Hospital on August 21, she found a man close to death and in extreme pain from waist-down paralysis. Days earlier, just weeks after sending his postcard, he had been hit at Falaise, Normandy, by a piece of shrapnel that had become lodged in his third lumbar vertebra.

Although *Victory Harvest* ends here, the story of this remarkable couple does not. They returned to Montreal where Charlie had multiple operations and two years of treatments at the Veterans' Affairs hospital in Ste-Anne-de-Bellevue, Quebec.

This was the beginning of a new life. With thousands of other war vets, Charlie had to learn how to function with substantially reduced physical abilities, and Marion had to learn how to work alongside him. As Charlie struggled to deal with his new life, he realized that the services available to war vets were unavailable to his civilian counterparts. He took on the task of obtaining better facilities and services for the civilian disabled. Under the auspices of the Rehabilitation Society, he rented a garage in Montreal and began organising training workshops and rehabilitation services. So successful was he that in 1953 he was offered what Marion describes as the "job of a lifetime complete with a salary beyond our imagination." But directing a major new organization for the civilian disabled had one hitch – although now able to get along on crutches, Charlie would have had to walk from the parking lot and in long office corridors in a downtown Montreal office building, an environment that was anything but hospitable to the disabled. He declined the offer.

Instead Charlie had another proposal, one that might better fit his condition: "You've always wanted to live by the sea," he said to Marion. "Let's go!" Marion agreed to go only if their friends Flo and George Whalley came with them. Charlie had met George on May 5, 1945, VE Day, when, both seriously wounded and paraplegic, they had shared an ambulance. Eight years of rehabilitation later, in 1953 the four made their way to the south shore of Nova Scotia. Using funds from the sale of their wartime house in Montreal, they purchased a handsome old log house on seven acres of white sand beach in the then still-active fishing community of Port Joli.

"Goose Haven" was a find. It had electricity, plumbing, a fireplace, and two small cottages. "We felt we could not just retire and rot," Marion told us, "so we enlarged and equipped the cottages to be rented." This was quite a "we," a foursome in which, as Marion explains it, "the boys organized, and Flo and I did the work with the assistance of the odd local carpenter." This work included building a second adjoining dwelling on the property for George and Flo in 1960.

In Nova Scotia Charlie re-launched his campaign for the civilian disabled. With the Paraplegic Association he conducted a survey of every disabled person in the Maritime provinces. He was away from home three weeks out of four. Decades ahead of his time, he was convinced that the disabled could be productive. With a capital investment of $100, he and George rented an old cement shed on the outskirts of the town of Liverpool and began K&W Bookbinding. Two years later they had a new building where they established a successful business which, at its height, employed over fifty disabled people.

This is where for us, memories of Marion and Charlie begin. In 1959 Wendy's parents bought an old house not far from Goose Haven. Her childhood memories are a montage of vital images – Marion and Flo in their overalls doing house repairs, hauling wood, fixing broken machinery, tending to their expansive and vibrant flower gardens by the sea; in their kitchens, sleeves rolled up, making jams and preserves, all the while conversing eagerly to visitors. But the memories that really stick are of the elegant dinner parties with fine crystal and china and candlelit tables, where the conversation was of poetry and history and exotic travel. Vigourous again, Charlie and Marion took three trips by freighter to the Far East, the Mediterranean, and Scotland and Norway. Despite wheelchairs, crutches, and the constant worries about various medical complications, there was always fun and laughter at Goose Haven. To a young girl, this was an exciting and exotic neighbourhood milieu.

The debilitating effects of their paraplegia began to effect both Charlie and George in the 1970s. They sold their business and both were often confined to home, often to their beds. Marion and Flo worked incessantly to make their lives as normal as possible despite the now more frequent, and sometimes extended, trips to Halifax.

George died in 1977. By the mid-1980s, Charlie suggested to Marion that a move closer to town (Port Joli was twenty miles from Liverpool) might be wise. When she finally agreed, they bought land on a rocky oceanside promontory at Hunt's Point, five miles from town. There Charlie designed a fine log house on Nova Scotia's South Shore and, from his wheelchair, directed local carpenters in its construction.

Two summers after we had "discovered" Marion's diary, we spent more time with Marion and Charlie at Loon Ledge. Charlie had come home from hospital just after our arrival on the east coast and was very frail. Our hope was to go systematically through the scrapbook with them. Though Charlie was not even supposed to sit up, he loved his stream of visitors and over several weeks Marion and he took us on a journey, week by week, page by page, item by item, through that huge, tattered old wartime volume of memorabilia. In the living room, we sat surrounded by paintings by Charlie's father (a noted Canadian stained-glass artist), stacks of books, birdfeeders in every window, fresh cut flowers on the tables. In such a setting of lives so fully and richly lived, it was easy to marvel at their adventures and their fun − as they interrupted one another to challenge an explanation or to clarify a detail.

As the pages that follow make clear, *Victory Harvest* is not the usual war story of danger and death. It is more than that, a celebration of everything that is about life − about sowing the seed, and reaping it, about being young and being together in love, about a lush landscape and the people that are its soil, about a country tested by fate and the collective will that was its salvation.

Of this place and these times Marion is a keen chronicler. But Marion and Charlie were not just witnesses to that time: they were its participants, and formed by it. As Charlie explained: "There came the interference of war and the fortunate event that we found ourselves still together in England, separated only by a few miles of country road and the exigencies of war. Being able to share these experiences was even more valuable than we knew at the time ... Now, forty-five years later these experiences are the very fabric of our lives. This was our romance."

Wendy Wickwire and Michael M'Gonigle
University of Victoria
Victoria, April 1997

ABBREVIATIONS

AA Anti-Aircraft
ARP Air Raid Precautions
ATS Auxiliary Territorial Service
AWOL Absent without leave
BDS Bomb Disposal Squad
CB Confined to barracks
ESWAEC East Sussex War Agricultural Committee
HE High Explosive
LDV Local Defence Volunteers
RAF Royal Air Force
RCAF Royal Canadian Air Force
RCR Royal Canadian Regiment
RMR Royal Montreal Regiment
WAAF Women's Auxiliary Air Force
WAC Women's Army Corps
WAEC War Agricultural Executive Committee
WD Women's Division
WLA Women's Land Army
WRENS Women's Royal Naval Service

Victory Harvest

CANADA TO ENGLAND

April 27, 1940. Montreal, Quebec

This must be kaleidoscopic, so much has happened, so much to record. Above all, Charlie has gone to war, my beautiful springer spaniel Doc is dead, and I am on my way over to my darling.

The weekend of September third, sparkling wines in firelight, sunshine, singing, "Something greater than the mind of man," and then the *Athenia*, the *Bismarck*, and the sober voice of Mr Chamberlain. Then Charlie haunted the Navy, but Canada's Navy was still in embryo. So one Thursday morning he telephoned home saying, "I've joined the Army." Four days later the First Canadian Division sailed and Charlie with them. And then my sweet Doc was killed. He and I were to have waited together and then I was suddenly alone. I found a tenant and we had no home anymore. I locked the door and never looked back to where Charlie had once carried me over the threshold, where our friends Jean and the doctor came, the doctor from whom our Doc, a little brown, wobbly puppy, had arrived as a wedding present, where Charlie's cousin Heather came for a weekend in August and stayed till Christmas, where the neighbour's children romped before our fire and the sun streamed into the kitchen, where Charlie made the coffee and phoned for beer and waxed my floors and we were terribly happy and sick with worry and always together.

Then Cousin Lilian was ill, Cousin Lilian who was never ill. Charlie wrote from Winchester with photographs and much description. I took his letter to her. She talked of Winchester to me, of the Cotswolds, of London, of great names and great people. She lived alone in her beautiful home but she was never lonely. Before I left she said gently, "You know, my dear, you should be in England."

"I shall be. I intend to work and save and I shall go in the fall."

"No. No, not in the fall, England in the spring. England in April. Now.

I can think of nothing I would rather do this year than to send you over to your husband."

I heard what Cousin Lilian said. I knew that she meant it. I felt unworthy and disturbed and full of gratitude and tried to show all these through my refusal.

A week later she said, "Have you decided to go to England? I meant what I said, you know."

I thanked her again but said that I could not possibly allow her to do so much for me, that I was grateful but that I should manage to go myself in September.

Cousin Lilian said, "Don't take off your hat," when I knocked at her door at eleven next morning. "Go down to Cook's and find out when you can secure a passage."

April 30, 1940. New York

Charlie doesn't know that I am in New York. Charlie thinks that I am quietly at home working to come to him in September. He doesn't know that I stood watching Brooklyn and the Harbour Front, and, tonight, from the roof of the Brooklyn Hospital, Manhattan blazing with lights. I turned excitedly to Dr Andrews, "New York by night: And next week I shall see London by night." Dr Andrews did not reply, he who had known London by night in the last war. I think I began my voyage there.

I should have photographed them all at the bus terminal: my friends, Charlie's friends, both our families. There had been no farewell for him. There is no pageantry in this war.

My seat on the bus from Montreal to New York was directly behind the driver and I sat with an ingenuous little French girl. She told me proudly that she could ride a bicycle with no hands. At Rouses Point the customs official pointed to the inspection tables. My bags were placed on them and I opened them.

"Where are you from?"

"Montreal."

"Where are you going?"

"England."

"England: Good God!" Then: "You're crazy, close your bags."

We have spent a quiet day for which I am grateful. I have seen so much and been so happy that it seems I have had my full share. The trip to England seems too much to contemplate. These days are but an interlude, an indelible but fleet panorama: Broadway ablaze, the view from the Empire State Building in the morning sunlight bringing a peculiar consciousness of the meaning of skyscraper; the quiet timeless "Little Church around the Corner;" the endless length and height of the apartment blocks along the Hudson; my first experience with subways; Fifth Avenue, Harlem; a drive on Long Island and the unforgettable fragrance of hyacinths around the fountain in Radio City.

And now I am going to send a cable, a very short cable, just "Sailing to you." After tonight I shall not need to send my love.

April 30, 1940. At sea

Can this really be me – alone on a wide, wide sea, with anti-aircraft guns mounted astern, submarine detectors on the forward deck, and three camouflaged bombers as freight amidships. What a shock it was when I saw them being loaded. I had expected to go in convoy, "Across the backboard sea in sombre echelon," or, if not, to sail brilliantly lighted, under a floodlit Stars and Stripes. But Mrs Andrews and Len, who had come to see me off, were stopped at a barricade scarcely inside the sheds at the docks. We had seen a blue plane being hoisted aboard a mustard-coloured ship at the end of the pier. I had hoped that that drab camouflage would not be on my ship, but as I walked alone through the long shadowy sheds I knew that it was.

Our departure from New York was unfortunate for us. Lunch was at one o'clock and when we came up on deck we discovered that we were on our way. Though we had just passed the Statue of Liberty there was a heavy haze and the skyline was a blur. We were particularly disappointed as we had been escorted out of harbour by surfaced submarines.

RMS *Samaria*

May 4, 1940. At sea

We are four. Four girls going to join our husbands, out of a total passenger list of one hundred and twenty-five. The ship normally carries thirteen hundred so it would seem that the opinion of the customs man at Rouses Point is shared by the general public. Each of us has a cabin to herself, save Margaret, Margaret Jones. Margaret is almost a bride. She has been showered and tea-ed, is carrying some thirty pairs of silk stockings, and sheds confetti at every lurch of the ship. Her fiancé is in a Transport Division and she has no idea of his whereabouts in England. All he has been able to give her is the GPO address. She was frightened and alone and terrified of sea-sickness and, to my surprise, exactly what I needed, not someone to care for me, but someone for me to care for. We met at lunch while still in dock and as soon as the engines began to throb she thought that she was sea-sick. We managed to keep her on deck until tea time but after life-boat drill she had her way. On such short acquaintance I could not force her to fight the feeling. I sought her out for dinner but she retired immediately after. I had a game of ping-pong with a lad of fifteen and went to bed about ten. Margaret emerged this morning amazed at herself and beginning to think that she may enjoy the trip.

We have two other table companions: Fay O'Connor, who has asthma and punctuates each sentence with squirts from an atomizer – once around the deck and she's done – and a fourth girl who has not opened her mouth yet. She has gentle eyes and good clothes.

"And the evening and the morning were the third day" – the most beautiful morning since the world began. We are lying on the bow of the ship, bare-headed, bare-armed, under a summer sun, with a warm breeze blowing. It is impossible, on a morning like this, to believe that war exists. There isn't a whitecap, nor any swell, just the broad shimmering band of sunlight on the water growing broader and less dazzling as the sun rises higher. Pillowed on our life-belts, we are conscious of the martial elements of the voyage, but we share the inevitable thrill of getting nearer to the midst of things.

Margaret lies beside me, her sickness overcome and her colour back. Fay O'Connor is asleep at my feet, breathing easily while the sun bakes the asthma out of her. The silent girl at our table has become our very charming friend. She is a German girl, by marriage a British subject, and she speaks with a fascinating accent. She says "To fi-ight – I ha-ate it. One must be a fighter or one must be a pacificist or one must hang oneself. That is all."

The days seem long and everyone is growing more strained. At night I lie wondering which things I should grab if the alarm were sounded, "Six short blasts on the ship's whistle accompanied by the ringing of all the electric gongs." And when the sun shines again it seems impossible that I should ever hear it. We are on our way, and though the four days to come seem unendurable, we can do nothing and I cannot help but enjoy the sea and the sky and the perfect weather.

Elizabeth and Fay and Andrea, the German girl, are each devoured by several fears. I know something of their stories and understand their worries. Elizabeth, who is to be married as soon as she arrives, met her fiancé only after the war began. She clings to the hope that he is still in England.

Fay is a widow. Her husband was gassed in the last war and later took his own life. She has a son in the Guards. Her asthma results

from her husband's gas attacks. Fay, who can scarcely breathe, is terrified of missing her son. She is an exceptionally admirable woman.
She smokes putrid, medicated cigarettes, inhales from her atomizer,
and flaunts a fine courage.

Andrea, the third and most attractive of our quartet, is the young
German girl. She lives a life of extremes and at the moment could not
be more miserable. She is very young, barely in her twenties, and is returning to her husband in the British Isles. Her parents, from whom
she has not heard since war was declared, are, she believes, still in Germany. She was in Spain at the outbreak of war and was taken aboard a
British destroyer, ending up in America where she has been lecturing
at a university in Alabama. She says that she has no home. Germany,
Spain, England, and America, each has a part of her. Her accent is
pronounced and is as captivating as she believes it to be despised. She
fears that she will be ill-treated in Britain and continually wishes that
the ship would sink and end her endless fears. We dare not leave her
for long as it is hard to get her back to an even sub-normal outlook.

On the whole we are four nice girls, of whom, unfortunately, only
three play bridge. As the third class lounges are way below decks and
hermetically sealed, which Margaret's stomach cannot take, nor Fay's
asthma, we visit in each other's cabins and walk or lie on deck. Mentally we are in a sad state. One rumour after another works its way
through the ship. Nebulous shapes flit through our minds, bits of gossip and disconcerting bulletins shred our fortitude. We manage to
laugh occasionally but our laughter is sad and short-lived.

Gas-masks were issued today and the ship is constantly changing
course. We fear each ripple on the sea. That the boys will be gone.
That the night is so long.

I still find it hard to believe that I am here, clothes slithering back and
forth as they hang on the wall, door and port open to a sunlit deck.
The vibration is negligible and I think that nothing can be more
soothing than the rise and fall of a ship. Soon I shall be with Charlie.
I scarcely dare to think of it lest the gods play some ironic jest.

We have had life-boat drill and gas mask drill and landing cards
were issued this morning. The delightful little Irish lady who shares
Margaret's cabin was worried about her passport. How we laughed
when I showed her where I keep mine. "Whoosh," she said, "What

ye don't know's not worth alarnin' dearie, Yoo'o didn't coom oop the Laggan on a bubble." She is a priceless person. We keep her talking as long as we can and love it.

Our little Irish lady was with me when we first glimpsed Ireland. "Sure and it's home," she said. Nothing else, but she was quivering. She told Andrea that she is going home alone and expects no one to meet her. "She is very sweet," Andrea said. "She is so poor." It was her way of saying "poor little soul."

We had a sherry party last night for Margaret. Poor child, to be married in a strange land, without a familiar face or custom. An odd little man, with whom we play bridge, was MC. He quotes poetry by the yard, strums the piano, chants monologues, and is a God-given fourth for bridge. He and a crony of his, of equally hoary vintage, were the two men of the party. They sang war-songs, told war-stories and thoroughly enjoyed amusing their four "sweethearts." The steward laid a white cloth and provided attractive little cakes and sandwiches. Margaret was surprised and rather wistful but winsome and gracious. Her charm lies in her quiet, slightly bewildered manner.

The hilarity reached its height when Fay, asthma forgotten, leaped on a chair and sang happily – "Let's all sing like the birdies sing – b-rrr-p." It was a beautiful full-bodied burp, coming before anyone had drawn breath for the first tweet.

The Chief Steward popped in and beat us all roundly at ping-pong and we saw each other to bed singing, "We all go the same way home." It was a good party and the only hours of foolish amusement which we have had on board.

This morning we have done nothing but gaze avidly at Ireland slipping past on our starboard side.

And now I must go in to pack, for tonight I shall be too scatter-brained. We are to go in on the tide and dock before morning.

May 13, 1940. 14 Milton Road, Aldershot
I find my new address very exciting and we have come, it seems, in time for the fireworks.

We sighted Ireland early on the eighth, and took the craziest course. We had been zig-zagging for days, watching the long angles of foam astern. But that proved commonplace travel compared to our manoeuvres when we reached the mine-fields. Sometimes we traveled in short zigs. Sometimes the sun lay astern, sometimes straight ahead, and we were constantly in doubt as to what land we saw, now to port, now to starboard.

About five o'clock a British plane flew out to meet us. She circled over and over us, dipping her wings. We had come a long way and felt very alone. "Now Britain knows we're here," was the thought in everyone's heart and we sighed with happiness.

That was a long evening and a longer night. At four a.m. I heard the ship's whistle, threw on a coat and stepped out on deck. There was a flaming red sunrise. We were anchored in the mouth of the Mersey. Some fifteen ships were around us, a jostling crowd after the wide sea, a destroyer, several freighters, mine-sweepers, and patrol boats. Unfortunately, the thrill faded as we rode at anchor until eleven-thirty. It was exciting when we got going again. We zig-zagged in small, sharp angles while two mine-sweepers circled round and round us. We were finally ashore about two o'clock, our first step on English soil with an English Bobby to greet us. We left the giant dull-painted ship with only the faintest sadness.

We found our baggage under our respective initials and feared being separated as we were so spread out. Andrea kept running back and forth between us, carrying a brief-case and her beautiful Leica camera, which she had just regained from safe-keeping with the purser. She was talking to me when she saw that her turn was next. I took her case and her camera and she ran excitedly back to her section, a confused mixture of excitement and terror, infuriated by our amusement. I made a bee-line for a telephone and was so excited myself that they were calling me to get into a taxi before I had sorted out my collection of strange pennies, florins, and sixpences. At Limestreet Station I got a message through to Charlie though I did not have time to speak to him. Margaret and Fay were already on the train and almost in tears with uncertainty. Then we discovered that somehow, inexplicably, Andrea had missed the train and I was still clutching her bulging briefcase and five hundred dollars' worth of Leica camera. We had all exchanged addresses so I was not particularly worried, but I was perturbed at having acquired so valuable a responsibility at a time when I was feeling most elated and irresponsible.

Here we were on a little miniature train, riding in a compartment with a shy little English soldier who was pop-eyed at our wild excitement. Rolling country, trees in full leaf, tiled roofs, chimney pots, even pinching could not make them seem true, gardens in bloom, trees in full blossom, and the almost impossibly green greenness of the pasture lands. Then suddenly we were in Euston and in the rush to get baggage I heard "Hello there!" And Charlie took over. After my call he had found a room for me in Aldershot and had come directly to Euston to await the arrival of our boat-train.

Then Fay's tall Guardsman met her, very tall, very impressive. And poor Margaret was left. We decided that she should wire my address to her Terry and then come on to Aldershot with us in the morning. So we went to a funny hotel in Woburn Place for the night, cabled back home, wired to Terry, and came on to Aldershot in the morning, to my new temporary home, covered with great purple clusters of wisteria, and with a fireplace in my room.

Newspaper headlines, May 10, 1940.
Before this the war had been referred to as the "phoney war."

Charlie had to return directly to the barracks so Margaret and I went for a walk. We were happy and thrilled and waited for Terry to make the chapter complete. We found a little tea-room, bought a paper and went in for coffee. It was May the tenth, and the headline was, "HOLLAND, BELGIUM and LUXEMBURG INVADED." Then "Britain and France send help. Allied Troops moving." and further down, "All RAF leave stopped." And also the British Expeditionary Force and the Canadian Active Service Force. In the centre of the page was the story of the first bombs which had been dropped on England. They were incendiaries and had fallen in Kent.

We could not eat and left the tea-room, but our walk had lost its savour. We saw groups of grim Canadians standing about and several excited MPs rounding up lads at the station. The first series of seven day leaves for the First Canadian Division since their arrival in England in 1939 had been scheduled to begin that morning. Both Terry and Charlie had leaves coming up the following week. Now all were canceled. Margaret's fears were reborn. Perhaps she was not in time after all. We walked quietly back to Milton Road. Suddenly Margaret stopped. There was a motorcycle leaning against the gate.

"I can't. I can't go in," she said.

I rushed in to my room. Tall and dark, with a twinkle in his eyes, a Canadian soldier rose to his feet. I shouted "You're Terry?"

"That's right."

"Well, hold everything," and I flew down to Margaret, pushed her in, and went back and sat on the doorstep.

We had lunch together and Terry stayed till six o'clock. I walked to the barracks in the afternoon. Rumour had it that the Canadians were to be off and away within twenty-four hours. An air-raid was expected and gas-masks were to be carried constantly.

Terry was taking Margaret back with him to Woking. I walked to the station with them. Terry had counted on his leave and had plans for a honeymoon on the Isle of Wight. All hung in the balance. It was a sad walk. Military police were calling, "All leaves canceled," and turning the boys back at the barriers.

Charlie was waiting for me when I returned and was free of duty until ten-thirty. We had a long walk and expected it to be a farewell as the whole Aldershot Command was buzzing with activity. Only four boys out of twenty thousand had passes for that evening. Charlie had one because I had just arrived. When he went back he worked right through the night. He said that there were forty-eight thousand rounds of ammunition to be loaded into machine-gun belts when he returned,

Sunday Charlie had a few hours off again and now no one knows what is to come. Rumours are many, facts are few. The RCR's (Royal

Canadian Regiment) have gone and the 48th, no one knows where. Hearsay has it that they have gone to Salisbury Plains and that the rest will follow. Again we hear that no more will pull out and that leaves will be restored, but no one knows.

It is a shame. Those whose leaves began Friday, when we arrived, all had received money from home and were turned back at the train. If they should get their leaves later the money will be gone. Some evaded the police, took taxis to London or borrowed civilians clothes and got out. They are all AWOL and in for trouble. Everyone is CB'd (confined to barracks) or on guard duty. An air raid is expected hourly and all are very prepared.

So it is a very disappointed and subdued Aldershot to which I have come, soldiers quiet and serious where they were gay and laughing the morning I arrived. Margaret is off in Woking and I have not heard from her. I dare not leave the beaten track between my digs and the barracks lest Charlie get a few hours off and miss me. We had hoped to go to Egham yesterday to see his aunt but he is not allowed to leave the Aldershot Command.

I am so thankful that I arrived in time. Perhaps in another week I should have missed him. He is so happy to have me and he looks so well. There is still a chance of his leave, but if that is not to be, we have had this.

I am sitting by Kay Scott's fire, as her room is larger than mine, while we wait for our husbands' return. She is quiet and friendly and is, as I am, the Canadian wife of a Canadian soldier. We walk to the barracks together at noon or explore the town together when the boys are not free.

Monday night, when we still had had no word from Margaret and Terry, Charlie, strictly against orders, and I took a bus to Woking. It was a beautiful ride, through winding lanes, with glimpses of old tile roofs through hedges and flowering trees. May is in full bloom, never have I seen whole trees covered with blossom, and to their red and white is added the yellow of laburnum, the hint of lilacs to come, and the waxen beauty of magnolia.

But unfortunately Terry was out and we did not know where Margaret lived. We talked for a few moments to two First Canadian Division boys who spotted my Canadian accent at once. One of them shook hands with me and said with soft nostalgic reverence, "Good-night, Canada."

Long restless beams of light swept the sky overhead as we came home. Charlie had to enlighten my greenhorn ignorance and explain that they were searchlights. We later walked from the bus to the depot in my first complete blackout.

The next noon Charlie rushed out to meet me as I passed the Garrison Theatre. He was waving a wire addressed to him and shouting "Get on that bus!" The bus stopped and I got on. The wire said "Wedding. Christ Church. 1500 hours." It was signed with Terry's name and regimental number.

I found the church. I found an old caretaker, shaving in a greenhouse behind it. He gave me the rector's telephone number. The rector gave me Margaret's address and I found her dressing, frightened and quite alone. But companionship changed things a bit, and she was the traditional lovely bride, smiling over her flowers, when I, my kerchief tied over my head, stood beside her, her matron of honour.

The church was large and we were only eight in all, but a very happy eight as we took the train to Waterloo and the tube to Picadilly where supper had been ordered and a magnum of champagne. It was a real war wedding. The boys dared not overstay their passes and we caught the 9:27 train from Waterloo.

May 21, 1940. Kenton, Middlesex
I had scarcely arrived and found so friendly a welcome from Charlie's aunt and uncle when I was whisked off to Euston station to meet Glen, Charlie's cousin, home on leave from the Navy. It was a lovely drive, through Hampstead Heath, where we saw Jack Straw's Castle, Wembly, Golders Green, and on home through the blackout.

Yesterday was a thrilling day. I telephoned Andrea and arranged to meet her in London, that we might spend a day together and I might return her camera and briefcase.

It was then that an unhappy incident occurred, reminiscent of early days on shipboard. Then, we, Fay and Margaret and I, when we had first learned of Andrea's German birth, had shared brief doubts. With true English phlegm, and too, with innate desire for fairness, also a vestige of our British ancestry, we decided, with little discussion and yet instinctively united, that we would give all that friendliness demanded, which was simple, as Andrea was appealing and attractive, but we would remember, too, the care which must be taken when talking to travelers in wartime.

And so, on this sunny morning, Andrea and I stood on the southeast corner of Trafalgar Square, pouring over Dad's old "Pocket Atlas and Guide to London."

"Can I help you, ladies?" I looked up and said thank you to an English Army major. He offered to walk down Whitehall with us and show us the way to Buckingham Palace. We had passed the Admiralty when he asked Andrea where she came from. Stiffly, and with a note in her voice which I had not heard before, she said, "I am a British subject."

"Yes, but you were not born in England?"

"I am a British subject."

Amicably, but with aroused curiosity, the English major pursued the subject. Andrea, whose moods I understood, was growing tight with indignation and something akin to self-pity. Finally she boiled over.

"I am not required to answer your questions. You have no right to ask me such questions. If you do not believe that I am a British subject you must call over that bobby."

"That," said the major, "is just what I will do" and called over a policeman who asked her for her identification papers.

She produced her passport and identity card. Both were in order. The bobby smiled, returned them to her, the major said, "Good afternoon," and the bobby directed us to Downing Street. Andrea was bubbling with rage. "He thought I was a parachutist. He thought, because I am flat-chested, that I am a boy, that I have destroyed my uniform and I am a Fifth Columnist."

We walked past No. 10 Downing street and back to Whitehall, and by the time we had stood a while on Westminster Bridge and Big Ben had charmingly struck three for us, the incident was forgotten.

A little higher up, Lambeth Bridge gave us another view of the Parliament buildings and then we crossed over to Westminster Abbey. An unpretentious door led us into the Poet's Corner. I saw Spenser first and then Jonson, "O rare Ben Jonson," Gray's and Milton's busts. Chairs were over the Tennyson and Browning plates. I wanted to move them. It was a most unhappy sensation to look down and walk upon the names and graves of those who have always meant reverence and inspiration.

Because of the service which was in progress our exploring was limited. We went out as we had come in and walking around the Abbey entered again to see the grave of the Unknown Soldier. I was very much moved by it and by the simple beauty of the inscription.

I went to tea with Andrea, to her temporary suburban home. She told me that she was unhappy in England, that she did not intend to return to her husband and thought that she would go to Canada. I sat at her desk to write her the letter she wished, inviting her to my Canadian home. She hoped that such a letter, from a Canadian citizen, would simplify the immigration question. I wrote "Dear Andrea –" and then looked up and smiled.

"I can't sit before you and write to you, I'll do it later and send it to you." And I must do it too.

This morning Charlie's cousins asked me if I would like to "walk across the fields to Harrow." They did not understand my incredulity and perfected my delight by explaining "Harrow, up there on the hill." And that is just what we did, walked "across the fields to Harrow."

The blackout curtains have just been drawn and the lights lit. I am delightfully sleepy. Tomorrow I go by bus from Ealing to Eastbourne. It is hard to believe on these beautiful sunny days that there can be anything to fear. Of the news, we listen and hope. It is all so terrible. Trainloads of wounded soldiers from France came through here today.

May 22, 1940. Eastbourne, Sussex
My first visit to Eastbourne was heralded by bad news, as was my arrival in England. Arras and Amiens have fallen. I have a postcard of Arras in 1918, a crumbled ruin, which Charlie's grandmother has just given to me. Her youngest son is buried there. And now the Germans march through again.

We have spent a sad and solemn evening. This family, Charlie's aunt and uncle, have lived for many years in Paris, and all their friends are now within the sound of gunfire. They fear for their friends, and we fear, as in these sombre days does all England, for our own shores. We are right at the foot of the downs, with the house backing on the sea. Beyond the garden, on the slopes between us and the sea, is a searchlight. These are good targets for Jerry. And of course the downs are

God-given landing places for paratroops. After lengthy discussions we are still undecided as to what should be done were they to land. Rumour is more rife here than in Aldershot, a hundred pounds offered for finding a mine on the beach, a thousand for sighting an enemy ship. But the rumbling guns across the channel are fact, as are the lights and fires which we have seen, and reported, on the downs at dusk.

We take the dog for a walk at night. Full moon, drifting clouds, and the sound of the sea rasping on the shingle beach, and across the channel we hear the burst of shells and see the flash and glow of explosions in the sky.

I had asked Charlie's uncle to find out how I could contact someone concerned with the Women's Land Army and today, after laborious searching and disentangling of red tape, he found that the woman I should speak to is almost his next door neighbour. I went to see her and have made application to join the WLA. I'd knew almost nothing about the Land Army – I'd seen it mentioned in the newspaper and thought of it again one evening in Aldershot when I was sitting around the fire with Charlie and some of his Canadian Army friends and their wives, discussing how I could find niche that would enable me to remain in England. The boys were all vehemently thumbs down about the Women's Services, the ATS (Auxiliary Territorial Service), WAAF (Women's Auxiliary Air Force) and the WRENs (Women's Royal Naval Service). But the WLA – they felt that that would be a reasonable way to contribute. Should I be accepted I am to be a dairy maid.

May 26, 1940. Aldershot
I have received a full and complete welcome in Eastbourne which I shall not soon forget, and was lunching with Charlie's grandmother when his wire arrived: "Come to Aldershot." Charlie's uncle checked trains for me while once again I repacked and via Brighton, Redhill, Victoria, and a final aggravating change at Woking I arrived at Aldershot at 10: 32 p.m. The blackout was almost complete. While I stood deliberating, Charlie emerged from a crowd of uniforms. He had returned from the north that morning and was off again on Monday "to nowhere."

We felt our way into the town through the silent blackness and at 14 Milton Road were able to arouse no one. We tried all the hotels but they were shuttered and barred. Aldershot has long been a garrison town and takes no chances. I had no place to sleep and I had had no dinner. We sniffed in vain through the blackout for a fish and chip shop and even the comfort station was locked. I definitely refused to spend the night on a park bench. But Charlie had a better idea. We walked through a gentle rain to the barracks. Charlie seated me on a rock outside the lines to wait for him. A little later he returned proudly with a can of sardines, two chocolate bars, two blankets, and a ground sheet. By midnight I had eaten and we had turned in, under a laburnum tree, in a field beyond the tennis courts. There were mosquitoes, and what we thought were catkins, dropping on us from the sprays of laburnum.

A cuckoo wakened us at five o'clock and we discovered that our blanket of catkins was little green slugs. Charlie rolled out and went back to the barracks, instructing me to cache the blankets, "But hang on to the ground sheet, because it's mine."

I did my hair, rolled and hid the blankets for future collection, and dutifully, but not without amusement and some misgiving, walked through the streets at seven in the morning with the precious ground sheet under my arm.

I sat on the white holy-stoned doorstep of 14 Milton Road to wait for the household to waken. An English major wakened me. I fell in when he opened the door for his morning paper. He helped me up, sat me in his best chair, and gave me a pear. Later I received a severe scolding from my kind landlady.

"Another time if you can't make anyone hear, you break a window. You can always sleep on the couch in the dining room. Under a tree! The very idea!"

Charlie arrived for lunch. We caught up on sleep. Had a long walk, collected some clean clothes from my bags at the station, searched for and found a hotel which would cash my travelers' cheques, and stopped in at the Dominion Soldiers' Club. Now we wait, with a bottle of Madeira, for Kay and Jeff Scott, before a very large fire in a very small fireplace.

June 8, 1940. Egham, Surrey
Charlie has disappeared again and I have spent a week with his Aunt Dora and her family. Margaret, Peter's young cousin, is ten years my junior, but I shed all seniority cycling with her tonight. Whatever

happens I shall never forget the fragrance of England, the scent of late-blooming laburnum tonight as we climbed a hill, looking over a hedge to clouds of rhododendron blossom, and then, new to me, the sweet scent of English honeysuckle. I felt my first nostalgic pang as we rode through tall woods and smelt the familiar scent of pine. Through the hedges the silver haze of grasses lay in the evening light between us and the distant ridges of blue hills.

We climbed a barbed wire fence to pick the first wild roses and I made the acquaintance of stinging nettles, a curse of which Canada is, I believe, happily free.

Our road was narrow and winding, there was a haze of heat in the air and the willow leaves were turned, suggesting rain.

We cycled for miles, Margaret and I, on the tow-path along the Thames, soldiers out in punts with their girls, and I not knowing where my soldier is. Somewhere in England, or – somewhere in France?

We went to Staines by bus and walked home by the river, swans drifting majestically, willows trailing along the water, and the river like a sheet of amber with the sun slanting on it.

I spent a day gardening with Arthur, who is my age. He had been on night duty, special police, for several nights and a few afternoons thrown in. He came off duty at ten one evening, very weary, and heard a lorry in difficulties on the hill beside the house. He went out to help and it was two o'clock before he came to bed. The following day, the gardening day, was his day off. He is his own hard taskmaster and dug a large area. So does an Englishman, and Englishwoman too, do a full day's work on a day off.

I have waited here for news from Charlie, but he has vanished into the blue, and I am, "in the army now," and must get organized.

Dunkirk has been evacuated and there is no sense of defeat, rather of pride and gathering might.

Then early one evening I telephoned Eastbourne and found that the application I had made had been accepted. I am now a member of the Women's Land Army. Just as I was about to cable home a wire came from Charlie: "Come to Aldershot." So by bus through Virginia Water and Sunningdale in the lovely English evening I have come again to Aldershot.

I have written to the family and told them that I must stay. I am strong and healthy and can work. I see wounded soldiers coming back and hear tales of their lack of supplies – I know I can help produce foodstuffs even if I cannot get them through. I feel like Rupert Brooke: "My present happiness is so great that I fear the jealous gods will requite me afterwards with some terrible punishment – death perhaps – or life."

I have been to Eastbourne and returned. I went to the WLA offices there and learned that I am to be sent to a private farm for a month's training. I was medically examined and filled in several forms.

Charlie's Uncle Alec and I had a long discussion one night. I am still known as the Fifth Columnist. I believe the joke developed from the fact that, as I have mentioned before, my arrival coincided with bad news, both my initial arrival in England on the day that the "phony war" ended and again when Germany began to advance so swiftly, just after I had come to Eastbourne for the first time. As yet Aunt Dado and Uncle Alec have not seen Charlie and me together and I come in for a lot of ribbing. After all, they say, they have no proof that I am his wife. I may have acquired her papers and am using her personality as the entrance into the family life of Charlie's relatives for subversive ends. I play up and ask leading questions about Eastbourne's pri-

Toilet paper, sent by Uncle Alec
for my collection.

vate life, from a tactical point of view. They shut up like clams with facetious deliberation, "Better not answer that till we have seen Charlie and made sure."

Through this teasing and the general awareness of Fifth Columnist activity in England we began discussing individual cases. Uncle Alec remembered Andrea and indicated how easily she could have been a member of the German espionage.

She had married, before the war, a British subject, thereby becoming British herself. She had been sent to a distant country and so was absolved of all possible complicity and suspicion. She returned to England at the outbreak of war, the British wife of a British subject. It was all very neat, he said. I was furious. She was very young, she was very charming, and she was my friend. Uncle Alec was delighted.

"That proves the fiendish success of German intelligence. Of course she is charming, of course she is young. How else but by such natural grace, such an ingenuous manner, could she be safe and satisfactory?"

I grew more loyal to her, more on the defensive. She had followed all rules on shipboard most scrupulously. "Of course she would," broke in Uncle Alec, "But what was it you said about getting through the customs?" I saw myself again, holding Andrea's briefcase and camera, while far down the shed, under her own initial, an official was inspecting her luggage.

"And didn't you say that she intended to get a divorce and wanted to go to Canada?" As yet I had not taken time to write that letter for which she had asked me.

"Don't you think that some unconscious doubt in your mind has made you procrastinate?" Uncle Alec persisted.

"No, I don't, I still intend to write it. Andrea is a person I am glad to have known. I have met few such charming people and I am not going to think such dreadful things of her."

"Very well," he said, "But I shouldn't write that letter." Nor have I had any opportunity to write it. We were busy all the next morning, and after lunch Aunt Dado and I had stopped a moment in the sun on the garden terrace when the telephone rang. It was a telegram from Charlie, "Meet me at Auntie Dora's tonight."

I arrived in Egham at seven-thirty to find an army truck at the door and Charlie and two of his friends waiting for me in the house. He had to leave at eleven. We went for a walk, had coffee and then he was gone. And again it may be to France, or it may be out East now that Italy is in the war.

To be in England, to be able to come to him. Cousin Lilian can never know how much she has given us.

Before I continue what must be a complete and distasteful ending to a very happy relationship, may I say that, if you, Andrea, should ever read this, I have spent time and thought before I reached the decision that finally I made. Whatever is the truth I have lost a friend.

I spoke to Arthur who is in the special police. I told him as a matter of interest of my shipboard companion. I stressed no points but I tried to omit nothing. And then I told him of the angle from which Charlie's Uncle Alec looked upon the story.

"I have been thinking the same thing," he said.

Later he told me that he had talked it all over with his superior at the station who had asked if I would consider having an interview with him. At first I refused. Arthur said that it was completely up to me. She was my friend and if I considered friendship to be of greater value than the possibility of danger to Charlie or the rest of the troops or to civilians, then I had the right to my faith in my friend.

But I could not know that that faith was justified. I asked Arthur to find out what would be done. He told me that an investigation would be made of which Andrea would never know, unless proof were found which would justify her internment. In either case, proof of her guilt or her innocence, I would be told exactly nothing.

For twenty-four hours I thought of it all, little things she had said, her fear of just such treatment as I was giving to her, her sudden angers, her immediate defensive responses. Were they genuine, or were they clever enlistments for sympathy and support? I could not know. I had carried her briefcase through the customs. Did that mean that she knew I would return it untouched? And why had she missed the train? I sincerely wished that I had inspected the briefcase. These doubts might then be resolved one way or another.

I did not know where Charlie was, but even though I did not, were I to spend the weekend with Andrea (which we had planned) would I not fear every word I said? I knew then, that even as Uncle Alec and Arthur had doubted, so too did I. The price was high, treason, and the complete severance of a friendship which I valued. But I was forced to realize that there were greater values than friendship, and that price I could not pay.

I spoke to Arthur as he went out on duty that night.

He had come in and gone to bed when I came down next morning, but there was a note on the table for me.

"Inspector Roberts, CID (Criminal Investigation Department), will be coming here at 9:30 a.m. to take a statement. I have gone to bed. Please wake me at nine o'clock. Arthur."

June 17, 1940. Eastbourne, Sussex

Every day hospital trains leave the coastal ports with wounded rescued by the "little ships" from Dunkirk.* I found to my personal dismay, on my return to Eastbourne, that my farming debut had been deferred until June 23rd. I have waded through a lot more red tape, have been fitted for breeches, shirts, shoes, and the most impossible hat. Now that the date is set and uncertainty ended I intend to enjoy the interim to the full.

I have spent the last few days digging the air-raid shelter in the garden. Apparently it was a thing of beauty last fall but it caved in during the winter. It's the devil to dig, solid chalk. I have to dig with a mattock. We have arranged a primitive elevator system for lifting out the chalk. Charlie's Uncle Alec and I plan and do the teamwork during the evenings and I dig away during the days. It is now seven feet deep. One more to go.

We were deep in it Saturday, figuratively and literally, when Charlie came through the garden gate. The family played the game right out. They ostentatiously watched my reaction to Charlie's arrival and his to me. Uncle Alec spoke to Charlie first.

"She is your wife, then?"

"What the heck, of course she's my wife."

Then the Fifth Columnist story came out. Charlie introduced me formally there in the garden, in my old shorts, covered with chalk, and there and then the work ceased and the weekend was dedicated to this, our first four-fold meeting.

We drove into Brighton, through Friston, across the Cuckmere, through Newhaven town, and across the cliffs at Rottingdean. We made no mention of it but each of us knew that under those cloudless skies, across that shining strip of channel, France was fighting a losing battle.

Charlie and his uncle were walking ahead on the beach at Brighton when Charlie turned and called, "Auntie." "I won't have it," Dado retorted. "I won't have a great six-foot soldier calling me 'Auntie.'"

---

* We later learned that 300,000 men of the British Expeditionary Force were rescued from Dunkirk by all the little volunteer vessels. 40,000 men were taken prisoner.

"Right then – Dado."

It had been rather ridiculous – she barely ten years older than I – but, more important, I felt we were no longer with "Charlie's aunt and uncle" but with friends.

No one stirred the next morning till nearly noon. It was raining and a suitable day for sleeping in and dinner at three. Two ARP (Air Raid Precautions) men came in at tea time to fit additional green gadgets on our gas-masks for "Little Arthur." That completed, we all walked to the bus with Charlie.

I have been digging all morning in the shelter and when I came in to lunch we turned on the BBC to learn that France has fallen. We were too shaken to eat, or to talk, and I can't write any more either.

The all-clear signal is sounding after my first air-raid alarm. The siren went at eleven. Where has the raid been tonight? Where is Charlie? What will the morning news bring?

We were all dressed to take the dog for a walk when we heard the low wailing whine of the siren. For about three hours we sat dutifully near the stairs, the strongest corner of the house, half asleep and incensed by the stupidity of it.

Planes went constantly back and forth over head, but no bombs fell and we heard no AA (anti-aircraft) fire. Finally we went into the garden, bright in the full moonlight. We romped with the dog, who had missed her walk, and as the all-clear would not sound we came to bed.

Shortly afterwards I heard the whistles and the raiders-past signal. I drew the curtains to find it full day and smiled to hear the neighbours saying, "Good-night," as they emerged from their shelters.

Somewhere those planes unloaded their bombs, and somewhere now is death and fire and grieving, and somewhere Britons are more grim and swearing anew to keep this island inviolate. I will not be accused of

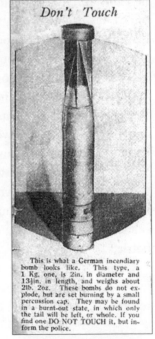

Don't Touch

This is what a German incendiary bomb looks like. This type, a 1 Kg. one, is 2in. in diameter and 13½in. in length, and weighs about 2lb. 2oz. These bombs do not explode, but are set burning by a small percussion cap. They may be found in a burnt-out state, in which only the tail will be left, or whole. If you find one DO NOT TOUCH it, but inform the police.

An incendiary bomb, like those dropping by the hundreds over the south of England. Buckets of sand and water were kept by every door.

Charlie and I, summer of 1940

histrionics. This morning I sat, conscious of my home, safe Canada, and listened while Alec and Dado spoke of where they could buy the necessary wood and wheels to build a small cart. If Jerry came, and we could not see what was to prevent him, food and blankets would have to go with us wherever we went. Dado had a few valuables which she would try to save. And yet homes and possessions sank in relative value. Lives alone were important. Because only by living could we hope to fight and work to repel and ultimately defeat the invader.

A plane is overhead now. God bless him. He had probably chased those Heinkels away and is having one last look around.

Tomorrow I say goodbye to Alec and Dado and tomorrow night I sleep at my farm, a long month's dream.

We have walked by the sea and walked on the downs and I have seen a dew-pond. We have driven to little villages and sat in old inn gardens. Charlie has been here and there have been evenings of gaiety and much laughter. But behind it all there is so deep an ache inside me. Among all the people we meet there is no sign of fear nor depression. Tomorrow their sons may go, or, having gone, a War Office wire may come. Tomorrow Jerry may come and they must leave their homes. Life goes on with kindness and humour and a quiet determination to take what comes and see it through.

Everywhere there are signs of war, anti-tank hazards along Pevensey Bay, great cement blocks which march along the shingle and cut across the country between peoples' houses and over their gardens. There are wires on tall poles across the roads and over the downs and farmlands to prevent planes from landing, guns along the front and sentries everywhere, on the buses, at the railway stations, on the down land roads, demanding one's card of identity.

We have been working all week on our dug-out and I have enjoyed it. I do what I can and when Alec comes home we work together till dark. It is all shored up now and tomorrow I must go.

NUNNINGHAM

Sunday, June 23, 1940. Nunningham Farm by Candlelight
Just time for a first good-night from my English farm, and I shall love it.

Monday, June 24, 1940. Nunningham Farm
Dado and Alec drove me here last night. We drove through straggling little villages and flat uninteresting country and my heart fell, then rose again, as the road began to climb between high banks and we

The Marshall house at Nunningham

turned onto a little village street, fragrant with roses in all the gardens and along all the walks. We turned off at the Woolpack Inn, and immediately the village was out of sight. The hedges on each side of us were covered with blossoming wild rose and the fields beyond them dropped away to blue hills in the shimmering distance. Before us the farmhouse and buildings lay in a hollow behind tall elms and a row of evergreens. Mr and Mrs Marshall came out to meet us. I hope that my relief was not as manifest as it was sincere. Alec had been teasing me about my old gray-bearded farmer and his work-worn wife for so long that I had almost come to believe in them.

When I saw them, Kath Marshall, a true Saxon, slender, and little older than I, and Walter, her husband, tall and lean, with blue Sussex eyes, each offering a quiet welcome, I realized with what apprehension I had entered this new life. I had not feared hard work or hard living, but I had been in dread of living with stolid, unfeeling people, whom I could not respect or from whom I could not learn.

I was shown my room and then we walked across the farm in the clear June evening. I liked Mrs Marshall's soft voice, very English, but gentle, with none of the intonations which so often make the English voice sound exaggerated and affected to the Canadian ear. I liked Mr Marshall's concise explanations of cropping and plans. We took a footpath which skirted a small hayfield close beside a wood. The wood was twenty acres, and young trees take twenty years to reach a useful size. Consequently, as an acre of wood was cut each winter, a constant supply of fuel, pea-sticks, and kindling (or light wood) was assured. I learned, too, that the wood was thick with violets and primroses in the early spring, and later, carpeted with bluebells.

In spite of my desire to begin immediately I was not wakened till eight yesterday morning – to the brisk chirrups of chickens and the lowing of cows. I have never been on a farm before and no child ever knew a more devastating excitement. I looked through my wide-open casement window, over the small orchard beside the house and the winding road. On a green bank is the stone parapet of the well with its windless, then a hedge and a sloping hayfield with clover and daisies blowing. The far hills are the Sussex Weald country beyond which lies London. Here there are no searchlights and no sirens, no concertina wire or tank traps, no soldiers or airmen, and only the occasional plane overhead.

At breakfast time I was presented to Peter, age two, who was very sleepy, incredibly fair, and very sweet in white sleepers and blue dressing gown.

I spent the morning turning hay. When it is mown it falls in long rows, called swathes, and is left to dry. Then it is turned with long-handled, three foot wooden rakes and left to dry again. Mr Marshall, John, the cowman, and I turned the whole field that morning though I was sadly inept. John fits into this rural scene perfectly. I wondered when I heard his name if, like Wordsworth's Michael, he had, "learned the meaning of all winds," and if he was, "watchful more than ordinary men." But John is just a lad, bronzed, slow to speak, quick to smile, patient and encouraging with me, and utterly in keeping with this fairy tale farm. I cannot believe the gods have been so kind – to be useful, to be near Charlie, and to be so happy too!

Walter and Peter

At three o'clock I was seated on a three-legged stool in the cool shadows of the old stone barn, having my first milking lesson. I was much more successful at producing laughter than milk. I was so afraid of hurting the cow, which amused Mr Marshall. "Don't worry about her, my girl, fresh milkers mostly worry about the cow hurting them."

After tea I drove up and down the hayfield in an old truck (excuse me, lorry, Mr Marshall meticulously explained the difference to me) sweeping hay. A ten-foot rake with long wooden tines and iron teeth was bolted onto the lorry. The rake slips under the hay and a great fragrant heap piles up before the lorry, which was carefully driven up to the stack and backed out, depositing its load before the men who pitch and stack. I was a mere parasite that night, watching and absorbing.

This morning, as we turned hay in another field, I was a little less fascinated by the hay, the great rakes, and my companions. I could take a moment to watch the rolling white clouds, the quiet fields, and the hills. I heard the soft call of the cuckoo and the clean swish of the hay as it fell. I mastered the movements of raking today and though I cannot yet keep pace with the men they are proud of me, which is the finest encouragement I could have.

In the afternoon I laboriously milked two cows while John did the other twelve. Tomorrow morning I intend to milk three. I will become a good milker or know the reason why. A lot of funny things can happen. Most of them did. I felt much better when John's cow put her foot in the pail. He has been milking for ten years, so accidents do not happen only to "fresh milkers," as they call me.

Tonight I met John's father, and "Ole Ted," Ted Gowlett, and another character who has surely, but as yet secretly, offered her challenge to me. Mr Marshall told me that tonight I was to work on the stack. From the collection leaning against it, Old Ted carefully chose, for its length and its smoothness of handle, a prong for me, then Mr Marshall turned to a peculiar orange contraption which I had not noticed before.

"What on earth is that?" I asked him.

"Tractor – Fordson," he obliged politely, but amazed, nevertheless, at the depths of my ignorance. He stepped to the front of it, and cranked till it fired and drowned out all conversation.

All evening, as I caught great pitches of hay at the edge of the stack, and passed them to the stacker, as I watched the sunset fade from the sky and the cleared hayfield lose the brilliance of its fresh green and the villages on the hill merge into the shadows, I saw that noisy, bone-shaking, fume-belching tractor (for the sweep was bolted to the tractor tonight) bringing in its load and faring forth again. And I vowed with every pitch I received and placed, that I would learn to drive that tractor.

John's father was the stacker and no slovenly work would suffice. The prong must be held a certain way, the pitch of hay placed at the stackers left or right according to the direction in which he worked. I learned that stacking is an art and the rick-builder a man to be respected. I learned, too, how beautiful the silence is when the tractor is shut off, and one by one little bird notes and the sound of settling hay and the rippling of the stream by the hedge come out of the quietness.

When we finally stopped at dark, my hair and ears and shoes were full of hay and I was filled with the sweet scent of it.

We came home through the pasture land where the cows were sleeping, climbed over the stile, and at the gate Gyp, Marshall's beautiful black and white border collie, came out to meet us. I remarked on her joy at her master's return. Mr Marshall said, "It's you she's coming to meet." And it was. So Nunningham has accepted me, and I am at home.

A lad with a wire from Charlie came into the barn while I was milking today. "Seven days leave. Coming to Nunningham." I couldn't finish my cow fast enough to run back to the house. Mrs Marshall assured me that Charlie was welcome and we were all very excited. As he had not said when he was coming I went back to work but I was not the most dependable of Land Girls. Mr Marshall said that I was so excited he thought that it was a poor idea to put me on a rick with a prong. The men teased me unmercifully but all went well.

The phone rang for Mr Marshall just as we came in. The innkeeper at the Woolpack asked him to come to the inn right away. I imagine I was tired or I should have seen the twinkle in his eye as he said, "Hop in the car and we'll have a quick one."

Of course, when we reached the inn, Charlie was there. He had stopped to ask the way and was nicely called for. It has been a gay evening.

July 9, 1940. By the stile, in the hay field
I have been here just over two weeks, so perfect and glorious a two weeks. Charlie had his leave, and we know that wars and oceans make no difference. We walk and talk together and the same quiet bond holds fast. He knows now where I am, how the clouds mass every changing hour and the woods form shady places on the sloping hills. Such finite miniature beauty – a tiny stream, a railed bridge, two planks wide, and railed at each end too, lest cattle stray, and with a great ivy-covered elm sloping over it. Behind a wooded hill rises with its slope a green lawn under the trees. Mr Marshall is running circles below it, whisking over the hay with a side delivery rake.

My little Te Deum is for so many things, above all for Mr and Mrs Marshall. Surely no happier home could have opened its doors to me, and for Charlie's week here with me. We had a day in Eastbourne together, went to market with Mr Marshall, and Charlie helped with the haying. Alec and Dado drove over on Sunday and we all had tea together on the lawn. Suddenly Charlie's week was over. We had a party the night before he left and the next morning I did not milk but took the bus to the train with him and saw him off. No longer did I fear to say good-bye to him. For while we are "hearts at peace under an English heaven," we each have our work. He enjoys caring for his guns and tanks, and I love every stupid cow I milk and every fragrant load of hay we stack, and I love these British folk with their gentle speech and smiling eyes.

We hoed all morning in the pouring rain. Mr Marshall continually told me to go in, but if he and John could stay out so could I. However, I think I shall never become skilled in hoeing. John's hoe slips back and forth with machine-like precision and never changing tempo and the weeds fall cleanly, leaving the young Swedes in straight rows. And he singles as he goes, leaving only the one desired plant. I direct my hoe painstakingly at each sprig of kilk (Sussex for charlock or field mustard) and trail of bindweed and, often as not, rip out half a dozen young Swedes as well. And as for my back, I think I shall view the world permanently from my right-angled bend. Swedes, by the way, are the pale orange-coloured root vegetables which we call turnips in Canada. Here they are mainly used for cattle food. Turnips for human consumption are white and more regularly spherical.

After dinner the rain proved too much even for the men. Se we cleaned out the potato shed and the loft. It was a dirty, dusty, but interesting job. I learned about several farm implements and we collected a beautiful pile of scrap iron for the government.

At three John and I left to fetch the cows for milking. I reached my goal some time ago, increasing one cow each day until at the end of a week I was milking seven and stripping them myself. So at last I am pulling my weight and Mr Marshall leaves John and me to the job.

Mr Marshall's mother came over tonight for tea. That great stack, the first one on which I worked, was on her farm. She brought me a note and a box of chocolates to thank me for helping with her hay. I had only been obeying orders and felt undeserving. How kind is this family, and how proud I am to know them.

I am feeling gloriously windblown and fragrant with hay and sun. We were haying down by the brook today and came home single file along the footpath. It led through a wheat field turning slowly golden, skirted a bank, feathery and blue-green with swelling oats rustling against the sky, a blue windswept sky behind great masses of radiant cloud. Then it turned into the cool wood, which has the cared for appearance of all these English woods. And then out beside the sunny wheat again, bordered with daisies and flaming poppies and growing through a carpet of scarlet pimpernels. I know now that these are unmentionables but my agricultural eye is still untrained and, layman-like, I see only their beauty.

We finished milking early so I cycled to the village, just as I was, in WLA overalls and my old McGill blazer, which Old Ted calls my monkey jacket. I had the hand brakes repaired on Mrs Marshall's bike, bought some chocolate, and paid a shilling for three peaches.

Now a soft rain is falling. Mrs Marshall is sewing. Mr Marshall is out collecting more scrap iron in the barn. And I sit here knowing a weariness and a content I have never known before.

And so the days follow one another, and I slip into the routine of which I am so proud to be a part. Each morning Mr Marshall wakes me. I dress quickly, tiptoe downstairs, put on my shoes which await me in a box just inside the door and try to keep Gyp from barking with delight. Then I collect the milking utensils from the dairy, skirt the fern-fringed pond under the willows, and "un-pinner" the barn door. Sometimes Mr Marshall has appeared by then, or sometimes I go through the barn alone to fetch the cows. The fields slope to the hills and a filmy mist lies in the valley. To the east a row of Lombardy poplars stands on a ridge against the sky and just beyond them is a windmill. In the west, and northerly, arable fields and winding hedges merge in the distance into the hills of the Sussex Weald. I think that that walk in the clear dawn is the loveliest part of the day.

If it is raining, or we are late, the cows are sure to be in the bottom brook fields, giving us an extra ten minutes walk. Gyp rounds them up for us. They are all shorthorns save one, a fool Guernsey who must always be collected personally. We walk back with them with one eye on Gypsy. She has a habit of swinging on the tail of any straggler and if that straggler is a cow heavy with calf, she must be called off promptly. Mr Marshall is silent, planning the day's work, while I plod beside him in my hobnailed shoes and khaki overalls, delighting in the scarlet pimpernels at my feet and the sudden rise and glorious song of a lark. Living in the momentary present, which no matter how momentary is very sweet.

Each cow knows her own stall and we hurry them in, and clip their iron halters. I do feel efficient and conditioned as I squeeze between them or push one aside.

Then we put on our white coats and wash our hands. The cows who give the most milk are milked first and we follow a certain order. Sometimes I sit quietly, my head against a smooth flank, listening to the ping-ping of the milk, streaming and jetting. Sometimes I watch the whitewashed walls of the old barn, and its old rafters and wonder about its history. It is over a hundred years old, an old tithe barn, with a wooden floor across the centre where the threshing was done (Mr Marshall told me that he had found an old flail in the loft) and great doors on each side through which a horse and wagon can be driven.

I finish my cow, dump the milk into the churn, wash my hands and go on to the next, smiling to hear Mr Marshall singing happily to himself behind his cow. Oddly enough, unconsciously and unfailingly, he sings hymns on Sunday but never on weekdays.

Then at seven the chain clinks as the pin is taken out of the huge staple and John comes in. "G'mornin', Mr Marshall." "Morning, John," and "Hi, John" from me to which he replies, "Mornin'," and with a grin, "No feet in t' pail this marnin' then?" "Why John, I'm a good milker now." "And that you are, my girl," from Mr Marshall, and we all get down to it again. My arms ache no longer and I can race to finish first and write the labels for the milkman who calls to collect the milk at eight. And I suppress my laughter at John's muttered invective as we hasten to let the cows out before they inopportunely heed the call of nature and give us a cleaning up job to do. I have learned with success to clap down a tail which begins to rise and push the old girl out in a hurry.

Then I'm off, for I have mash to mix in the tidy granary and the chickens to let out and feed. I always say good morning as I open the slides to let them out of their coops, at which Mr Marshall, coming in to breakfast, laughs heartily. Then I wash the milk pails. Cold water, then hot and soda, and rinse, one brush for the inside and one for the outside, dry them and stand them upside down on the scrubbed table. And so to breakfast and am I ready for it! Then follows the order of the day, turning hay, stacking it, or hoeing if the weather has been wet – the one thing so far which I hate. Mr Marshall is amused and is kind, and I am very spoiled. He says he knows a good worker when he sees one and manages to find another job for me if he can.

I break off at three and go proudly on my own for the cows. Today I left the sunny hay field behind and climbed the gate at the wood, proof that I am not yet truly one of the agricultural community, for farming folk never climb gates – perhaps for an inborn consideration of the gates, perhaps because it requires less energy to open it and walk through it. Similarly, it is characteristic of a farmer always to wear a hat and always to carry a cane. The cane, as everything in farming, has a reason. It can be poked in a field and the soil roughly tested or it can poke out a blocked drain. No farmer walking across his land "of a Sunday" would dream of leaving his cane at home.

But I confess that as I neared the western side of the wood where the sun shone through the leaves, filling the wood with little golden pools, I again climbed a gate. Two rabbits sat up, watched me a moment, and then hopped off. We had thrown one aside earlier in the day which had been killed by the mowing machine. At first I felt miserable about them, but now I realize that killing them is unavoidable. They cannot see in the long grass. The tractor moves fast and the mover cuts clean. Besides, they are infernal pests, one of the three R's: Rats, Rooks, and Rabbits, the farmers' enemies. When I finally got the cows in, fetched the pails and filter, I had milked ten of them before John arrived to help.

Mrs Marshall and I mowed the lawn tonight and Mr Marshall pointed out a hill to eastward where the Saxon camp had stood and where Harold made his last stand at Senlac in 1066. It grew dark early and is now a wild rainy night. Everyone else has long been asleep. I must put out this Aladdin lamp, which is another chapter in my education, and take my candle upstairs where the wind and rain are nearer and comfortable reminders of nights at home, camping under canvas.

July 17, 1940. Somewhere in Heathgate Parish
Mr Marshall is a member of the War Agricultural Executive Committee (WAEC) which has undertaken a thorough survey of all agricultural

lands in England. Each farm or stretch of land capable of cultivation must be made to produce its maximum. The WAEC assesses the possibilities of each farm. Guidance and advice offered on poorly managed farms, if not taken voluntarily, is later enforced. Every rainy day, or spare moment on evenings or weekends, sees Mr Marshall visiting one or other of the farms in his district. When possible I accompany him, mostly because he is kind and knows how much I enjoy driving through these English lanes and having the opportunity to learn farming conditions and problems by hearing them discussed first hand. And secondly, because each farm surveyed entails the filling on of several forms and questionnaires, which I am able to do on the spot and save him time and secretarial work on his return. At the moment I am waiting in his car while he hunts through farm buildings for the owner of the farm. When they return I shall be permitted to walk across with them while they inspect various fields with regard to the ploughing up of pasture land.

I look above a hedge across sloping lawns and groups of chestnut trees to a field of wheat in the valley. A man driving a flock of sheep has just passed, funny jiggley little things, bouncing along with black faces and black legs. Some of them are covered with red patches, so the old trade of Hardy's reddler is still plied. How these days bring books alive to me. Many things which had been merely names before, I now see and use daily, a handbill, a swap (as a sickle is called in Sussex), and now the reddler, an archaic and antipodean figure, today is endowed with reality.

The morning has been beautiful, England's fine misty rain falling softly, which seems unworthy of notice but which soaks to the skin when one works all day in it. It is clearing now, shreds of tattered gray cloud are drifting overhead, and blue mists cling under the trees and along the woods. I can hear a tractor working somewhere out of sight and it is thrilling to know that I could now meet it with some claim to acquaintance-ship.

Later. At Wren Wallop
I am sitting on a gate while Mr Marshall tries to persuade Mr Abbott to plough and utilize a derelict field. Apparently this field has been a local eyesore for many years, and more than that, a menace, as it is full of docks which seed neighbouring fields. I enjoy listening to Mr Marshall.

He's a younger man than all these farmers yet they all seek advice and information from him. He is practical and unassuming, knows the answer, complete with facts and figures, or tells the inquirer exactly from whom he may learn what he wishes. One question he always refers to me – and I am smug about it too!

"What about leather jackets, Mr Marshall?" Leather jackets are the larvae of the crane fly. At this question we both smile, and Mr Marshall turns to me, "You tell 'em, Polly."

"One pound of Paris Green to twenty-five pounds of bran. Moisten with a little water and use before rain or heavy dew."

At the moment Mr Abbott is betting a little spitefully on what he considers the rate of depreciation of a tractor – and now, hooray! Mr Abbott has just given in, very grudgingly. He is going to plough up his field of docks. My Mr Marshall wins again.

Back at Nunningham

This has been an exciting day. It began at 6 a.m. I milked a cow which I had seldom milked before. She is low slung and I was too high on my stool, so I fetched a low box and carried on. Old John Lovell, a local ancient, dropped in for an early morning visit and was muttering something about, "Coo's fut in t' pail." He's well over eighty, speaks very broad Sussex and unless I pay close attention I cannot understand him. So I missed the point of his remark and Mr Marshall said nothing. However I know now. One second later the confounded cow had her foot in the pail of milk. I was too low. Ordinarily when a cow kicks, her foot hits the side of the pail which one can snatch away before it spills. But if one is too low the foot goes inside the pail and, well, as Sussex folk say, "There it is." I have been teased all day. "Polly has no more milk when she's finished a cow than when she begins."

And now for my good news which I have been hoarding. My month's training is nearly over. And so I am due to go to an unknown job. But harvest time is near, so Mr Marshall wrote the WLA to ask if I might remain here another month as if would not be detrimental to my chances of a job. Today the reply came, and I stay.

Today, between high hedges with glimpses of thatched cottages and the level marshes and one splendid view of the castle, we drove out on WAEC business to March Farm, where we found our man and were deploring the state of the "dicks" (dikes) when we heard a plane very low above us. It was a German one. We saw it circling about a mile to the west. Suddenly it dropped four bombs. We heard the explosions and went wild with excitement. Two spitfires appeared immediately, one circled below and one alongside. One or other was lost in the clouds most of the time, but we heard three bursts of machine-gunfire and waited hopefully for the Junker to fall at our feet. Finally the dogfight grew too distant to be heard.

We ran back to the car and drove to the Woolpack where we knew we would hear where the bombs had fallen. Sure enough, Fatty Cornford was there and had just returned from The Merry Harriers near Heath Cross. The bombs have fallen on Cralle Place Farm quite near there. No one was hurt and the only damage was to a barn which was empty.

I have been sitting on my window-sill, watching the sunset beyond the fresh green of the cleared hayfields and picking hay out of my socks, a constant and damnable job.

Tonight a sorrowful and apprehensive Land Girl was to have left Nunningham for her unknown permanent home. Instead she has had a weekend of happiness and content. Yesterday morning we cut hay in the Long Brook Field, and, as it was Saturday, loafed pleasantly till milking at three-thirty. In the evening Mr Marshall took Peter and me with him, and walked down to the Glebe Field, to "put a pole in a haystack." A sheet, a large green tarpaulin, is thrown over the stack for protection from rain until the stack is threshed. The pole goes under the sheet to raise it a little and allow for air circulation. When we came back, windblown and pleasantly tired, I went upstairs to shed my overalls. Mr Marshall called me, rather peremptorily I thought, so hair down and shoes off, I came and there was Charlie, very tired, very hungry, and very broke. He had hitch-hiked from Epsom where his regiment is camping on the downs.

We had a quiet pleasant evening and a good sleep. I did not get up for milking as Charlie had to leave at nine o'clock.

I drove to Ninfield, later in the morning with Mr Marshall and Charlie. Peter accepts me too and, as I have never lived with a young child before, his trust is a new and well-prized possession. There are certain things which he allows no one to do for him save me. "No," he will say, "No, Mummy, Auntie do it." I am sure that my dignity and pride at being an auntie, even a courtesy one, must stick out all over. I carried him through an oat field yesterday and afterwards I leaned against a gate and closed my eyes while waiting for his Dad. Peter said, "Poor Auntie, so tired," at which I smiled and opened my eyes again. "Oh – Auntie wake up." He speaks clearly and precisely and is just two. He slept on my shoulder this morning, content and relaxed. Coming home Mr Marshall said, "See the stocks," and there they were, on Ninfield Green, set up centuries ago by the roadside, with holes for two pairs of feet and shackles for four hands.

Peter and I collecting eggs

We had tea at Chilthurst, Mr Marshall's mother's, and went for the most beautiful drive in the evening. Occasionally over the hills we could see Pevensey and the channel, where every day we hear the sounds of Jerry attacking our convoys. We drove inland, through the tiny village of Dallington with its old houses clustered on a hill about the tall-spired church. Roses and clematis climb over all the houses, beautiful with their heavy timbers and leaded lights. We drove down the castle road but the castle is no more and the hedge too high to see the ruins.

I wish Charlie could have been with us, but having him pop in last night was so exciting. He has gained nearly twenty pounds and swears that I have done the same.

Today I drove the tractor. Mr Marshall stresses the fact that I may say I can drive the tractor but I am not a tractor driver. I can start it and stop it, steer it and change gears, and I have long been able to see to her needs – fuel, oil, and water, but I know little of caring for her and if she refused to go I should know nothing of the causes of her indisposition. But I drove the tractor today.

It was a morning for sailing, fresh, with a clear blue sky and great heaped clouds. All the mighty words apply, towers and battlements and ramparts, rich and brilliant in the sunlight. We hand-raked a little hay field, turning the dry, fluffy crop, then John drove the horse-rake leaving long rows of haycocks. I drove the tractor for Mr Marshall to pitch hay on to the wagon behind, where Old Ted stacked it. There was a strong breeze blowing and the hay was very short and was blown all over. There was much merriment over the ineffectiveness of Mr Marshall's pitching. We laughed and sang gaily until milking time.

Tonight I dressed in civilian clothes and drove forth as Mr Marshall's secretary again. Often as we crossed a hill the sea swung into view, through a gateway or over a hedge, a blue and tranquil sea under a pale shell-like sunset.

I prowled around an old oast-house while Mr Marshall was talking to a farmer. I have seen many here, but this was my first opportunity to explore one. An oast-house is a kiln used for drying hops, usually round, of red brick, and with an inside diameter of twelve to eighteen feet. After rising about sixteen feet the walls taper to a point. Across the top of the perpendicular section is a wire grill, on which the hops are piled. The fire is laid below and the smoke escapes through a vent about two feet wide at the top, which has a cone or sleeve, like the wind-stock on an aerodrome. I was very interested, particularly as I believe that this room in which I am sitting was originally an oast-house. Mr. Marshall has not yet told me the history of Nunningham. I must hold him to it.

This morning was rainy, canceling all our haying work of yesterday, so we spent the day de-carbonizing the tractor. Soon I shall know the old girl inside and out. Later I drew three buckets of water and lost my temper over the rickety well-cover. So I fetched a hammer and nails and fixed that once and for all, and repaired two or three chicken coops into the bargain. This evening Mr Marshall and I rounded up a lot of tackle which has done its work for the season. He drove the lorry and I the tractor. We went down to the Brook Field and loaded the sweep onto the lorry while I hitched the side-delivery rake onto the tractor and brought them back to the farm. We collected a drudge, a queer iron mesh affair, and harrows and a shim, which is a sort of plough-shaped horse hoe, and the mowing machine, all from various fields, and put them under cover in the buildings near the barn, all in the clear evening light, under a pink and blue sunset sky. It was as if we were under a delicately coloured china bowl, which after a gray drizzly day was especially lovely.

We came in, and after a good feed of chocolate, felt very greedy but satisfied. Everyone is in bed and I must go too. These days are peaceful and beautiful, and just over the hill are tank traps and anti-parachute defenses and four miles away the South Coast, which is a forbidden area. Planes pass overhead, Jerries as often as not, and searchlights reach up their long fingers.

The new budget is out. Every garage for miles around was out of petrol today. People are buying before the price rises; everywhere we see khaki and airforce blue. The farmers behind us on the hill tell tales of watching convoys attacked in the channel. We work hard and happily, with occasional rain but mostly glorious sunshine and I feel that come what may these have been spacious days.

The cow calved this morning and we shimmed swedes. I led the horse up and down the rows and Mr Marshall guided the shim. I am not a skilled horse leader, but fortunately old Snowball knows her job and teaches me as she goes along. Tonight I took Gyp for a walk and picked a whole basket full of mushrooms. It is raining again, and we are feeling very flip and casual, filling in WAEC forms on the dining room table with a lot of foolishness. Mrs Marshall and I are trying to persuade Mr Marshall to drive us to Eastbourne and Pevensey tomorrow. We want to have tea at the old Mint House, but Mr Marshall is demurring on the grounds that it is unethical to take young Peter into a danger zone.

A damned cow (and I mean it) kicked me right across the barn today. Other than that there is little to report. The weather remained unsettled and thundery and I spent the afternoon holding bolts and spanners while Mr Marshall and Old Ted overhauled the binder, and cycled up to the village every little while for bits and bolts.

Then at milking time I was walking between two cows to fasten their collars, and suddenly I was in the opposite side of the barn. I have a bruise and shape of Cherry's hoof on my thigh where she hit me, and something like housemaid's knee on the elbow on which I landed.

I hope the time will never come when I grow so contented and conditioned that sensations fail to register. I made a flying visit to the bank today and on the return trip I felt so completely adjusted and at home. I caught the bus as if I had caught that bus for years. I swung off at the Woolpack, walked past the Cock Robin Tea Room to the stile, and home across the short cut. I hesitated at the second stile for a moment, looking around Professionally at the potatoes, well-advanced on my left, and the oats greening ahead. I can scarcely believe that less than two months ago I did not know the difference between hay and straw, let alone wheat and oats. I cut through the gap in the hedge, crossed the garden, slipped the key from its hide-out hook, which informed me that Mr and Mrs Marshall were both out, unlocked the kitchen door, left my purchases on the mangle table, and put on my rubber boots. Cigarette in one hand, milking utensils in the other, I went on to the barn. It is all habit now, but I still retain a delightful glow. I am here in England, Nunningham has taken me to her heart, and we are each dear to the other.

I went through the barn doors, happily swinging my pails, deposited them on stools and churns, and went on to the pasture for the cows, recognizing that I am taking a small part in helping England prepare for what is to come.

August 1, 1940. Nunningham
Mr Marshall, out of the kindness of his heart, feeling that there was little profit and less future in it, tonight gave me my first ploughing lesson. I am amazed and frightened. Never again, when I see a farmer ploughing, shall I think that he is driving along in half somnolent content. "No man putting his hand to the plough and looking back is fit for the kingdom of God." I now understand why. A moment spent in facing backward to see how the furrow looks is the moment the tractor wheel takes to climb out of it. The keeping of a straight furrow seems an impossible feat. A slope or a hollow, or a bump in the field, and away she goes, bulging out to one side or the other. Shrieking at each other over the din of the tractor I tried to ask questions and Mr Marshall to answer them. I gather that on a slope the plough slips down and the furrow slice must be made wider, in a hollow a different lever raises the share to keep the work level. Similarly, over a hump the lever must again be used lest the plough drive through it and cut

very deep. Going up hills or down calls for different plough settings as do changes in the consistency of the soil. All these things, and more, apart from steering the tractor must be mastered. As yet they are merely theory to me.

Steering the tractor was all I could manage tonight. Mr Marshall attended to the levers and guided me in turning. There is a lever which trips the plough in and out of the furrow, as you enter from, or pull out onto, the headland. How do you mark out a field, why do you plough across instead of up and down, all these and a hundred more things I must ask and learn and achieve in practice. Mr Marshall says that tractor driving is not a job for a girl because, though she can pull a wagon around, and run messages as it were, she cannot manage the more skilled jobs. Possibly I cannot, but I mean to try. Not for nothing did this noisy, fume-belcher toss her head at me during my first week at Nunningham. I accepted her challenge, and not easily shall she defeat me.

I am lying in a corner of the Big Pasture, again realizing that I may share in this incredible peacefulness and beauty. I have the hour to spare between lunch and milking time, which is granted on weekends, and I cherish it carefully as did Pippa her day.

Old Cherry, our calf's mother, has come to me, partly out of curiosity, but also to reproach me for loitering here when she is anxious to be led home to her child. The old oak tree which gives me shade and a comfortable back stands on the edge of a grassy hollow which used to be an iron pit, in the days when Sussex was the seat of the iron industry. Now the old pit is a rifle range, taken over by the Home Guard. There is a second pit in the pasture, deeper and forming a pond, around which most of the cows are lying. Those on foot have come over to me and nose me interestedly. Pushing cows away requires more effort than I had bargained for. Mr Marshall was right. He warned me not to make pets of them, which I have done. Each cow gets a bowl full of cake, "kyke," as John calls it, which is a compressed, mostly linseed, high protein concentrate made into half-inch cubes. I usually carry a pocketful for which the cows nudge and nuzzle me as a horse would for sugar. Some little time ago I began to perceive the value of Mr Marshall's warning when the cows which I was milking would try to get their heads around into my pocket. Now I have further proof, for there is little peace for me here in their midst, with one licking my legs and another my neck, while they sniff and push to reach my pocket. Cows do not lick gently like dogs. Their tongues are more like rasps.

I have had two "soul destroying" jobs, as Mr Marshall calls them. Yesterday we were singling kale. Kale is a vegetable used for winter cattle food. This variety, known as marrow, grows up to five feet high, with a stalk as thick as my arm and leafing out at the top somewhat like broccoli. We had been busy haying and had let the kale get ahead of us, so that instead of easily pulling out little finger-sized plants these required a fair amount of strength. The rows were long, the sun was hot, and Old Ted and I spent the whole day at it. During one breathing spell, as we stopped to straighten our backs and roll a cigarette, Ted told me what he thought of the job. "I wouldn't pull kale," he said disgustedly, "for any other bugger but Wal – ter Mar – shall."

Ted and I are great friends and great is my pride in knowing that I may say so. It was he who christened me Polly shortly after I came, partly, I imagine, because he was shy about using my own name as the Marshalls do, and partly because he had no intention of calling a stupid city ingenue, such as I, by the title of Mrs.

Ted tested me in many ways – all the farm equivalents of sending me for a left-handed monkey wrench. Usually I have caught him out, but sometimes only by the twinkle in his eye or the tone of his voice, for squats and speens and spuds are names I have never known. Now no job is too simple or too difficult for Dan to teach me. When I handle a tool awkwardly Dan takes it from me – "'Ere Polly, 'old it this way, look, like this," twisting it dexterously. "And this – now you try it. That's right, turn yer l'il ole wrist, a little more, now you goo on, an' min' ye don't kill yerself." He watches me a moment and then leaves me to it.

Ted is about sixty, lean and sinewy and there is nothing he cannot do well. He is impatient in some ways, with people mostly, intolerant of laziness, stupidity, or snobbery but like Walter Marshall, who is even more impatient indoors, he has infinite time and interest for any work on the farm. Nothing is too trivial to do well. Knocking-off time may come and go but if Ted or Mr Marshall are in the midst of something they will see it through before they stop. "Nothing is worth doing which is not worth doing well," Mr Marshall has often said to me. Rain may be falling heavily, and darkness too, but Ted does not get out his bike and prepare to ride home before he has cleaned his spade and his fork or any tool he had been using or cleaned and covered carefully the farming implement. And he is making it his job to see to it that I become a member of the same thorough, dependable, proud fraternity.

The second soul-destroying job is digging potatoes. Shortly their harvest will be the order of day and now Ted and I are digging a road through them so that the potato spinner may begin its work with no damage.

Today I was given strict orders to be on time for dinner as Mr Marshall had to go out immediately after. Consequently I asked Old Ted for the time. He looked at me severely. "I knowed a little ole party once, always wantin' to git off she was, so I put a spud (a spud is a fork, a four-tined fork, known as a four-speened spud) right through her hand, I did. She couldn't git away fer a cupla days. Her mother asked me where she was – then I 'membered. I'd left Maud – Maud 'er name was, pinned in the 'arms [haulms – tops of potato plants] up there in that ole tater patch. She worn't too bad neither. Bit weak maybe, but she was a'right. People aint 'alf crule enough these days you know. 'Cours they'd arrest yer now. But 'twern't like that one time o'day." All Ted's instructions to me are camouflaged in similar tales.

I was almost buried in hay one night when I got under the grab. We have a pulley arrangement on a pole, with Snowball the old mare attached to one end of the cable and a large wire grab, similar to a dredging steam shovel, attached to the other. Someone fixes the grab into a huge pitch

Taking Snowball to pasture
after a day's work

of hay and leads Snowball away, and up onto the stack goes the hay. Through inattention I let it release its load over me. Ted warned me to keep clear of it. "I knowed a little ole party, one time o'day, got lost in a stack. Never found her till they was carvin' up the stack next winter and they sliced at 'er. Kep' beautiful she did, wunnerful how sweet she was. Course I don't min' if you gits built in – but I was sorry for her. Left nineteen children, she did. When she didn't come home to get dinner they all just pined away and died. Turrible thing, ain't it?"

When I jumped off a stack, via a loaded hay wagon beside it, Ted called sharply, "Don't you never do that again, Polly." I realized then how springy the hay is and how easily one may bounce off again. Ted "knew a little ole party once – she died a-doin' that." He went on thoughtfully. "And you're dead a turrible long time."

My luck was certainly in the day I was sent to Nunningham. The Marshalls, Walter and Kath, are two of the best friends it has ever been my good fortune to possess. We laugh at the same things and we understand each other's silences. Ted is an interesting, amusing, and valuable "mate." But, as never with Walter and Kath, we sometimes misunderstand one another, though in ways that do not matter, as they do not affect our work. For instance, poor Lucy, an old cow to whose presence in the herd I have long objected, finally was pronounced tubercular by the inspector and the "knacker man" was to call for her. Just after milking a day or two ago, a lorry backed up to the big barn door. I told Lucy that it was the best thing for all concerned and patted a last farewell. A rope was fitted over her horns and she was led out on the ramp leading to the lorry. The driver must have been holding the humane killer in his hand but I was too busy, watching Lucy and wondering how the crane on the lorry would be utilized, to notice it. Suddenly the driver shouted, "Stand clear." I thought, "Heavens, Lucy knows me – I needn't worry. I could lead her up more easily than you could, my friend," when suddenly he placed a snub-nosed pop-gun at her forehead and fired. She slumped, kicked, and I let out a cry and ran for Walter and Ted. Walter realized that I was surprised, that I had expected Lucy to depart alive, to be disposed of later. He knew that I shook and cried a little because it was a bit rough to see the old girl, whom I had milked daily, shot down at my feet. I think he felt a little badly too – though it may have been pounds, shillings, and pence which hurt him the most.

But Ted was very scornful. I had reverted to a spineless city wench, which he had suspected all along, scared of a gun, even a dummy pop-gun affair, upset by a dead cow. It was quite a while before he got over his disgust and disappointment and I crawled into my old niche again.

That took place the first of August. I wonder if this will be as exciting a month as July – we have had dogfights overhead almost daily and Jerry's total losses for the month are 240 planes and 600 airmen. These raids over our lands have got our blood up and we are delighted to hear those figures.

We had enough rainy weather, between finishing the hay and the beginning of harvest, to go over the binder completely. Ted and Walter told me over and over how it worked, how the long knife cuts the standing corn as the mower cuts hay, which falls onto the canvas belt on the "table" and is carried up between two other belts and shuffling boards which push and press it, evening the butt ends. They showed me where the arm comes over, threaded with binder twine, and ties the corn in the centre and finally, when the weight of the corn presses the trip, the bound sheaf of grain is shot clear. I followed their descriptions with great interest but even then I was not prepared for my reaction.

It seemed that I had never seen anything so glorious. Ted was on the binder and Walter was driving the tractor. Kath and Peter came down to the corn field to watch the beginning of this year's harvest. As the first sheaf shot out onto the ground all the storied richness of golden harvests came before me. No longer need I know vicarious pleasure, the glory of the harvest was mine A thankfulness, a plenitude, a deep delight filled me. Before me lay the fields of tall wheat, crackling in the breeze. Under blue sky and brilliant sunshine, the tractor firing evenly, the binder clicking and switching and then sheaf after sheaf, so neatly, so quickly, shooting out onto the stubble in long rows – stiff golden wheat, with here and there a cluster of daisies, a few poppies and the lovely but pestilential purple of thistles.

John showed me how to shock and we worked round and round behind the binder. Since then we have cut several fields of golden wheat with no litter at all, and last of all the soft feathery oats, and then on to shocking it, standing the sheaves, not more than six of oats and eight or ten of wheat, to dry before they are stacked. Ted says oats must "stand three Sundays," wheat not so long. There is a little hollow on one side of the sheaf where the knotter depresses the straw. The sheaves are picked up just below the heads of the grain, one in each hand, and hanged down firmly, butts apart, heads mingling, with the little hollows to the outside. John's father is most particular on that point, because if there is rain that hollow forms a little runnel for drainage.

Great is the disgrace if, on the morning after a field has been shocked, many sheaves are found to have fallen. We do have a few each day and Ted and John swear that they are mine. My denials are strong but they know and I know that they are probably right.

Cutting wheat
at Nunningham

August 8, 1940. Epsom, Surrey
I left on Saturday noon to spend the weekend with Charlie, and what a journey it is. First the bus and train changes in Sussex with which now I am familiar, then I find that I arrive in East Croyden station and must taxi, walk, or tram across the town to West Croyden Station for the Epsom train. And after three or four stops change again at Sutton for a very short run into Epsom. All these changes keep one constantly on the watch. There are no names on the stations; the large boards have been removed as Jerry can read them from the air. With time the one-inch lettering can be discovered and deciphered on the backs of benches or under the station eaves just above the "South for Sunshine" posters. But one must, as the English folk say, "look sharp," as there is little time. The trains glide gently to a stop. In one short moment the travelers have left or entered the compartments and the train is away again. At night it is a real game, but English travelers are helpful and friendly. No sooner do I begin to peer through win-

dow blinds searching for the tiny light or listening intently to hear the station master calling his station than some fellow traveler enlightens me, either, "Here you are, then," or "It's all right, you've three more to go." Then I settle back in the darkness, for on coast trains there is no light whatsoever. I may talk a little to my guide in the ghostly blue light which is permitted on inland trains.

Charlie met me at Epsom Station and took me to the White Hart, where I met Howard Graham, who was to be my host for the weekend, and Bill Peacock, a tall quiet soldier from Charlie's regiment.

We all drove to Leatherhead and Dorking and then, after a drink at the White Horse near Box Hill, to the Cock at Hedley. Charlie was exploring the dim recesses of the great open chimney when we were all startled to hear, "Give us a penny,"coming from the shadows. A parrot hung in his cage in the fireplace. Some locals who sat in the window-seat called with a chuckle, "Give him one."

Charlie offered the penny which the parrot took in one claw, saying "Thank you," to which Charlie replied, "You're very welcome."

"Bugger you," said the parrot to the waiting silence in the lounge.

August 10, 1940. Nunningham

Next morning Charlie took me to the camp, on Epsom Downs, just behind the race course, where I met several of the boys, saw their tents and slit trenches and "Boxcar," the company pup who recently delivered thirteen puppies. We walked across the deserted racecourse and met Howard and Jean at the Derby Arms, just behind the grandstand.

I shopped a little in Epsom, hopefully buying a bathing suit. I say hopefully, for all the south coast beaches are barred to the public. Then after tea at Nell Gwynne's tearoom, my train was due.

Charlie at Epsom Downs
race course

To my amusement, when I asked a guard at Sutton on which track the Croyden train would come, a lady stepped forward saying that she lived in Croyden and would direct me. We boarded a train at her direction and after a few miles I noticed a strange station and said, "Mitcham, I didn't come through Mitcham on my way to Epsom."

"Of course you didn't," she said, "We're on the wrong train."

The next stop was Streatham where we got off and came by tram to Croyden. So I seem to find my way about England. However, we enjoyed our meeting and I had my first ride on an English tram car.

I am very weary tonight and suffered from hay fever or, as it should be, oat fever. The sirens have been sounding warnings and all-clear signals all day today. We have no local siren but we hear them follow one another around us from various districts. Walter Marshall bellows, "Shut off that tractor!" and we listen. If it is the all-clear, a long steady note fading to a whine, we start up the tractor and carry on. If it is "Wailing Willie," the rising and falling warning signal, we also carry on but we work watchfully and excitedly. The skies are high and blue and almost constantly filled with spiraling vapor trails. We saw thirty-seven Jerrys in formation today and several hundred black and flashing specks above them, too high to count. Since listening to the news we know that they were returning from the bombing of Croyden. My trip was fortunately timed.

We saw some Spitfires, "a couple or three," as Ted says, disappear among the flight of Jerrys and almost immediately one broke out of formation and came toward the crest of the hill. We saw it dive, sail downwards, dive again, and suddenly tip over the windmill, to crash into the trees. Later we heard anti-aircraft fire but the planes had gone out of sight.

We miss a lot of excitement working with the tractor as we can hear so little and our work keeps our eyes down on the field. Unless the planes are very low or very numerous, we find that we have missed several skirmishes overhead. The men swear that they can distinguish our planes from Jerry's by the hum of the motors but my ears are not too acute, though I do know now which is gunfire and which the sound of bomb explosions.

John told us at milking time this morning that the plane we saw fall was a Heinkel 110. A friend of Walter's captured the pilot. We had quite a raid during the night. It stopped the clocks at two minutes to one. Jerry is making quite a social event of milking. John rides through the village to work and brings us the latest bulletins. Several ceilings had fallen and windows were blown out after last night's raid.

One bomb fell in the park where Kath and I had been to a country fair one evening last week. The beautiful old house was luckily undamaged.

I telephoned Dado and Alec tonight to see if they were safe as there have been raids in the Eastbourne direction all day. A plane was blown up over the town and came down in bits. One pilot came down by parachute. Alec saw him land. The other tried to do so but his parachute failed to open and they took his body down from the ridge of someone's roof.

Sunday is not a day of rest on the farm, but it is a day when pressure is removed. Breakfast is a little later, one leans a little longer on one's dung-spud, talking with no prod of conscience, and the early afternoon is a drowsy vacant time when one disregards the little murmurs of mending or letters or the stronger calls of cycling and the paths through the woods.

Today we began earlier, as John does not come on Sundays and Walter and I do the milking ourselves. I fed the chickens, carried water, and tidied my room before breakfast. Kath slept in a little so I set the table. After we had finished the dishes, when I was washing the milk pails, I noticed that the stains on the filter, which I had thought to be permanent, could be removed by scraping. I spent an hour working on that small job while Walter enjoyed an extended after-breakfast snooze. Then we cleaned out the cow stalls and pumped water, three hundred gallons into the barn tank – a daily chore. I fed the calves, spotted and put away some hay rakes which had been left to rot in the rickyard, and then went into the kitchen to watch Kath dexterously clean a duck.

Sunday dinner is becoming the approved time for air-raids. We no sooner sit down than, much to Kath's disgust, the air is filled with the drone of planes and we troop out to the ridge behind the house to watch the activity. As they roar overhead Walter insists that we run for cover to the chosen spot under the stairs. No bombs fell today but there was a mighty AA barrage. When we returned to Kath's nice dinner, long cold, little time is left for milking. As soon as the dishes are done it is into overalls again and get to it.

We had tea with Walter's mother today at Chilthurst and then made a few WAEC calls. Kath and Peter and I sat talking to Mrs Weldon at

Home Farm, while Walter walked across it with Mr Weldon. Kath spoke of several bomb craters we had seen on the way over, none very wide or very deep. (Walter says that is because the ground is so hard, which also causes the violent explosion.) Then Mrs Weldon asked us if we wished to see a crashed Jerry. It was the Heinkel 110 which we had seen break out of formation last week. Mrs Weldon said that she had been out in the fields with the children when about forty planes came over, very high. She paid little attention until she heard machine-gun fire directly overhead. Then she and the children ran for the orchard to take shelter under the trees. When the dive-bombers had passed they began to walk toward the house and reached the farmyard just in time to see the Heinkel skid over the roof, black smoke pouring from its tail, and make a beautiful landing in the field.

Walter and Ted and I were shocking oats just below the wood to-night. It was a beautiful evening and spirits were high. Ted was full of tales and Walter and I laughed heartily with him. He had just made some remark about jumping over a shock which I said he could not do. The sheaves were very heavy-headed and all of five feet in height. In addition, we had stood them six and eight long as they were ripe and dry.

"You've got duck's disease, Polly," Ted said, "Just like me." And with a sly little smile, only five foot four as he is and sixty years and all, he cleared the sheaves easily. He and I then turned to Walter. Walter is over six feet, but he has a quiet dignity and is usually above such foolishness. However, the night was fresh and clear and the harvest progressing more than satisfactorily and Walter gave us a quick wink and I think surprised himself as completely as he surprised us by easily clearing the shock. My attempt a moment later was a miserable failure. Kath arrived at that moment and joined in the delighted laughter. She had come with a message from Charlie, who had telephoned asking me to meet him at Uckfield. I sat in the midst of my fallen sheaves thinking that that was very disturbing. I could not get to Uckfield tonight, I did not know the way and anyway I could not get back again. Kath said that Charlie gave no particulars but said, "Tell her to meet me at the bus station in Uckfield tonight." Ted said, "You got twenty minutes, Polly, if you want to get that bus. Don't sit there shuckin' out them oats."

I ran to the house, washed, dressed, cycled to the village, stabled Kath's cycle behind the Woolpack, and just caught the bus. I had to change twice. But two hours later, I was sitting on the bench outside Uckfield bus station with ice in my veins. Charlie was not there. Did his phone call mean that he was going abroad? Did his absence mean that he could not get a pass for tonight? He was company clerk and might have called because he had had advance notice and then was unable to get away.

Ten minutes, twenty minutes, half an hour I waited. Charlie arrived ten minutes before the last bus. We ran up to the nearest pub, had a short drink, and I caught my bus. I was sole passenger on the top deck and slept full length across the seat all the way home.

To spend ten minutes with Charlie I had spent four hours traveling, the first two dizzy with apprehension, because he had been studying maps and had decided that it was possible for us to meet at Uckfield in an evening.

August 22, 1940. *In the harvest field*

The corn is all cut. Corn, a word which in this sense comes with difficulty to my lips. Here in England it retains its old Anglo-Saxon meaning of grain, a seed, whereas in Canada and in the United States the sense has narrowed. Corn, at home, means only sweet or Mexican corn, and the collective word for all cereals is grain.

I am sitting on the tractor seat, writing during stops, while I drive the wagon up and down the rows of wheat and then bring the full load close up to the stack. I am not very skilled at pulling up close yet. Ted is stacking on the rick and we have just heard the siren and the distant hum of planes. Ted says that if they come overhead he's for the ladder. "Better be a coward for a few minutes than dead forever."

Day after day now I steer the tractor while Ted or Walter or John load and stack. John's brother and father are added to the team, working on the rick as they did in hay time. We work all morning and on through the afternoon under swift white clouds. The men bring their tea, and Walter and I go home for a short half hour and then work on through the quiet evening till after sunset.

Now they are topping off a stack, so I must wait for the wagon to be unloaded. Soon we shall begin a new stack and work in shifts again. Hay stacks are rectangular, but corn stacks are round. A foot is made, as for hay, of hedge "brishings" or bracken, and then the sheaves are laid, heads in, round and round. Some stacks are begun with a standing sheaf in the middle to keep the sheaves sloping to the sides. The diameter grows gradually to the edge of the roof where the stack begins to taper sharply to a point. The stacker is proud of his judgment when he gauges the stack so that it will be completed by the last sheaf in the field. He has assessed his crop and built his stack exactly.

John passes the last sheaf of the harvest up to me.

To keep the corn dry until the rick is thatched, the top is covered with litter – coarse hay, bracken, or last year's straw. But there will be little thatching this year, as the threshers are due today.

Shortly we shall be off again. Walter is to drive, with John and his young brother Alan pitching, and Old Ted and me on the rick with John's father pitching up. We shall go on until it is too dark to see.

These are rich and gracious days, with Jerry to add seasoning. There has been another form of excitement too. News gets around the village when Walter is about to finish cutting a cornfield. Three or four old chaps with guns turn up, and Kath's brother, who enjoys the fun, her father too, sometimes – a fine-looking old gentleman with snow-white hair and side whiskers. These and a great collection of youngsters appear as the standing corn grows less. With each round of the binder the group presses closer, with guns and sticks. Soon the corn grows too thin to hide the quivering rabbits which huddle further and further from the knife. As the corn becomes a row thin enough to see through, they bolt, the guns go, the boys shriek and fall on the rabbits, another and another of which darts under a sheaf which is quickly rolled off. Shocks are pulled down and the excitement continues until the last blade of corn is cut, the last scared rabbit has bolted. Sometimes the spoils number a dozen, sometimes one or two, but the expectation and the chase bear no relation to the bag.

Rupert Brooke said that, "One misses the dead in the New World." "Look as long as you like and you shall not see a white arm in the foam." I now understand his feeling. These woods are filled with the shades of poetry and history. The ancient Britons who built Pevensey Castle and the Saxons who lived about Battle Abbey found game in our woods and fish in our streams. Nunningham was woodland in their day, part of the old forest of Anderida. William landed and foraged here for his three thousand men. Harold camped behind us and his standards flashed in the sun. There "was a legion's camping place when Caesar sailed from Gaul," and eastward on the downs are "the lines the Flint men made to guard their wondrous towns."

I slept well and soundly last night, and found that Kath and Walter and all the village lay awake because of the sirens and the constant woom-woom of German planes all through the moonlit hours.

September 4, 1940. Nunningham
This morning, rested and light-hearted after two comparatively peaceful nights, we swung through the milking, singing lustily, Walter and John and I. Breakfast was over, pails washed, and chickens fed when suddenly the heat struck us, breathless and humid. We worked all day under a merciless sun, carrying fence posts and barbed wire to repair old fences and build a new one. Half the big pasture is being ploughed for wheat, Walter's contribution to the ploughing up campaign, and a new fence must be placed across it.

These have been busy days, days full of rich, sunny weather, and my arms full of golden sheaves, wheat first and then rustling silvery oats. We spent days binding, and then shocking – or stooking – and lastly, carrying, as the proper term seems to be. Finally a large round stack stood in each cleared stubble of field, fields growing quietly green as next year's "seeds" come through.

I am constantly confronted by the miraculous dove-tailing in farming work. A judicious blend of first-class grasses, clovers, the rye grasses and cocksfoot or timothy, is sown over a young wheat crop, to mature during the spring following harvest. The straw from the grain is utilized, wheat straw for thatching or litter, that is, bedding down the stock in winter, and oat straw for subsidiary feed. The litter is absorbed by cow dung and returned to the land. Hedges are trimmed and the hedge brushings or "brishings" become a base of ricks. Waste from one process becomes a basis for another.

Harvest was no sooner in than the threshers came. Those were the days! Walter wakened me to begin milking at five o'clock. Breakfast was at six-thirty. The threshing-machine arrived the night before and had been set up by its own gang. It is run by a steam engine and we had to fill countless milk churns for its water supply. Then, of course, there was an hour of adjusting extensions – hip boots, wrenches, strong language and much mud, and finally the pump worked again.

With the possible exception of carting peas, threshing is the filthiest, dustiest job I have encountered yet. In addition there is the interminable noise. Two men work on the wheat stack, feeding the threshing machine. Sheaves are dropped to a platform on the top of the machine where the bond cutter cuts the binder twine and tosses the loose grain into the sifting, fanning compartments. The results appear in three places, first the corn, at the back, then the straw which comes out in front, and finally the chaff is blown out underneath.

The corn comes through four chutes, two of head, or whole heavy corn; and two of tail, the light and broken kernels. One man has a full job at the chutes. He hooks empty sacks under each and removes and ties the full ones. There is a special way of tying. And then the sacks are loaded on to a trailer for storage in the granary. A bat is used for lifting and two men can heave the sacks with ease. I have done the job alone, once for a whole morning. A sack of wheat weighs two and one-quarter hundred weights, oats one and a half. Barley weighs two hundred weights and beans and peas the same as wheat, though sometimes fourteen pounds more. Walter told me that the different weights are the result of corn originally having been sold by the bushel, leveled and struck. Then the government standardized the system by selling by weight.

The second process completed by the thresher is the separating of the straw, which is tied in large bundles and pushed out the front of the thresher. One man pitches these trusses to two others who build them into a straw stack. When the corn stack has been threshed a large straw stack is standing in its place. And lastly the chaff, or cavings, is sifted through the bottom of the machine, enveloping everyone in dust, broken bits of straw, and husks. Some poor soul, sometimes I, must spend whole days raking the heap clear lest it choke the machine.

The threshing machine is an itinerant and one is more or less forced to avail oneself of its services at the convenience of its owner. We were fortunate this year: our turn came just as harvesting was over. A slight break might have been welcome but the satisfaction of having the stacks safely threshed and out of danger from incendiary bombs is a wonderful thing. My days while the thresher was here consisted of milking early, pumping, carrying tea to the men two or three times a day, and working on either the corn or straw stack. Afternoon milking was mine alone. To fetch, milk, and turn loose again a herd of cows is an achievement far beyond my dreams of three short months ago.

A day or two ago I heard a lorry lumbering past the house from the farm. Looking up from dinner I saw a quiet look of content pass between Kath and Walter Marshall. "It's the corn," Walter explained to me. The lorry made several trips that day, loaded high with fat, heavy stacks and with each one I felt the same surge of pride. I saw the long hours of ploughing and sowing and harrowing, and the hours I know of cutting and carrying, and too, those of which I know little, of planning and watching and deciding. And now the year's most important crop is harvested and safe.

I spent last Sunday in Eastbourne with Dado and Alec. Alec has finished our dug-out and we opened it officially with cocktails there before dinner. He has creosoted the inside, and the heavy rafters and walls look like old oak. It has a cement floor and built-in seats – old spring seats from a motor car. There are little cupboards set into the walls for playing cards and games and for glasses and bottles. And Alec has put in an electric light system. There are candle brackets for auxiliary lighting, and shelves which, on Sunday, each held a bowl of sweet peas. When I went down the sun was slanting through the emergency exit and our air-raid shelter looked like an old inn with the dark wood and gleaming leather and the sun shining on the sweet peas. Then I saw the pick and shovel on the wall and realized that they were there in case one had to dig oneself out.

We spent a lazy afternoon in the sun and Dado and Alec drove me back to Nunningham. Shortly after they were safely home, the excitement began.

We all sleep downstairs now. Walter feels that it is safer. He and Kath sleep with Peter in the dining room, and I on the livingroom floor with Mrs Marshall, Walter's mother. Peter's cot has been brought down beside the fireplace and every night we bundle down our mattresses and bedclothes, and take them up again each morning at breakfast time. We do not feel that the need for precaution merits having the beds in the way all day.

Mine, a single mattress, is a simple job, but bringing down the Marshalls' big double one is quite a performance.

Sunday night we completed the moving procedure and were undressing upstairs when we heard the planes going over. We all ran out in pajamas and dressing gowns, to our "observation post" by the well. From a black moonless night the change was startling. There were over a hundred searchlights lacing their long probing beams in all directions overhead. As the house stand on a slight rise in a valley and our horizon is far distant hills, we have an excellent view of air activity. The planes were going over in relays, very quickly, and very high. One group of searchlights would follow a flight, hand it over to another reaching set, and then swing back to pick up the following formation. The anti-aircraft barrage was very heavy and almost constant. Suddenly in the direction of London I saw a sheet of light spread and hang in the sky. At the same instant Kath and Walter were exclaiming about flares. For several moments the sky remained brilliant with them, red and white, in various signal groupings, while in all directions lingering sparks of light drifted downwards from exploding shells, and at short intervals the lightning-like flashes were repeated over London. We heard several heavy bumps but the AA fire was so heavy that we could scarcely distinguish the individual sound of bombs.

As there seemed no sign of the raid easing we went to bed, I, accustomed to traffic and night noises to sleep deeply till morning, but Kath and Walter to watch and listen and have but little rest.

We are all sitting around the dining room table, reading or writing. A moment ago I heard a plane's steady drone over the house and said, "There's one." Walter did not lift his eyes from his book as he replied, "I know." There is no need to say more. Saturday afternoon I was invited with Kath to tea with a friend of hers. The house was an interesting one, old, of mellow brick and tiles, built partly over a waterfall. Unfortunately we sat around the fire too long, discussing the modern innovations, so that no time remained to explore the house, or to climb the tower to see the view. We hurried home as it was first aid meeting night for Kath and she was anxious to put Peter to bed – which she did but it was not for long.

I helped Walter with the dugout when she was gone. Churchill's talk had ignited him. No sooner was it over than he was out with pick and shovel, digging into the garden bank. Walter has stoically resisted all urges to build any type of air-raid shelter, considering one useless unless we slept in it every night. But now, with invasion imminent, and with us in the invaders' path, the picture is different. We may have to dig in while the battle rolls past us.

It was a blowing, darkening night as I filled sandbags. I thought of Nunningham and of how I have grown to love it and of how all the electric gadgets, the oriental rugs, and the planned kitchen which we had seen during the afternoon left me uninterested and unwarmed. I remembered that when we came down the lane and the long gray house took shape against the misty hills, Walter and Gyp at the gate to meet us, I felt again a sense of peace. I pushed Peter's pram into its corner and stood still. Here was no anxiety over a scratch on a polished table, or a rubber heal mark on gleaming tiles. There was no unmistakable pride over the possession of a bathroom or of back stairs. There was just Nunningham, her dreams and growth slowly maturing, just the little corner of England that is home, to me, Gyp and Peter, Kath and Walter, paths and woods I knew, the dark shadows of the barn in the early morning, the silhouetted well's windless against the sunset. I could not bear the thought that Nunningham should suffer and I hated the scars in the bank that we were making.

It was growing steadily darker and I was holding sacks for Walter to fill when suddenly – BOOM! – in the next field to us, and we saw the long column of smoke. Walter ducked, pulled me down, then gasped, "Get that boy!" I ran in and upstairs in the dark, picked up Peter, throwing a shawl around him. It was quite dark now so I dared not take a light as we had not blacked out. I sat by the chimney in the big armchair. Walter drew the curtains and lit the lamp. No other bomb fell, there was no other sound. No plane had gone over before the explosion so we decided that it must have been a time bomb. Kath returned and we had cocoa and a sandwich, lugged down the mattresses, and went to sleep. We discovered this morning that our bomb had been a Land Mine, set off by the LDV's (Local Defence

Volunteers) for experimental purposes, and we were furious because we had not been advised.

It was a rainy morning. When we went for the cows Walter strayed off to see what damage the bomb had done, so I milked alone till John came. The rain grew steadily worse and after breakfast when it became obvious that nothing much could be done, I made a dentist appointment and cycled to the bus. The coast towns now are very lonely places. Hastings and Bexhill are being evacuated and Eastbourne has long been devoid of children.

When I returned Kath was busy pasting strips of cloth on the windows according to the BBC anti-splinter recipe, and not too happy about the problem it would cause when window washing. We talked of the day when we could remove it. "We won't remove it." Walter was in the easy mood of an active man on a rainy day. "When that time comes we'll jolly well smash the windows."

The work on the dug-out goes on. Kath and I are sitting under the apple trees tonight, while Walter and our Michael dig. Walter explains that it will be timbered, then recovered with corrugated iron to protect us against falling dirt from the sandbags above it.

"Of course," says John hopefully, "It ain't no use against a direct hit." Walter laughs and asks cheerfully, "But why should the Old Man pick this spot to drop an egg?"

The sun is warm, and the breeze fresh. Great columns of white cloud, full of sunlight and gray-blue shadows, are moving across the sky. I am on top of the bank, with apples bumping on my shoulder, and Gypsy, soft black and white, at my feet. All the little fields lie golden inside their hedges and we hear occasional planes and spurts of machine-gunfire overhead.

Later

Walter announced that the dugout was completed. Kath and I crawled through the sandbag maze and sat politely on the seats provided. We were very interested but felt formal and somewhat like guests, while Walter and Ted strutted about, proudly explaining how strongly the roof was built and how the bank formed the best of buttresses. We heard a plane overhead. Unconsciously, we filed out and stood idly watching it as we talked. Then Ted gave one of his snorts of rage.

"Look at them two b—'s," he said. "Come on – " I just had time, as we were shoved back into the dug-out, to see two bombs, seemingly a yard apart, released from the plane. Walter ran frantically to the house for Peter, then stopped and fell flat. The two explosions were fairly near but not close enough to rattle the windows. I think we all realized, after Ted's shout, that the plane was moving westward and was past us when the bombs were released.

I wonder if the shelter will be of any value. Will we ever be in it if that stray comes our way? But Walter would say that it was not built for that purpose. It is there in the bank, for us to go to ground, "If the Invasion Comes."

Kath and I scored a small victory* today over Walter's cautious and dutiful desire to "stay put." I have been begging him for a long time to let us all go out to dinner some Sunday. He weakened sufficiently, after breakfast, to allow me to call the White Friar's Inn to make reservations for today.

We rushed through the work in the barn, washing cow stalls and feeding calves, and rushed in to dress. By then Walter was regretting his decision to leave home. Kath had dressed Peter and was bathing herself in the kitchen. Walter and I stood in the sunshine, talking through the open door. He felt that all was not well. Something was in the air. We finally agreed to abide by one proviso – that he drive up to the village for news and if there was anything in the wind we would defer our trip. Kath and I could see that he was very disturbed, and though we did not wish to go against his judgment, we could see no reason for his fears.

I was in the bath when he returned, the old tin bath filled from the steaming copper. Walter banged on the door.

"You'll have to wait," I said.

"Wait? – Oh no I won't. Get out of that bath, my girl. You want to go, not I."

"We can go, then?"

"I imagine so."

---

* How small a victory we learned much later. That Sunday was September 15th, known in history as the Battle of Britain Sunday.

"Kath – Kath, we can go! Come on in Walter, I'm respectable."

We drove through the winding lanes, dined in an old paneled room with intricate timbered beams, sat in the sun in a formal garden and Peter and I lost ourselves in the narrow turnings of boxwood maze.

Planes flew over, high, shining specks in the blue sky. Again and again we heard the steady humming throb as they went inland in large formations. At last, when the sound of machine-gunning told us that our boys were up to meet them, Walter could keep still no longer.

"Come on, girls, it's time to get back for milking," was all he said, but Kath's eyes met mine. We knew that he meant he must take us home. To have his farm and his family apart from each other was too great a responsibility.

Some time ago, when we were threshing, I was pitching on the straw stack when some temporary trouble with the machine gave us all a ten-minute break. I was about to climb down to have a cigarette (no cigarettes on stacks) when I heard old John Lovell, who had been bond-cutting, talking to Ted. Ted had been pitching off the corn stack, which was now level with where John was standing on the platform of the thresher. He was leaning on his prong, giving the impression that he was bored by John's tale but too lazy too move out of hearing.

John speaks very slowly, mumbling his words under his long white mustache. I understood that he had been down on the marshes one morning during the early days of the raids and some planes had gone over.

"Oi seen them pla—nes goo over, but Oi never kno—ed they was Jer—ries, till Oi heard the bu—m fa—ll." Ted caught my eye and winked and just then the threshers set the machine going again and the incident was more or less forgotten. Though Walter and Kath both heard the story.

Last night I was awakened at three-fifteen (I had put the flashlight under the bedclothes and looked at my watch) by the successive waves of Jerrys overhead, en route again to poor London. I listened for a minute to their distinctive woom, woom and then suddenly I heard swish, and a prolonged hissing noise. I tensed immediately. At last they had found us, here it was – incendiaries! That is all one can hear, just a swish, as they spurt and flare a minute. One is not dropped alone and so, as I was certain that there was one on the roof, a tile roof about which I was not worried, I jumped from my pallet on the floor, to see if there were any on the stacks, before I alarmed the household. As I jumped, I caught one toe in the other pajama leg and went down with a crash that shook the house.

I listened, still no sound in the house, still the interminable hum of planes. Picking myself up, I drew the heavy curtains and looked out, to see bright starlight, still trees and the sleeping valley.

I tip-toed back to bed, explained to "Grandma" (who comes up from her lonely farm every night to sleep), and we giggled with relief for a little while and were soon asleep again.

I was up at six and, lest I disturb Mrs Marshall, dressed in the dark and tip-toed through the dining room to wake Walter. Now that he and Kath must sleep with Peter, the alarm clock has been surrendered to me. In the kitchen I put on my rubber boots, drew the bolt softly, and Gyp and I collected the pails and went through the barn for the cows.

It was a misty morning with no sunrise and the cows vague shapes on the horizon. I have learned to bend and squint along the sky-line to count their nebulous forms. I had milked three or four cows before Walter arrived, just in time to get into his white coat before John came in. We all milked silently for a little while, than I heard Walter and John discussing the night's activity and John's denial that anything had fallen nearby. As John went out to the loose box to milk a cow that had recently calved Walter said, "Well, one fell, John, and it was close 'un too, because it shook the house."

As I walked past John to pour my full pail into the churn I said, "But it wasn't a bomb, it was me." And I told him.

He must have told Walter because I heard them both chuckling, and later when I was pumping up the barn tank. Walter winked at me over his shoulder, "I heard a bu—m fall," he said slowly, as he took his jacket from the nail beside the barn clock.

Life these days is little else but potatoes and mud. Walter has engaged a Mr Foord and his two sons and two horses to help lift the potatoes. With John and his brother and dad, and Ted, Dave Hunnisett, who is of Ted's vintage, and two others from the village and me, we are twelve. Mr Foord drives the spinner up and down the rows and the potatoes are whizzed out of the ground and hit a mesh screen to fall back along the rows. We grovel along, working in pairs, each pair with a Sussex trug basket. When the trug is filled we shoot the potatoes into sacks which stand at intervals beside the row. Each pair of workers has so many feet of the row and no sooner has he cleared his segment than the spinner has been down the next row and potatoes lie thickly as far as one can see again. And woe betide one if one lags, or the horses must stop behind one and wait. Such is the height of shame!

It is a long, dreary, back-breaking job. We have had wet weather. The trug picks up a heavy layer of mud. Boots develop two- to three-inch soles, which, no sooner has one scraped them off, adhere again. Fingernails are completely ringed with black and one's hands dry and crack. Gloves are useless as they are soon wet and then thick with mud. Nevertheless, when the long day is over, when I have fed the chickens and watered Mr Foord's two beautiful Clydesdales and turned them out into the pasture, riding one and leading the other, when Walter lets me drive the tractor while we go back to the "tater field" and he and Ted load up the sacks which have been filled during the day and we store them in the potato shed, then as we say good-night in the twilight, we all feel pride and satisfaction. There is not the glory of the corn harvest in the humble potato, but as we turn towards home, in the dark which comes early now, there is a comfort in the knowledge that we have safely stored five or six more tons of spuds. And the warmth of the fire and Kath's quiet welcome, her flaxen head lifted from her mending, seem doubly sweet.

While we were "tatering" this afternoon, working in a swift mechanical daze, Walter ran across my vision waving and pointing. One by one we all saw him and ran headlong for the hedge for we saw what was driving him. A small shining plane had left the formation high overhead and was diving straight for our little group on the sloping field. We all ran, crashed into the holly hedge, muttered disgustedly at the prickles, and crouching, looked up, expecting to breathe our last amongst a shower of machine-gun bullets. Just before the plane reached us it pulled out of the dive, rose sharply, and plummeted straight down to crash a mile or so away on the other side of the village.

As it went low over our heads, we had seen the circles on its wings, gasped with relief, and run from the hedge cheering. Then the smoke poured from it as it rocketed up and we stood quietly and helplessly watching. No one spoke as it crashed and we went silently back to work.

October 3, 1940. Nunningham
The potatoes are lifted, for which we all give thanks, but now they must be sorted, seventy tons of them. It is a relaxing comfortable sort of job after the hustle of lifting them. There is no more working at top speed to clear your patch before the spinner is upon you again. Here we move slowly, working under cover. John empties one sack into the large sieve or riddle. Any too large to go through go into a sack. Those are "wares," the best potatoes, and are weighted for sale. Ted has the smaller riddle. Those which go through are "chats" the smallest of all, and we feed them to the cows. The middle size, which will not go through Ted's riddle, are seed potatoes. I weigh and tie up as the sacks become full, stacking them in rows, and Walter carts them away on a trailer. Everyone is pleased to work quietly and I listen delightedly to the tales and arguments I hear.

I have been wearing my heavy Land Army boots lately as we have had wet weather for some days. When I complained that my feet hurt Ted said, "Wash 'em," and chuckled, "Walter, you tell Polly about ol' Jim." Jim, I learned in time, had worked for Walter's father, and was a very unsavoury character who was constantly complaining about his feet. One day Mr Marshall suggested to him that he try a handful of salt in the water when he washed them. Jim looked blankly at him.

"No trick to it, Jim," said Walter's father, "just put a handful of ordinary salt in the basin and soak 'em."

"You mean wa—sh 'em?" said Jim in amazement.

"Of course I mean wash 'em."

"Well I dunno's about that," Jim said uneasily, "I ain't washed 'em for years and years."

This morning after regular milking, chickens, and breakfast at eight, I filled three churns to take by trailer to Dave Hunnisett who needs it for thatching the big hayrick down in Hollytree Field. I lingered a little watching him rake out his long bundles of selected straw and climb slowly up the ladder to work.

It rained gently all day and we all riddled potatoes till John and I left at milking time. I was adjusting the disc in the filter when BOOM, BOOM, BOOM – three bombs fell just over the hill. They always come on rainy days, the dogs, sneaking over just above the clouds. I ran in to Kath and Peter, but we heard no more so off I went for my cows. Planes circled overhead for some time, but though John and I made several surveys we saw nothing and no more bombs fell.

Last Monday was the Marshalls' wedding anniversary. Grandma Marshall and I were anxious to plan a surprise for them. A party was out of the question as we are so far from the village that no one would care to wend his weary way home in the blackout. Nor would any of Kath's friends leave the responsibility of their own young children to anyone in these disturbing times.

We decided to have our own party. Grandma would make a cake and some sausage rolls and I would get new mats for the kitchen which I knew Kath wanted. How to get them presented the problem. Walter would not allow Kath to go far from the farm because of the air activity so I could not suggest a trip to town. And going to the village was equally difficult as Walter has a few necessary calls and usually does our shopping for us.

However, I did manage to find an excuse and cycled up one rainy morning. I bought the mats and also a cheap kettle, the only one to be had. Kath has a lovely copper one but it requires a lot of polishing and Walter complains of its slow-motion spout. I left them at the store and arranged that John should pick them up and hide them in the barn. We later put them in a sack and hid them in the loft.

After milking on Monday I brought the sack down and hid it under a pitch of hay. When Walter came in to tea I thought he looked amused but he said nothing. Our surprise might have been given away had not Charlie telephoned just then. He was cycling, was about five miles away, and would we save him some tea? While we waited for him, Grandma and I held a hasty consultation and decided to keep our surprise till supper time. "Supper" in English country life is the equivalent of our bedtime snack and often, especially when we have been working till ten-thirty, is a very substantial meal.

Charlie's arrival added the spark which lifted our little party onto the plane of real festivity. I had bought a bottle of sherry and Grandma had made sandwiches as well as sausage rolls and a cake. Kath was pleased with her gifts. Walter had discovered them, heaving a prong into the hay while feeding the calves, hence his look at tea time.

Charlie had great news. He expects to have leave shortly and we hope to go to Scotland. And it must come soon, for my time here is over, the harvest is safely home and the potatoes too, and any day I may hear that I am to go off to my new job.

Charlie had to leave at five o'clock in the morning. It was a true soldier's farewell. The alarm went off while it was still pitch dark. We dressed and tip-toed past Kath and Walter, asleep on the dining room floor. I prepared Charlie's breakfast by candlelight and then drew the bolt softly. I stood at the garden gate in my old Land Army overalls and waved good-bye as his tall khaki figure disappeared in the chilly, gray shadows of dawn.

October 19, 1940. North British Hotel, Glasgow
Charlie's call came through the day before yesterday and I met him in London, and also met Penny, Corporal Andrew Stanton Prendergast. "His leave began at 0800 hours, with mine," Charlie explained. "He's coming with us." Our holiday mood was firmly established when, after greeting me conventionally, Penny gravely drew from behind his back a corsage of chrysanthemums, each as large as a cabbage. I am just five foot. Penny waved a conjurer's hand and a bootblack who, incidentally, was sharing our mirth, produced four enormous pins and I was duly attached to the chrysanthemums. The boys added my baggage to their own and we marched out of Victoria Station with all Britain at our feet.

Our train was due to leave at 7:15. The plan was to take our luggage direct to King's Cross to be free of it. We were amazed, as we crossed London, to see the ordered and controlled manner in which the unbelievable bomb devastation is being cleared away. Squads of men were at work everywhere refilling road craters and demolishing dangerous buildings.

At King's Cross we found that there was a relief train leaving immediately and we felt it wise to take it and so be away from London before dusk, partly because if there is a raid on the train will not depart and partly because one has, when on pleasure bent, no right to chance injury and give the workers and wardens extra work.

The siren went just after we had pulled out. We held our breaths but the train did not stop. Before we were beyond London we had to draw the blackout curtains and from then on the journey was long and tedious, for us and for our double ration of compartment companions, soldiers, sailors, and airmen.

We changed trains at York and had two hours to wait. We felt our way between walls and buildings in the dark rainy night in search of food. Ultimately we reached the hotel to which we had been directed – or perhaps it was another.

We were to have had an early night last night but the small matter of Penny's sprained ankle decreed otherwise. We buttoned up our collars and braved the downpour in search of a chemist's shop. Then with Penny's ankle comfortably strapped and our coats whipping around our wet legs, we decided that a toast was in order, a good stiff toast to Bonnie Scotland in her own Scotch whiskey. And would you believe it, we tried five pubs, five large urban pubs, before we could get a foothold in one! We agreed that Glasgow on a Saturday night was the drinkin'est town we had ever struck. The pub into which we finally managed to squeeze was a huge place. It had three large horseshoe bars in the middle of it and I am sure it was an hour before we managed to come into direct contact with one of them. This was brought about because suddenly we found ourselves in the midst of a welcoming clamourous crowd.

"Good evenin'. Good evenin' to ye."

"My brother went to Canada."

"My son is in Canada."

What'll ye have? What'll ye have?"

The Canada patches which Charlie and Penny wore on their shoulders were the "Open Sesame" to the hearts of these Glasgow men. Sparkling little glasses of whiskey appeared on the bar, as far along as I could see. It seemed that we were the first members of the Canadian Forces who had been so far north, and it seemed too, that the warmth and affection which our Dominion holds in the hearts of these Scottish men is second to none. It was much later when we parted, with many goodnights and pledges of goodwill.

The boys decided, on our return to Penny's room, that so much Scotch must be followed by the inevitable beer chaser. I, a simple milkmaid, could no longer endure the torture of my confining foundation garment and had withdrawn into the bathroom to remove it. A sharp knock sounded on the bedroom door just as I returned and, surreptitiously, I slid my girdle under Penny's pillow.

My deep breath of relief was swallowed in a gulp of astonishment. The door opened silently and an apparition, such she certainly seemed, glided into the room. She was six feet tall and her black skirts touched the floor. Her pleated cap and long apron strings were stiffly starched and shone like white china. She had sharp black eyes and a look of disdain on her motionless face. Her white-cuffed hands held a small tray with six splits on it. When Penny took the tray her hands fell to her sides, and with head held high she turned, as if on oiled castors, and with no sway of her skirts, no evidence of walking, she glided smoothly out of the room. We looked at the beer, at each other, and it was a long time before we could stop laughing.

The night was still young. There was an old sailor in the hotel bar which we visited next with a smooth, full moon face and a white fringe of curly lamb's wool whisker bordering his chin from ear to ear. We delightedly watched his vain but good-humoured efforts to fish the red and green cherries out of the bottom of his glass.

Later in a jubilant moment, Penny kissed me.

"Penny kissed me, Charlie." Charlie winked at me.

"I know," he said, "Leigh Hunt." And we linked arms and marched through the corridor chanting:

"Penny kissed me when we met,
Jumping from the chair he sat in;
Time, you thief, who loves to get
Sweets in to your list, put that in!
Say I'm weary, say I'm sad,
Say that health and wealth have miss'd me,
Say I'm growing old, but add,
Penny kiss'd me."

At the end of each line we picked up a pair of boots from someone's door and put them opposite another door where there were no boots.

But the highlight came next morning at breakfast. The waiter, a very punctilious waiter, had stepped up beside Penny and offered an

impressive gilt-crested menu. Penny waved it aside and began to un-
button his tunic.

"While I think of it," he said, "You forgot something last night."
He drew forth my girdle and passed it across the table.

"You left this under my pillow."

The waiter, with a deeply injured look, walked sadly around the
table to Charlie, who managed to stife his laughter and order breakfast.

Truly, when we "have a couple o' drinks on a Saturday night, Glasgow belongs" to us.

Cousin Elspeth met us at the bus terminal and from beginning to
end it has been a perfect day. We drove along the Clyde, looking down
over hospital ships and destroyers, and Charlie pointed out where he
had docked nearly a year ago. We left the bus at Tarbet, on Loch
Lomond, and at the hotel found that we were too late for breakfast
and too early for lunch. We had a sandwich and walked the eight
miles along "the bonnie, bonnie banks" from Tarbet to Ardlui. There
was a strong wind blowing with, as Elspeth said, "a smir of rain."

Through the madly tossing pine trees we could see the spume flying from the white crests of the waves on Loch Lomond, with high
gray-blue walls of mountain beyond. We were unable to see Ben
Lomond through the rain and low cloud. Occasionally the mists
would draw away and reveal magic little islands on the long vistas of
folding hills, and then they would be blotted out. We passed a boy
and a girl cooking bacon under an overhanging rock. We hung, prac-
tically by our heels, to drink from an icy mountain burn. Elspeth
showed us where Wordsworth met his "Highland Girl" and I too,

"Methinks till I grow old
As fair before me shall behold
As I do now, the cabin small
The lake, the bay, the waterfall."

Night, inky black night, had closed in completely when we reached
Ardlui. Fortunately the inn abutted on the road or, blinded by sheets
of rain, we should have missed it. There was no sign of a light within
which did not surprise us. We had become accustomed to finding en-
trances through many ingenious blackout systems. Dark and desolate
outside, the interior, when we had found a way in, seemed even more
forlorn and melancholy. We wandered through dark corridors knock-

ing and calling but no one answered us. It was an uncanny, mysterious place. We felt our way through doors and hallways and every door we opened caused a draught. Finally, following a glimmer of light, we opened a door which led us into a vast kitchen. The little girl who was sitting beside the fire showed neither surprise nor welcome. She led us through her ghostly inn to a large empty dining-room and lit the fire which was already laid.

We sat on the floor before a shiny brass fender and ate ham and eggs and scones and honey. A framed address hung beside the mantel stating that Queen Victoria had dined in the same room. We wondered if Her Majesty would have minded that we ate with so little state. We had walked eight miles through wind and weather and would have perished had we sat even as far from the fire as the nearest table. I was glad that only the Queen's menu hung on the wall. Her portrait would surely have been disapproving and disconcerting.

We had to walk a little way in heavy rain for the bus. Sleepy, wind-blown, and very happy, we returned to Glasgow about ten o'clock. Elspeth and I sent the boys to sleep together and intend to talk for hours.

October 26, 1940. Nunningham
Our glorious week has ended. I spent our last day in Glasgow shopping with Elspeth. I have been here in England for nearly six months now, with clothes for only a month's visit, and while I could not help feeling that we were seeing very little of Glasgow, the rain continued steadily and it was too foggy to see anything anyway.

We met the bus for dinner, at Whitehall, and were amused at a naval officer who looked sternly down his nose at Charlie for ordering a German hock.

Our train left the next morning at five o'clock. We could find neither taxi, tram, nor bus and stumbled through the black rainy night with our baggage. Elspeth looked sad and lonely at the station. She had insisted on coming to see us off and we hated to leave her behind in the mist and the rain. So often a hope and a friend fail one. But, as she wrote to me today, "Somehow I wonder when folks take up a thread of friendship again. But there is simply no doubt in my mind."

We slept till after daylight on the train, breakfasted, and then stood at the windows, too excited to remain seated, watching crag after crag, moor land and sheer ribbon-like burns, falling from heights lost in the clouds. The colours were so beautiful, yet so muted after Canada's flaming autumn brilliance. Foaming streams rushed past the train, little black-face mountain goats clung to the hills, and wonder of wonders, as we alighted at Fort William, the clouds parted and we saw Scotland in the sunshine for the first time.

With Charlie at Fort William

Elspeth had told us to find John, her brother, who is an engineer with digs in Fort William. When we reached the house his bright and alert landlady said that of course she had room for us. Charlie and I were given a room which looked over Loch Linnhe, where two Sterling bombers flashed in the sunlight.

We set out immediately to climb Ben Nevis. His 4406 feet interested us little. We did not care if we reached the top but we felt like climbing. We bought bread and cheese, ham and olives (rationing seemed to be no problem in Scotland) and then, because the hour was late, we took a taxi to Spean Bridge and stepped out gaily into the rough wild country and the wonderful sunshine.

The pathway which leads to the ben is worn and wide and, though steep and winding, easy to follow. Rushing torrents roared beneath us. We passed giddy little gray-faced Cheviots, with light feet and swaying wool, and the friendly rough-coated Highland cattle, with their broad-sweeping horns, and Aberdeen Angus with no horns at all. The Highland cattle were easier to approach and stood to be scratched more contentedly than my own shorthorns at Nunningham.

Our feet were soon wet through from spongy moss and peat bogs. Ben Nevis himself and all his gentle-looking neighbours were lost in mist. There was no view. We climbed until we were chilled and misted ourselves with the clouds settling upon us and then decided that though the air and climb were good, somehow this was not the day for our meeting with Ben. We spread Penny's gas cape, ate our lunch quickly, wrung out our socks, and began the easy descent.

We passed some tinkers at the bottom, cooking over an open fire beside the high arch of the bridge – shades of "Romany Rye." I wanted to cross over to speak to them but Charlie hurried me on.

John met us on our return, and we sat by the fire, talking far into the night, often unsure of John's meaning, as he poked quiet fun at us in his burry Scottish voice. One time he told me to "mind the ashtray as it was a bit shuggily." That conveyed exactly nothing to me.

"It's shuggily," John explained. "Coggily, ye ken, a mite wobbly."

Next morning we drove through Fort William and John nodded to every passer-by. I said, "It's a good feeling to have lived in a village long enough for all the folk to greet you."

"Och, aye," replied John. "'Tis bonnie."

He drove us that day along Loch Linnhe and Loch Ness, past Fort Augustus, now a Benedictine monastery, and past Castle Urquhart, a stern ruin rising from a rocky point on Loch Ness. Whoever brought disaster upon Castle Urquhart deserved his victory. I believe that John said that it was Edward I. To have stormed that cragged and barren shore needed fortitude and genius.

We saw no sign of the Loch Ness monster. John said that it was his belief that he appears only on pay nights.

After lunch at Inverness John drove with careless speed along our road, which twisted and veered between dizzy heights and sheer cliff edges. In one spot two ancient Scots in smocks and tam o'shanters and long plaid scarves barred our way. They were trying to load a deer onto a little donkey. They struggled for a while and rested for a while, blocking the road completely. Charlie and Penny helped them thanklesssly.

John, Penny, and I at Inverness

Charlie and I on Carr Bridge

We stopped at Carr Bridge where the road crosses the new single span and walked a few feet downstream to the arch of the old one, still serviceable, with its beautiful curve a perfect semi-circle of smooth cobble-like stones.

We passed Ruthven Castle just as sunset was fading. It stands, another fairy-tale castle, with twin towers on a high mound, in the midst of quiet pasture lands. James VI, later James I of England, was imprisoned there and there is tale of a lover who leapt from one tower to another to avoid discovery.

The next day was our last and John offered to drive us to Crianlarich to meet our train. Mrs McNab sat darning Penny's socks while we made our plans. When I said, "No, thank you," to porridge, she said, "Then you'll have no eggs and bacon." I had porridge.

My Scotch blood throbbed as we drove through gloomy and forbidding mountains at Gencoe. Someday I will return, and if one of the small white cottages will have me, I will learn to know these rugged hills and the story of their people, who were my people. It was there that the proud MacDonalds were treacherously slaughtered by the Campbells. We drove through narrow passes and under the shadow of the Three Sisters.

At Kinloch Rannoch, the lake, though it was a misty cheerless day, seemed friendly and restful and brought out, in sharp contrast, the dreary and barren desolation of the Moor of Rannoch. Here and there gray skies glinted on little squares of water where peat had been cut. We saw ptarmigan, grouse, and pheasant. Charlie took a picture of four little stags.

We waited for our train at a tiny station above a rushing stream and regretfully watched it approach between towering snow-capped peaks. Again we stood at the windows, the glorious Scottish Highlands fading in the evening light, with here a turreted castle and there a deep gorge until, as we neared Glasgow, we saw again the silhouettes of destroyers against the last bars of light in the sky.

Our journey to London took from 4:50 p.m. until 3:30 a.m. the following morning, with again no sleep in the crowded compartment. Eventually we had orange juice and bacon and eggs at Lyons Corner House, when Penny called the waitress and said brightly, "Bacon and eggs for three."

She looked questioningly at our empty plates and stood silent. Penny repeated his order as if she had not heard. Slightly confused, but conditioned to taking orders, she took our plates and returned with the bacon and eggs.

The siren sounded when I was in a little shop in Piccadilly. The shop girl started and disappeared, to some subterranean shelter, I suppose. Nothing happened and I went into the street to see a little man nailing a "Business as usual" sign onto his window, which had been bombed out the day before, while still the warning wailed on.

We saw department stores with a floor or two missing or a corner knocked out, but trade being briskly carried on in the basement. The bus in which we rode had only two glass windows remaining, and they were covered with shatter-proof netting. We made our first acquaintance with Billy Brown, of London town, the little man in the bowler hat of government cartoons. Here he was sketched pointing to a torn corner of the window netting and saying,

> If you'll pardon my correction,
> That stuff is there for your protection.

Underneath this some wag had penciled,

> I'm quite aware of that, old top,
> But I can't see my bloody stop.

A similar parallel is to be seen on rural buses, where a modernistic poster demonstrates the proper way to signal a bus to stop in the dark.

> Hold your light down, in your hand,
> The driver then will understand.

Again there is a penciled comment,

> I know he will understand, the cuss,
> But will he stop the bloody bus.

But the prize rhyming jingle is a heartfelt plea from the fuel conservation people, who beg that:

> If it's heat that you desire
> Poke the missus, not the fire.
> If you lead a single life
> Poke some other bugger's wife,
> Poke his wife or poke your own,
> But leave the bloody fire alone.

At Victoria, where my train left before Charlie's, the first person we met was Alec. It was a happy meeting for Charlie and I were glad to know that he and Dado were still safe. We traveled together and at Haywards Heath I went with him to the garage for his car, and he drove me first to Uckfield, where we had tea at the Maiden's Head, and then home to Nunningham.

If you've news of our munitions KEEP IT DARK Ships or planes or troop positions KEEP IT DARK Lives are lost through conversation Here's a tip for the duration When you've private information KEEP IT DARK!

Penny pinched a copy of this for me

I had missed a lot of excitement here. Three bombs fell in the Shaw Field, one an oil bomb which had burned fiercely but had done no damage, and the second, an HE (high explosive) had killed a cow, by no means the cow we would have chosen to have killed but a fine young one just due to produce her second calf. And the third is a time bomb which has not gone off yet.

Last night I was lying on the hearth rug between Kath and Walter, reading Lorna Doone. I must have fallen asleep, for I wakened suddenly to see Kath and Walter scrambling into the safe corner. "Bonk" came the second bomb, then "bonk," closer, and again closer, "bonk," the fourth one fell. I had never heard any quite so close and we were giggling foolishly with relief when the telephone rang. It startled us more than the bombs had done. Walter had the receiver off the hook before it had ceased to ring. We all heard, "Incendiaries on your farm," and then Walter and I were out like a shot, out into a weird night, glowing with a thousand fiercely brilliant flares. The chicken houses and arks were blank shapes against an eerie green sky. Behind them hundreds of little dancing lights defined the area of a stubble field and the rising curve of the road. Walter snatched up the shovel and rake, long age placed by the door in readiness for this night, and then follows the sound and the fury.

Walter ordered me in, and I saw no more. I raged and I fumed but I obeyed. This was my first incendiary raid and I was not permitted to extinguish even one small bomb.

"You silly little fool," Walter told me when he came in. "If Jerry had come back and dropped some big stuff by the light of those incendiaries, Kath would have had her hands full with the baby. Your job would have been to turn the cows loose. Understand?"

I felt full of shame and very stupid. To cheer me, Walter told me that the first incendiary which he had put out lay just by the stile in the potato field. I went out and found it this morning and it is now my personal candlestick. It holds a candle beautifully in its burnt-out fins.

There were two deaths in the village from the HE's we had heard and several houses were damaged. Walter saw the furniture in one house, deeply pitted with glass because the windows blew in. He was so concerned that he and Old Ted have spent the day building a two-inch thick shutter which requires two men to put into place at blackout time.

Three times, since I have been writing, bombs have fallen, but they were a mile or two away. The windows have rattled, and even the back door, solid oak, with its new ten-inch bolt. The old one, heavy, hand-wrought iron, was blown off, staples and all, in a raid a week ago.

November 5, 1940. Nunningham

We had been dung-carting Saturday morning in the light rain. By noon we were forced to stop as the storm set in in earnest. We were sheltering in the hovel by the barn when Ted and Walter caught sight of old John Lovell, trudging up the path from the woods, with a bundle of faggots over his back. John wore a long belted smock and corduroy trousers, tied below the knees with pieces of string. I found myself thinking that I might be a subject of King Alfred and wondering if I should see the brass collar of thralldom under John's long white hair and side whiskers. Then I heard Ted saying that John had been drunk on his wedding day. As the old man walked slowly past the barn Walter called out, "Come on, John. Come in to the dry and rest a bit."

"Aye," said John, "Aye, Good day all, an' a wet 'un 'tis too."

"John," Walter looked at me, with his eyes twinkling, "What's this I hear about you being drunk on your wedding day?"

"Course I were," John was out of breath, and spoke slowly and hoarsely. "Course I were. There was one on 'em holdin' me up on one side an' one on 'em holdin' me up on t'other. If I hadn'a bin drunk I wouldn'a never 'a' got ma—rried."

It was still pouring rain at tea time when I was out feeding the fowls. I heard the crunch of a cycle on the beach road and Charlie's gay hello. A weekend after a week's leave was a very special surprise. Unfortunately, the rain kept up continuously, so that except for milking times we stayed happily by the fireside. I felt miserable on Sunday evening when Charlie cycled off at dusk in the slanting rain. However we had a lovely weekend and Hitler was kind. Usually I worry about Charlie traveling in the dark but Sunday was the first night in fifty-six during which London has had no alert.

All in a great hurry, and filled with foreboding, I am to leave Nunningham and fare forth on a new job. A call came from West Sussex for me. I communicated the information to Mrs Mullins, who told me to forget about it. She said that it was not a job which she wished me to take. She knew the facts and would advise West Sussex that I was not to go. She said that it was not a worthwhile job for a good worker, and secondly, that I would not be happy there.

However, twenty-four hours later Lady De La Warr telephoned me herself. She explained that other Land Girls had proved unsatisfactory in the job in question and it was difficult to prove whether the girl or the job itself was at fault. As I was older, and presumably a little wiser, she asked if I would go. Apparently I was under no obligation to stay if I judged the work to be unsuitable. And so now I am packing and saying farewell to all things lovely.

The rain falls softly and I am full of tears tonight. All the sweet silly things come back to me – Walter's talks about chicken and cattle breeding. "Wait until tonight," he would say, when I would ask pertinent questions, and then with Kath to join in the lesson, we would have long discussions. I think of all their forbearance, Walter's and John's and Ted's, when I forgot to tie up a cow or to close a gate. And of Old Ted, his nose down a rabbit hole fearing that he must dig out his ferret, of the glory of wheat falling beneath the binder, of rows over Lucy (a cow named Alice whom I re-christened because of her leucorrhea), the long lovely walks to or from the hay or corn fields in the hot summer noons, of my struggles with the tractor, which I still have not mastered, of leaving here for our glorious week in Scotland and coming home with gladness to a full welcome, and now, here in this old kitchen, where we have our baths so hilariously (farm life often demands passage through the kitchen regardless of who is in the bath) and where we sat for many evenings, cold and uncomfortable, on nights of heavy raids, waiting for young Peter to fall asleep in his crib. Here by the old chimney piece and the copper, waiting again for young Peter to go to sleep, must I say my valedictory.

I thought I had grown too old, that two people could mean so much to me, and here I sit, with Kath and Walter grown so very dear, one on either side of me, and know, as I knew one day I must, I shall no longer call this home.

We have been laughing tonight about the time I gave up smoking. Ted said that I could not do it. I told him that I had no intention of doing so as I enjoyed smoking, but that I would quit for a week to prove to him that I could. I did, and by the end of the week I had become completely unbearable. I fought with everyone in sight, I aired all my agriculturally acquired proficiency in swearing, and some from way back, and I stamped off to bed in tears every night. And so

Walter said that wherever I went, or whatever I was doing, I could come back to Nunningham any time, for a day or a week or as long as I liked.

"This is your home in England, Polly, and I want you to know that – on one condition."

"What's that?"

"That you don't give up smoking. Because we can't stand it."

SOUTHWATER
AND NUNNINGHAM

November 20, 1940. Southwater, near Chichester

Mrs Marshall Thomson, my new employer, met me at the train in
Chichester and we proceeded in state in her big Lagonda, turning in
between open wrought iron gates just at dusk. Since then the high
brick walls and laurel hedges have hemmed my prison, a most beautiful prison, with vast Regency dining room, shimmering chande-
liers and exquisite china and a graceful Boulle Commode used as a
serving table. The drawing-room is Louis XV, brocaded walls, roses
and cupids on the pale carpeting, furniture inlaid with mother-of-
pearl — all in an atmosphere where there is no grace and beauty, nor
any simple kindness. In my room there is a thick butter-coloured
carpet, with a modern continental bed, obviously custom-built, as it
is about seven feet wide. I have lime-green sheets and butter-
coloured blankets. My photographs, and actually my books, look
uncomfortable.

I was given the alarm clock that I might wake in time for milking,
but I was offered no guidance. I found the cows in about the tenth
building I explored. There was a raid on so I dared not use a light. At
breakfast I was given a rough list of my duties, but no one has been
near me to see if they have been carried out. I had never looked a pig
in the face before, but I have now learned the hard way how to get
into their pens for feeding and cleaning without letting the pigs out,

and how to keep them back while I get their mash into their troughs instead of all over me.

My days are endless walking back and forth, feeding cows, pigs, chickens, and geese, with food for each type of stock stored near a different one. Where Walter had a huge granary, stocked to overflowing, here we run out of pig food one day, chicken grub the next. Mrs Marshall Thomson dashes into town each day and returns with a half hundred weight of meal or mash or corn. Today I reported that only one bale of hay remains, a day's feed for the cows.

These folk once had money, and they want me to realize it, too. I have heard of Mrs Marshall Thomson's youth on the continent, of their sixteen servants, of colossal parties and jewels stored in bank vaults. I have been told of Mr Marshall Thomson's war-destroyed business and of the disloyalties of their respective families. I am sincerely sorry for their fall from high estate, but I also believe that no Land Girl is justified in putting in her time, utilizing her training, to help the Marshall Thomsons keep stock, which in peacetime was only a hobby and which they are trying to carry on in wartime solely to augment their own rations. The work itself is routine drudgery, with no form of relaxation. Mrs Marshall Thomson is short-tempered and erratic, and I shiver in my shoes, more from surprise than fear when ever I hear her shrill, "For God's sake – What the bloody hell – ?" I never know if she is apostrophizing me or her Great Dane, which she seems to find more of a nuisance than a friend.

Day's Routine.

7:00 a.m.   Up. Dress. (In complete darkness, no blackout in either bed or bathroom.)

Fetch cows food from granary, 4 buckets, light cowshed lantern.

Feed cows.

Back to house for milk pails.

Clean out worst of manure.

Wash cows udders and hindquarters.

Milk.

Take milk to dairy.

Two trips from granary with mash for pigs.

Feed chicken and geese.

8:30 a.m.   Breakfast.

Make bed and tidy room.

Wash milk pails, udder cloths, and separator.

Groom cows, wash brush and currycomb.

Take cows to pasture. (Too cold to let them out before breakfast.)

Fill troughs with drinking water. (Dragged by bucket up icy mud bank.)

Get sack of hay for horse.

Walk 300 yards to horse stable, feed him, clean out his stall and take him to pasture.

Bring down fresh straw for him. (I cannot carry bedding and feed in one trip. Later I intend to harness up that old horse and make him carry his week's supply — if there ever is that much.)

Clean out cow stalls — 8 wheelbarrow loads of dung

Cart it to midden (indigenous for dung pile) 100 yards away.

Wash out cow stalls, breaking ice on tank and carrying water from tank 50 yards away.

Fetch fresh straw.

Fetch fresh hay. (Both of these at Nunningham are in the barn.)

Clean out the pig pens.

Clean out the little pigs house. (There are about 40 little pigs and their shed is about three feet high, impossible for me to stand upright.)

Clean out the chicken houses.

Clean out the geese houses. All long trips to dung pile with barrow.

Mix pig food for evening. (Has to soak.)

Mix cow grub for evening. (Sugar beet pulp, also must soak.)

Mix mash for chickens and feed them.

2:00 p.m.   Make myself a sandwich. (Mrs Marshall Thomson says lunch is only a habit and ignores noontime completely.)

Till three-thirty the days vary little. Once I even went beyond the brick wall to order hay from a horrible man down the road. One day I burned a couple of chickens which had died.

3:30 p.m.   Feed the sows.
Feed the little pigs.
Fetch the cows from the pasture.
Fetch their food.
Fetch the milk pails.
Wash the cows.
Milk. (My hour of peace.)
Take milk to dairy. (As it is in open buckets, it must be removed from dust in cow stalls immediately.)
Feed cows, corn, bran, etc.
Give them hay.
Bed them down.
Water them.
Shut the door!
Bring horse from pasture to stable.
Take down his morning hay and water him.
Feed the chicken and geese.
Shut them up.
Mix cow food for morning.
Mix pig food for morning.
Wash milk pails.
Wash myself, and wait, starving, for dinner at eight.

10:00 p.m.   Clean out cow stalls again.
Water cows. (Break ice on tank again, and eight long trips with two buckets, back and forth between tank and cow shed in the dark.)
Bed.

Ninety percent of that work is re-crossing footsteps. At Nunning-ham everything is on the way to a job. Here there is no method or planning.

At the end of a week I told Mrs Marshall Thomson that I would stay only till she could get someone else. At first she shrieked at me,

"What is it you don't like? Is it me? Is it the food? It is the work? Is it the farm?"

Later she grew very calm about it. She said that she had known I would not stay and that she ought to have a man. However I was not to escape so easily. I had apparently hit her between the eyes. It was she who had dismissed the previous girls. This was a different affair altogether and the next few days were very uncomfortable ones, made more unhappy for me by my personal doubts. I had joined the Land Army. Here was my chance to grin and bear it, to see the job through. But I could not convince myself that, in this case, martyrdom was worth the candle. The WLA person to whom I wrote was very indignant.

"I know that the job has its differences," she wrote, "But, so you will find, have all jobs. It does give us a bad name if girls are constantly leaving their employers."

I had pretty well convinced myself that I should be more miserable if I left than if I stayed when I asked Mrs Marshall Thomson if she could arrange with someone to milk one Sunday that I might have the day off. On large farms milkers usually get alternate Sundays. But on small, one Sunday in three. That was all I asked. Mrs Marshall Thomson looked at me in amazement.

"My dear girl," she said. "Farm workers don't get time off." Well, she was right. Hers did not anyway.

December 5, 1940. Southwater
Life goes on, with no sign of anyone to replace me. And there is no relaxation such as I knew at Nunningham with "my ordinary farming-class friends." Of course, we of the "professional classes" (I am claimed by virtue of a university degree) look down our noses at respectable farming folk, who pay their bills, improve their land and equipment, and work shoulder to shoulder, employer and employee together, each taking pride in his work.

I find that even the bombing here does not interest me. As long as we are not hit I do not care where the bombs fall. Actually we are rather on edge tonight as there is no air activity at all and the peace is uncanny.

Kath and Walter have just telephoned. They are coming to see me on Sunday. I have arranged with Mrs Marshall Thomson that if I get up at four and have all my work done, I may go to town with them for lunch, provided that I am back again by three for milking.

December 31, 1940. Nunningham

With the help of Walter and Mrs Mullins the day finally came when I left Southwater. Walter and Kath arrived for their visit. We had dinner at the Dolphin and Anchor and after telling me all the Nunningham news, they drove back to the Southwater with me. Mrs Marshall Thomson seemed to have as little use for Walter when they met as he had for her. He and Kath followed me as I went about my afternoon jobs.

All my replies to his questions brought the same remark from Walter. "Humph, that helps the war, doesn't it?" Finally, when he asked what became of the milk, I said, "Butter."

"What does she do with the butter?"

"Sells it to her friends."

Walter lifted young Peter off the gate where we had been leaning, "You get the hell away from here, my girl," he said, as Kath and I stepped out to keep up with him. "Get back to Nunningham and we shall begin again from there."

That night I wrote Mrs Mullins, told her that Mrs Marshall Thomson was making no effort to replace me and that the local WLA secretary disapproved of my decision to leave. I offered to resign from the Land Army if I was letting it down by leaving Southwater. She replied immediately, and asked me not to think of resigning, and to go back to Nunningham and then to let her know as soon as I could to come over and have tea and talk about it. I cried that night.

Mrs Marshall Thomson called me a quitter at parting, and said that she had previously been under the impression that Canadians had guts. Then as the taxi arrived she whispered to me to tell the driver, a local man, that I was going away on leave.

"Don't tell him you're leaving, I don't know what he'll think."

Why she cared I do not know, but at least I was spared the blasphemous tirade I had been dreading and we parted with a cheery handshake.

I was a very ashamed and subdued Land Girl for the first hour or so of my journey but, as I left Southwater well behind, I concluded that it was Mrs Marshall Thomson, to whom I owed nothing, whom I had let down and not the Land Army, which was organized for service. And I found comfort in the knowledge that Walter and Mrs Mullins agreed.

As I passed through Chichester I regretted that I had lived near the town for almost a month and had barely glimpsed the Cathedral, nor had I any opportunity to see Goodwood, Boxgrove Priory, or Bosham, each of which were in cycling distance, but not a Saturday afternoon had I had.

Later I caught a train but my baggage did not. I did not care. I was free. Southwater had never existed and my baggage would turn up sometime. When I reached the little market town near Nunningham I could hardly contain my excitement. There was a time bomb on the regular route and we had to go by devious back roads. Double decker buses were never meant to travel these sunken Sussex lanes. Branches whacked against the windows of the upper deck with a racket like machine-gunfire. An old man on the front seat bobbed up and down at every crash and the little girl opposite him nearly exploded with mirth. The louder the clatter of branches on the glass the lower the old man ducked and the wilder were the little girls' squeals of glee. I think that the old gentleman would have been happier had the window smashed so that he could have lost his temper in irate complaint. To add to his fury and our fun, the lady behind him had a terrified pup in a basket, whose yelps coincided with the crashes. I was nearly hysterical myself when the bus stopped at the Woolpack.

I ran blindly down the lane, in sudden utter terror lest Nunningham had been only a dream, or lest Hitler had had a go at it, but as I turned the corner, there it lay, the old stone farmhouse, with the willows behind it and the lovely hills in the evening light.

Kath was drawing the blackout curtains as I came running in. Peter said, "Hello Auntie, wind up my tractor." Walter and John were milking and later Walter drove me up to see Old Ted, whose delighted welcome made my homecoming complete.

"Little ol' devil," he said, "Reckon our Polly's glad she's back, eh Walter?"

And he knew he was right. Ted never calls me "little old devil" unless I do something right or show some unexpected glimmer of intelligence.

Even old John Lovell understood. I was helping Walter fill the tractor next morning when he came down the footpath.

"G'marnin', Mr Marshall."

"Morning, John."

"I see you got your la—ady back agin."

Walter laughed, and grinned at me, "A bad penny turns up," he said. "I knowed she'd coom back."

"You did, John. How did you know?"

"Oh, Oi knows them folks, Ah, Oi knows 'em. A body must be dam' ornery if they don't do nuthin' right."

From then on life was as before. Walter took Kath to Lewes one day and I stayed with Peter, and I went to Eastbourne and had lunch with Dado and Alec. On Christmas Eve we all found time to go to pick holly growing on our own farm.

Charlie's scheme, on which he had been for over a month, finished just in time for him to come down for Christmas. He arrived after tea on Christmas Eve and we all decorated the house. Life was sweet.

Kath tied up some bunches of old balloons. Several burst as we blew them up and the rest went off with healthy explosions during the night.

Kath and Walter sleep with Peter in the shelter, which was built while I was away. It is the finest indoor shelter I have seen. A door was cut through the diningroom wall into what had been a frost-proof room for seed potatoes. It is flanked on four sides by other rooms, all of which are contained by the outside stone wall of the house. Walter lined it with eighteen-inch reinforced concrete walls and ceilings, forming a room just big enough for a double bed and Peter's small crib. The completion of the shelter is of inestimable comfort to us all. No longer do we have the bothersome moving of mattresses twice daily and Walter, who took unto himself, and bore heavily, the responsibility of all our lives, feels that he has done his utmost. Now, as we sit by the fire, Peter is safe and our place of refuge is close at hand.

Charlie and I made tea at five-thirty Christmas morning and took it in to Kath and Walter, that we might all share in Peter's excitement before Walter and I went milking. Poor Walter had bought Peter a special toy tractor, but Peter had asked only for a book. This he saw immediately, among all the other gifts at the foot of his bed. Again and again Walter said, "Look at your tractor," but Peter replied, "No, thank you, Father Christmas brought my book."

I had hoped that we would go to church, but Walter had given John the day off, and by the time the cows were fed and the cow stalls cleaned out there was no time. We were to drive up to the village for

Grandma Marshall and of course it was inevitable that we call in at the Woolpack. It was Christmas, I was a returned wanderer, Charlie a welcome guest, and the celebration was a very gay one.

After a complete Christmas dinner there was just time to open our gifts before milking. Several of Kath's friends dropped in during the evening and we played games, roasted chestnuts, and talked by the fire.

Next morning Walter drove Charlie to his early train while I went milking. Later, when I was pumping up the barn tank, I realized that the swift semi-rotary motion was not the best thing for my watch. I stripped it off, finished pumping, fed the chickens, and went in to breakfast. As I washed my hands I discovered that my engagement ring, which I had been wearing for Christmas, was missing. I know it came off when I took off my watch, but John had cleaned out the cow stalls while I was feeding the fowls and there was no sign of it. We checked where I had scattered the chicken food, we went through the trap for liquid manure and since then, for five days, I have sat on the milking stool, and gone through the dung pile, lump by frozen lump, with a trowel and a wooden spoon and fast ebbing hope, not to mention much kind-hearted teasing from all who pass by on the footpath.

Somehow only one thing hurts, the fact that it is Charlie's ring and that he was so proud of it because I was proud to wear it. It is not easy to explain how I have gone to bed each night and wakened each morning glad to be alive and unharmed, and yet quite reconciled to the fact that I may, at any moment, lose everything that I have with me. Each day I feel more selfish when I think of how other people are suffering. My belongings seem unimportant. If a bomb hits Nunningham, Kath and Walter lose everything they own and even more, their home, but what do I lose? A couple of suitcases! Our home is safe, waiting for us in Canada. I have a second chance, a sort of reprieve. The invasion scare proves what I mean. "We had better leave the silver," Alec had said. "It won't keep us warm. We'd best take heavy coats instead."

Walter scolded me very severely once, when I said how badly I should feel if Nunningham were hit. He said that so long as we all got out of it alive he would not care.

"Oh, but you would," I argued, "You'd hate to lose your old chest," and I named several other prized possessions.

"I don't care," he said sternly, "if every stick is destroyed so long as Kath and Peter are safe. Material things don't matter one scrap, my girl, and the sooner you realize that the better."

I think that these lessons have made me grieve less for my ring, although I feel badly because of my carelessness and because of Charlie.

Walter says that we must go off to bed. It is only ten-thirty and when I said, "Aw Walter, it's New Year's Eve!" he said shrilly, "I expect the New Year will come in all right without me stopping up. And now good night to you and Happy New Year."

We have had quite a bit of snow lately and I find that I have an ache for a kindred spirit. How they all hate snow! I have tried to do a little missionary work but I am a complete failure. The snow blocks the road and the milk lorry cannot get down. We must take the churns up to it on the tractor. The ground is frozen so that ploughing has been held up for two weeks. The cold freezes the pipes, the snow bothers the chickens so that they will not come out to feed and the eggs fall off, the kale is frozen and cutting it is a miserable job. To Walter there is no beauty in anything that is such an unadulterated nuisance, and no pleasure in weather that is so darned cold.

I can see their point of view. All the seed potatoes have had to be moved lest they freeze, the barn pump is frozen, and it is not much fun bringing in a pitch of hay in a high wind. Hay blows off the prong all over the rick yard and I double up in amusement and elicit bitter remarks from John. The situation is serious, because the ploughing is getting behind, but the grumbling is all good-natured. "You can have that country of yours, if this is the kind of weather you have." And of course I feel the cold as much as they do, which causes them amusement. I brought no fur coat or overshoes and so, like them, I am thrown unprepared into winter, and the joke is on me too. But it will not be next year. English folk carry on, year after year, with unheated bedrooms and spring and fall clothes, expecting to get through the winter with no really cold spells. They fooled me this year, but only this year. Next year I shall prepare for winter.

Winter is still with us. I was wakened in the current manner, by Walter thumping on the ceiling below. (On Christmas Eve Charlie and I slept in the room over the dining room, which, because the chimney passes through it, is comfortably warm. I have remained ever since.) Each night I put a shoe on my bedside table as I blow out my candle. Walter bangs on the ceiling below to waken me in the morning, I push off the shoe in response and three minutes later I am collecting the milking pails from the dairy. Walter, not infrequently, goes back to bed, confident that once I am awake I am on the job. He says that I am the best getter-upper he ever saw on week days, and the best sleeper-inner when I may.

This morning, however, he stayed up and we stepped out into the moonlight together. It had snowed a little and the world was a magic place. The willow branches, tipped with moonlight, sparkled against the white roof of the barn. Unfortunately Walter slipped just then and spilled the water for washing the cows. I laughed at his vocabulary and he swore again, "Shut up, you'll wake the baby." He was laughing too by the time I had refilled the pail and he had lit the barn lanterns. We had just buttoned on our white coats when John arrived. As John dares not use his motorcycle because of the icy roads and must walk the two miles to work, his good mornings do not sound very convincing these days.

February 1, 1941. Nunningham
Charlie wrote a while ago that he might be moved, but gave no details. I arranged with Walter to take a few days off to go to see him, in case the move was north – or even further away. The regiment had been moved from their camp into billets in Sutton when the cold weather came. Charlie met me at the station and guided me through the residential district. He had told me that he could find a room for me, but I was surprised when we turned in the gateway of a beautifully kept, gracious-looking house in a large garden. My previous rooms had been in Cheam, in a tiny spotless house. We were greeted by Mrs, Young and Mac, their black scottie, in what was to be the beginning of a wonderful friendship.

Charlie's billet is two doors away, in a house where the owner has evacuated to a safer area. Mrs Young, who knew that the boys were denied the use of the hot water system, offered the use of one of her bathrooms to Charlie. Upon occasion she had asked Charlie to tea, and given him the freedom of her garden, where he might read, in his leisure time. When he was unable to find a room for me (my rooms in

Cheam were occupied and, as usual, there was no room at the inn), he had called at Mrs Young's for advice. She immediately invited me to stay with them.

I spent five days with Mr and Mrs Young. Charlie would come in for tea and stay until seven, returning next door for the night. The days were busy ones for him as the regiment had left town and he was one of those responsible for closing up and accounting for all keys and damages in the properties which the boys had occupied. He was bursting with pride over the final figures, eight hundred men in forty houses, for a period of eighteen months and the damages amounted to only eighty-six pounds.

A day or two later we had a pleasant surprise. Penny, whom I had not seen since our trip to Scotland, had been in hospital for some weeks with an injured foot. He was now discharged and had been sent back to his unit to report. He knew that the boys had gone and was delighted to meet Charlie. The two of them burst excitedly into Mrs. Young's and took me out to lunch. We went to the "Cock" and I learned how Penny had had a six hundred pound armoured plate dropped on his foot. We sat talking over a drink and Penny jokingly asked the waiter for a steak for lunch. Half an hour later, to our amazement and consternation, he returned and said, "Your steaks are ready, sir." We followed him upstairs to the dining room, hoping that, if steaks really did exist in England, we had enough money to pay for them.

I left on Saturday morning in time for Saturday afternoon milking and managed to walk into the barn in my working clothes just as Walter was finishing his first cow.

Young Peter's vocabulary, for a child not yet three, is amazing, and like most English children, he speaks with such clarity and precision. He ran into the kitchen yesterday to Kath and me.

"Mummy," he said, "There's a lady on the wireless, talking about hygiene." Kath and I stared at him. That was a big word for a small boy.

"Well," Peter's pride was injured, "She said that she was going to talk about hygiene." When he goes out he wears blue mittens my aunt sent to him and often he says, "My mitts came from Canada. Auntie's auntie made them."

He showed his mother a picture of a bombed-out London street. "Houses damaged, Mummy," he said. "Bombs did it." Kath looked at me. "Where ever did you hear that?" she asked him.

"Over the wireless," which may not have been true but was a logical reply.

He helps me dusting. One room had a little knothole in the skirting-board which Peter discovered.

"Auntie!" he said emphatically, "Bunny hole." Then down on his knees he explored it very carefully and said seriously, "Nobody home." He, as I am, is very interested in rabbiting.

John initiated me into some of the tricks yesterday afternoon. Our equipment consisted of several old corn sacks, one containing nets, one, tied in the middle to keep them apart, for the ferrets, and lastly, the empty one for the rabbits. We were doing the holes along the lane. First we spread the nets across the holes, several at a time to save trouble as the holes may be connected. Then John introduced the ferret. "Put him in the burry" as John said.

We heard a squeak.

"Stand back," John ordered. This, he explained, was so that the rabbit would not see me, for then he would slow up and the net not draw up tight. I obeyed orders and poor little Brer Rabbit went head first into the net which drew tight around him. He rolled down the bank and hung dangling on the string which John had fixed to the hedge. We grabbed him and then noticed that the ferret had gone back into the burrow. John shoved the rabbit and tangled net into my hands and then quickly put up another, just in time, for out bolted another rabbit. We caught five altogether and then had to leave to go milking. Walter says he has known as many as seventy nets to be set up to a barrow or rabbit warren.

John goes rabbiting every week now, ferreting with his brother on Saturday afternoons and shooting with Old Ted on Sundays. He sells the rabbits for two to three shillings, which brings him a nice little sum for a day's sport, and Walter is grateful. He says rabbits and rats took more food than the German U-boats in the last war.

And we are very glad of the rabbits for food too. The first time I ate rabbit was in Aldershot and I was very nearly ill. I felt as if I were eating a cat. But I have grown accustomed to the idea now and Kath cooks them deliciously. She fries the legs and back to a golden brown, then

Kath feeding the
chickens

bakes them in a casserole, with stock, onions and herbs. Even if there
were no meat shortage I should enjoy eating rabbit as Kath cooks it.

Here in the country we do not suffer from a boring diet. Kath is a
wonderful housekeeper. The larder is filled with salted and bottled vegetables and fruits. And there is fresh garden produce throughout the
year. But the meat situation is the same for all. We are allowed about a
shilling's worth per person, per week. Last week and the week before
we could not get that. The butcher, Kath's brother C.D., had barely
enough to give each customer a small roast and then close up for a
week. One day Kath sent me to get any meat I could. All C.D. had was
sausages, which are poor fare, only forty percent meat permitted by law.

"Did you make them yourself?" I asked.

"Yes."

"Well, that's something. At least we know what's in them."

No reply, merely a quizzical frown.

"Do you eat them yourself, Mr Snatt?"

"Good God, no! Wouldn't touch 'em."

Jerry has been over and there has been a lot of excitement tonight.
This has been interrupted several times while I followed Walter's orders
to retire to the shelter. At least twelve bombs fell fairly near this evening
and there was some machine-gunning, which means that our boys
might bring down a Messerschmitt on the doorstep, so possibly discre-
tion is the better part of valour. This is the first night since I have been
back from Southwater that we have had such constant air activity.

None of us has been able to settle down to any work so Walter has been telling me about Nunningham. He told me long ago about the name, which is an Anglo-Saxon one: "ing" is a suffix meaning belonging to, and "ham" means home. So my beautiful farm, the home of Kath and Walter, who have given me, and Charlie too, a haven of contentment in this time of war and of danger, has an Anglo-Saxon name which means simply, "home belonging to Nunn."

Nunningham was, some years back, part of the castle estate of seven farms which are now independently owned. Sometimes I think that, almost unconsciously, certainly unvoiced, Walter would like to buy those farms and unite them all again. That he could, if he set out to do so, I have no doubts. He is already managing acreage equal to the combined extent of the old castle farmlands. And it

Nunningham farm, the loveliest spot in England

was not many years ago that he bought Nunningham, with a heavy mortgage, I imagine, though I have not asked. I know he owns it outright now. When he and Kath were first married he had no help. He would have the milking done and all the chores and then harness the horses and be out in the fields ploughing by seven o'clock in the morning. After dark he would milk again, and often Kath, looking for him after ten o'clock, would find him asleep over the barn pump. Kath shared too in the building of the farm. There were paying guests, sometimes all that the house would hold, right up till the time when Peter was born. Each year saw some improvement, some new addition. Fields were drained, bridges built, a new well dug. One year John began to work here, then Old Ted came, more cows, the tractor.

Walter, in spite of his agricultural integrity and hard work, is still the traditional farmer. Affairs in the house take second place to the needs of the farm. Today, for instance, Kath reported a missing sheet. This a second casualty. The clothes poles are beside the pond, and, after the complete disappearance of a tablecloth some years ago, Walter promised to move the poles. As farmers do, Walter really intends to move those poles. Perhaps now that the pond has also digested a sheet, the job will be done. We shall see.

February 15, 1941. Nunningham barn doorway
It is a perfectly glorious spring day and I have stolen a moment to absorb the beauty of it. Gyp lies at my feet and the only sound is the breathing of the cows and the occasional rattle of an iron collar.

Ted is pitching straw from the big stack beyond the barnyard, and his unbelted coat is blowing into the swift white clouds. The blue Sussex wagon is almost loaded, outlined against the rising hills.

The breeze is so warm I find it hard to believe that it is only February. This morning when we came out milking dawn was just breaking. There was a ring of pale light around the hills and the pond shimmered, eerie, wan-blue, behind the motionless willows.

We have had no sun for weeks and weeks, five Walter said, and the sunrise created a new world. It feels like spring just to watch the lifting of the straw in the barnyard as little breezes come under the gate and to see the sun on the warm dusty colour of the thatched ricks.

Gyp has an impatient eye on a chaffinch on the barn rafters and the time has come for me to get busy. I must clean and pulp some mangles and pump up the barn tank before milking.

Walter is ploughing now from dawn till dark and John is spreading beach, as the pebbles from the shore are called, on the bad spots in the lane. Therefore the cows and the barn are my domain. Hitler, raids, and the threat of invasion cannot spoil the tranquillity of these spring days, with the milk yield good, winter wheat showing three inch spikes of green, and field after field combed new and orderly under the plough.

How strange it is to realize that a plough is a weapon of war. Nothing seems more the epitome of peace than the sight of Walter slowly crossing back and forth on a far hill, with a flutter of swirling gulls in his wake.

Well, I've done it. For three days, since the air has been warm and sweet, I have ached to "take the blithe adventure of the fugitive," to leave the work I have loved, the fields and the woods, to find the open road again where there was just me and I might belong all to myself again.

To leave directly after milking was the only way to make the best use of daylight. I knew that the suggestion would cause an upheaval. The bomb in the pasture had much the same effect.

"Would it put anyone out if I went for a walk and skipped tea?"

"Miss your tea? I never heard of such a thing. You come right in and have your tea, my girl. It'll be light after. I have to go down to the pasture – you can have your walk and come down there with me."

I said I was sorry but that I was going anyway. I wonder if I could have explained adequately. To Walter, tea comes after milking, just as soon as one can wash one's hands, as inexorable as fate.

I take root. I feel that I belong to Nunningham. I exult in the wheat, growing green and straight, in the fields fresh-furrowed and ready. I love the woods and the cows, and the lovely old barn with a special love. But all the while I know that my pride is a pseudo-pride, the cows I call mine are Walter Marshall's, my room is not my own. One day the telephone will ring and I shall go.

So, as for walking down to the pasture tonight, that was exactly what I did not want – a ten-minute walk on familiar ground, with familiar companionship. I had to get away, alone, beyond the old horizons.

I walked past the barn, through the big pasture, and over the new ploughed piece where Walter recently ploughed up an old horseshoe. He says he knows it to be a very old one, partly by its almost circular shape and partly because he is almost certain that that field has never been ploughed before. Farm records show that it was pasture land as far back as 1835, which means that it had not been ploughed during the Napoleonic wars, and therefore Walter feels it unlikely that it was ever ploughed before that date. I intend to take the horseshoe to Eastbourne for comparison with the old ones there.

I climbed the stile to the lowest brook field and walked across it to Nunningham River. When I crossed the bridge I was off Nunningham land. I sat on the rail for a little while, leaning against the old ivy-covered elm. How different is this English spring to spring in Canada. Here hedges and trees are always green with ivy and the grass green as in summer. The ivy in full green leaf dulled the thrill of discovering how fat the buds on the elm had grown.

Nunningham Stream lay far below the bridge, between banks which the centuries have deepened. I walked along beside it, losing the footpath and climbing a wooded hill. Then, crossing a grass field and two arable ones, I found a dead magpie, a rabbit trap, and a hen's nest with two eggs in it.

Darkness was filling the valley when I came to where the hedge and the stream met in a little wooded corner. I climbed a worn stile and, at an unexpected angle, came upon an old stone bridge. The sun went down quietly and the west was ivory and gray, barred with clouds of shading blues, and the wind was salty, blowing straight from the channel. Every turning of the road brought different silhouettes against the sky, tree branches soft with buds, steep-roofed cottages, and then the high, hedged banks and the road filled with darkness.

Night came quickly and when I passed the clump of spruce which we can see from Nunningham, I looked east to where she lay in a shadowy hollow, under the first piercing star. Birds were singing sleepily, the wind rustled the tree-tops, and a flock of sheep were making a little soft noise beyond the hedge.

I walked on past the house where Walter was born and, a little further, the home of Kath's family, and then turned left along the highway which parallels the sea. By then Orion was very brilliant. I saw Lyra and Cassiopoeia, but dared not look up any longer as I was on a main road in the blackout.

It seemed so short a walk to bring so much content. I was filled with peace as I came down the lane, with the first glimmerings of moonrise in the sky.

I was feeding the hens yesterday and Walter was ploughing. I saw him wave to someone whom I could not see, and stood waiting, with my trug full of corn, to satisfy my curiosity. In a moment or two, around the bend in the lane, came Charlie.

He helped to collect and wash the eggs and then came and talked to us while we milked. This morning he helped to clean out the barn and to bring in a cow and her calf. The cow had been out in the loose-box for calving. She was very frisky and tried to get over the dung-pile. When Charlie asked if she could jump it Walter only grinned. She did, clean over, about an eight-foot jump.

Charlie was tired and finds Nunningham home. We sat all day by the fire and enjoyed the peacefulness. He is so much nearer to me now that he can stay till nine o'clock, instead of leaving at two, as before.

March 13, 1941. Nunningham
Two weeks ago Ted brought me the first snowdrops and crocus from his garden and last Saturday he knocked at the door at dinner time.

"Polly, you say you ain't never seen no primroses. You goo down behind the Shaw Field stile arter yore dinner, and look by the hedge – you'll find 'em."

We found them, soft and pale and lovely as this English spring which is stealing upon us. And meanwhile all my letters from home tell of heavy storms, of snow shoveling, and of sliding weekends. And here with all the leaves unfolding it seems that we have had only a taste of winter. I have been waiting all these many months for winter to come and now the time has past and I am not sorry. The nights have been long and dark and I am weary of the chill and blackness, and ache for sunshine and full busy days again.

I am becoming a child of the soil and I realize as never before how civilization keeps one all out of tune. In my days of city life the hours of sleep differed little in summer or winter, when social activities continue in to the small hours of the morning more often than not. But here our way of life and our energies are in direct ratio to the hours of sunlight. In summer Walter is up at dawn, and works lustily and cheerfully till after dark. He will have supper at eleven and be an alert and interesting companion till Kath insists that it is long past bedtime. In winter it is he who sends us off to bed. He is difficult to rouse in the morning, finds the day's work heavy and exhausting and, after dozing in his chair after tea, is ready for bed by nine o'clock.

I must say that I am becoming converted. In summer, like all growing things, man has the urge to go and to do. In winter, nature sleeps and man has less energy, less driving power. I note with interest that while Walter eats five slices of bread for tea on weekdays, on Sunday he never eats more than two. We city people eat from habit. Walter

eats to supply energy. I am convinced that we use the word civilization in an inverted sense. We city folk eat for the sake of eating, play
bridge because we have nothing better to do, drive ourselves unhappily at work which we do not enjoy, solely for the purpose of acquiring
sufficient money to get away from it all for weekends, for two weeks
in the year, and ultimately to retire and play golf and vegetate, and
this we call civilization.

Country folk work with a steady swing during the hours of sunlight, sleep deeply, free from insomnia, through the quiet night, eat
when they are hungry, and know a peace and a satisfaction, a perme-
ating sense of security which all the tram-catching, committee-meet-
ing, convention-attending cycle of urban life can never claim.

I had a letter from home recently, in which the writer deplored my
lowered standard, claimed that I was wasting the advantages and education which had been given me, certainly intended for better ends
than cleaning out cow stalls. All this because I had mentioned that, as
in Walter's opinion girls are not fitted for the heavy work of tractor-
driving, I have determined to become nothing less than head cowman.
I hold no brief for cowmen as such, possibly the average cowman has
little to recommend him to my city friend. Nevertheless, to be a good
cowman requires intelligence. My friend desires clean milk. To understand the principles of clean milk production and to maintain them is
a job of which he may be proud, be it milking, or thatching or ploughing. He derives satisfaction from his skill and from his ability to create
which routine office work cannot give. He does not return home, as
the city man does, mentally tired, nervous, irritable, and bored, requir-
ing some form of amusement to occupy a restless mind. No extrava-
gant entertainment, no stimulating conversation can give a city man
pleasure equal to that with which a country man looks forward to his
own fireside.

So large a part of the city man's pay goes in keeping up with the
Joneses, so large a part of his energy is used in whacking a golf ball
or in making six diamonds doubled or in watching his diet because
of ulcers. The cowman derives his pleasure from a steady milk yield
and the sight of his herd grazing contentedly in good pasture, and
if, on a Saturday night, he loses a game of darts in the local pub he
will stand the winner a pint, not write him a cheque for a week's
salary.

Perhaps had I known the peaceful serenity of Nunningham sooner I would have been spared the gray hairs which Old Ted discovered with disgust, this morning.

"You want to git rid o' them gray hairs, Polly," he advised. "You couldn't say you was brown-haired if you was fillin' in a passport or some such thing. You're just roan, you are, that's what."

Some observant person listed our three last American visitors in one of the daily papers:

Summer WElles

Wendall WILLkie

Walter   WINant

I sincerely hope that the augury may be fulfilled.

April 1, 1941. Nunningham

Today I have sent home two Sussex trug* baskets. Kath and I finally found time to visit the little trug-shop on the Lewes-Hastings road, near Herstmonceux, where they are made.

I quote from the folder of T. & R.T.G. Reid, Cooper's Croft, Hailsham:

They make trugs for use, baskets that will last for years, instead of trash that will wear out in a season or two. My own garden trugs have been in use for twenty years, hard use. They are made from willow and bound with chestnut, both tough and enduring woods. The willow is split into broad laths, bent to sharp, bound with selected chestnut and then firmly nailed together. The result is a cheap and almost indestructible basket, engaging to the eye and a joy to the possessor. And so, if you want an honest basket, get a trug.

London Daily News

These trugs I use daily. There are one or two in the house, a large square one for wood by the fire, several in the granary, and several

---

* The word trug comes from the Anglo Saxon "trog," a trough or wooden vessel. Obviously to "trug" something along comes from this source.

more in the barn. They are used throughout Sussex, for shopping, for mending, and for garden tools and produce.

April 8, 1941. Cheam, Surrey
Charlie's long looked-for leave begins tomorrow, and he has had our tickets made out for Bristol. Thence we go west for three or four days on the North Devon coast and spend the balance of the time with Charlie's grandmother in Monmouth.

I found my little rooms in Cheam unoccupied and Charlie and I spent the evening talking to Mr and Mrs Carter, with whom we stay. Mr Carter was in Mesopotamia and Persia and Iraq in the last war and he and Charlie have much to talk about. Mrs Carter and I knit and discuss the present wartime shortages.

I gave her a bad fright tonight. Mr Carter was out on Home Guard duty and I had not pulled my blackout properly. At ten-thirty the crowd from the pub came singing down the road. Someone yelled, "Put out that bloody light or we'll throw a brick through the window." Mrs Carter called up in great distress. I put out the light immediately, and waited while she went outside to check for chinks before I turned it on again. Broken windows are almost impossible to replace and also one incurs a five pound fine if there is a streak of light showing from any part of the house.

Mrs Young had lunch with me today and I returned with her. Charlie later joined us for tea, and tomorrow we leave for London and the West Country.

April 10, 1941. Clovelly, near Bideford, North Devon
Perhaps in peacetime trappers and holiday-makers may destroy the charm of Clovelly, but they can do no permanent damage. When they are gone the narrow cobbled street (the guidebook calls it Cliff Staircase), the cottages built tightly above one another, the flowers which clamber over them and fill every crevice and cranny, are untouched and unchanged. The little herring-boats still come in, seeking the sheltering arm of the pier and the spray rises against the cliffs, westward past the lifeboat station and eastward towards Bideford.

The name Clovelly is thought to come from Ceave Leigh (A.s. *cleof*, promontory, and *below*, protection, shelter). Certainly the Devon, "All along, down along out along lea," must tie in somewhere.

From every house one must go "up along" or "down along" to its neighbour. There are one to two side streets, little mews or cobbled pathways, where more stone or plaster houses are clustered together under their borders and garlands of flowers. Charlie and I spent an enchanting afternoon finding, at every turn, new vistas of the sea, fanlights and friezes of freshly carved wood over the doorways of simple cottages, wisteria and aubretia in every fingerhold and every variety of climbing rose.

We went underneath the arches of the Red Lion in to the courtyard, where we clambered over intricately made baskets which I learned are lobster-pots, and made the acquaintance of the patient little donkeys which are the pack-horses, taxis, milkmen and even garbage collectors of Clovelly. We climbed "up along," looking backwards at the brilliantly coloured vista of roofs and flowers, curving through the fissure in the cliffs to the sea, and turned right, walking on red Devon soil, until we reached Clovelly Church.

I was interested to see the old hour-glass by the pulpit, and the old Saxon doorway and front. At the end of each pew were tiny, horribly uncomfortable shelves where poor little orphan apprentices had to sit. And I thought of the coombes we had explored and of the wild Doone country when I saw the heavy racks in each pew for pikes and guns.

But I think the memory which will remain with me longest is that of the grave of a young Clovelly airman, who died on active service in this war, on the day, now over a year ago, when Charlie sailed for England. In those days, when Charlie was on the sea, this young Devon gunner, with an old Devon name, was brought home to rest under the yew trees, near the sea, in beautiful Clovelly. On this stone surround were the words, "One of our pilots is safe."

Even here, so far from the South Coast raids, from barbed wire and tank traps, we may not forget that England is at war. All morning, and in the afternoon, when we walked in the opposite direction, patrol planes flew back and forth along the coast-line, and once we looked down onto the top of a bomber flying below us as we stood on the edge of the 400-foot cliffs.

We walked to the west, through the deer park, past the Angel's Wings, a little wooden summer house, sheltered by several pairs of carved wings, to Gallantry Bower. There is a controversy concerning the name of this glorious high promontory, which sweeps down, a clear unbroken four-hundred-foot drop to the rocky pebble beach below. The Carys of Clovelly and, since 1738 the Hamlyns, have possessed, and still do to this day, the right to pass sentence to hang. Thus it is possible that once a gallows stood on the smooth green lawns which stretch to the overhanging cliff. The alternative story, and certainly a no less dramatic one, has it that a lover pursued his lass to the cliff edge, and being too late to save her from leaping, gallantly hopped over himself, resolved to be with her in death if all else were denied.

It was there, as I lay on the smooth green turf, head and shoulders over the cliff edge, with Charlie standing, unhappily, a little way back, that the great bomber flew below us, tilting its wings in salute and seeming to scrape the bare rock face.

We went on down a steep path, and up again to the next jutting cliff and against a strong head wind, walked around the verandah of a Lock-out post. Following a steep trail to the beach we came into a little cove. The ruins of a pottery kiln are there and a little cottage. We jumped from rock to rock out to Neptune's Reading Desk and came back as the tide drove us farther and farther in.

April 30, 1941. Nunningham
Mrs Mullins telephoned last week and said that she had a job for me, with a Mr Brian Moss. After having been once bit at the Southwater, I was twice shy of Mr Moss and his Green Farm, so Walter promised that he would drive me over first and give me his seasoned opinion.

We traveled through country which is beyond Walter's jurisdiction, that is, in his WAEC capacity, and turned, finally, along a sunken lane, as genuine a "Smuggler's Way" as I have seen. These roadways were cut deep into the banks so that smugglers, with their laden pack animals, could pass to and fro without arousing the curiosity of the countryside.

Walter stopped to ask the way at a small thatched cottage, snug behind a flowering hedge and two blossoming red may trees. A girl in Land Army uniform, holding a baby in her arms, told us that Green Farm was a black and white Sussex house about a mile down the road.

Walter and Kath were aware, I say with some amusement, of my delight when we saw the house. It stood on a high bank, above a newly dug garden, with a winding driveway leading to the side of it. The house was long and low, of white plaster, with heavy timbers, creosoted to a weathered black, and a simple brick design in the over-hanging facade of the upper story. The open casement windows on either side of the front door had plain royal blue curtains, while cop-per bowls and candlesticks gleamed from the deep window ledges. The front door was painted black and had a small, stone crest, a peculiar gryphon sort of winged animal, set in the wall above it.

Kath and Walter knew that such a house would fascinate me and said that the thought of living in it would greatly dull the pain of my dreaded departure from Nunningham. I said that I thought they were most unkind but, as usual, probably right.

Mr Moss and his mother proved to be peculiarly self-satisfied people, both round and shiny and apple-cheeked, Mr Moss about my age. Both seemed quite unappreciative and unconscious of their lovely house.

Mr Moss took Walter and me out to see the cow stalls, which were new modern buildings a little way down the road. He has forty cows, mostly Ayrshires and Shorthorns, and two colossal Friesians, a breed I have not seen at close quarters before, and one lovely little Red Poll, just due to calve.

Milking was in progress, and though on the whole the stalls were spotless, airy, and hygienic, my eyes met Walter's several times as I noticed things of which I knew he would disapprove – the condition of cow flanks, a foul udder cloth, and the rusty milk pails hugged be-tween knees under soiled milking coats. Perhaps Green Farm did not don clean milking coats until Monday. I hoped as much.

Mr Moss told us that he had a tractor and that he expected me to drive it. I was about to express my enthusiasm and also to confess my limitations when Walter's confident assurance of my capabilities took my breath away.

"She can manage very well – harrowing, hay-raking, corn-carting, and she's done some ploughing."

Was this Walter Marshall, who swore at me from dawn to dusk, who had never let me use the tractor except in an emergency, or when I argued till he could bear it no longer? All the way home I longed to ask if he had meant the things he had said, but I dared not risk batter-ing the armour he had given me for my new adventure.

I said good-bye to Nunningham this morning. Walter sent me to Grandma Marshall's with a message and I walked home across the fields. I crossed the old bridge on which I am forbidden to drive the tractor. Its repair has long been one of Walter's someday jobs. I picked a few silvery blossoms growing beside it, which Old Ted says are wild garlic. Along the river meadows the banks are yellow with primroses and fields nodding with daisies. I climbed the stile and put up a pheasant at the corner of the wood. I tried in vain to find her nest and walked on, unable to avoid crushing violets at every step. I gathered some feathery pink Milkmaids, or Ladies' Smock, and in the shadow of the wood, some wild orchids.

One corner of the wood had been cleared and, as I looked between the clumps of ash and alder, I marveled that shadow could give to old stumps and bits of wood so heavenly a blue. But as I stepped into the sunlight to cross the open part the air was filled with fragrance and I saw that violets, hundreds and thousands of tiny wood violets and the tall scented ones, covered the clearing with a thick unbroken carpet of velvety blue-purple.

I added a few to my collection and continuing on the path through the woods, came to where the sun shines through an open glade. There the ground was covered with primroses, each plant a fluffy, big, yellow ball of bloom. A cuckoo called, blithe and independent, and then, as I neared the pasture side of the wood I found that I was not to leave Nunningham without seeing what I has so long dreamed of, Nunningham Wood, a waving sea of bluebells. So often Kath has said, "Oh I wish you could see Nunningham Wood when the blue-bells come," and today they are out and far more lovely than I had dreamed.

I shall take with me my little nosegay of Nunningham's wild flowers, together with a few of Kath's polyanthus and the forget-me-nots which Old Ted brought to me tonight.

GREEN FARM

May 7, 1941. Green Farm
I do not like milking Friesians, great, bony things they are, with thin hard teats. And I am not sure yet of the Ayrshires. One and all, they were strange with me today, and would not let down their milk, but I think that I shall have no difficulty. I had to learn how to use a milk sterilizer and a cooler but a few people around here are going to learn to wash their hands and their cows and to use clean udder cloths before long too. Mr Moss says that that is up to me. If I will keep the cloths clean, he will see to it that the men use them. Poor old chaps, they will too. Fred Poplett must be all of eighty and Mr Burke older still. Mr Burke makes me think of my Dad. He is sturdy and given to little speech and, like Old Ted, he knows how things should be done. But unlike Dad and Old Ted, the poor old man has had his day. Fred is sleepy and sloppy and mumbles constantly. We three, with Mr Moss, must see to the wishes and needs of the farm. I can see where I, even such as I am, will be of some value as an auxiliary tractor driver.

I have had a pleasant day. I took the old mare to the village to be shod this morning. I rode her happily for a mile or so until a car passed. Then I had to pick myself out of the hedge and catch my old mare again. I met Iris Wolfe, the Land Girl from whom we have asked the way a week ago. Her husband is overseas and she has a small son, but manages to find the time to milk at the farm near her cottage. She is a quiet practical girl and we hope to see more of each other.

After lunch I helped Mr Moss to put a new draw bar on the roller and then he helped Fred and me with the milking. Mr Moss's attitude to his cows is quite different from Walter's. He likes them, makes friends with them and sings loudly and melodiously as he goes about his work. Already we get along very well. He will toss me the udder cloth as I return from pouring my brimming bucket into the cooler and grin broadly. Strains of, "To be a farmer's bo-o-oy," float past him as he goes to the little shed to milk the two odd cows there.

He and Mrs Moss went out tonight. I washed the tea dishes for them in the old fashioned whitewashed kitchen and then came up to my room to complete unpacking.

I have a tiny iron-backed fireplace with a broad mantel where my books and blue Devon mug look happy and content. There are heavy timbers in the whitewashed walls and broad oak beams in the ceiling. I wonder about who has slept in this peaceful little room and what thoughts were theirs as they looked through the diamond-paned casement to the pale sunset beyond the apple blossom.

Last night Mr Moss took me down to the "Yew Tree," a little pub under the shadow of willow trees, and actually "down by the old mill stream," which is the meeting place for everyone in this scattered district. We sat on benches under the willows and talked over mugs of ale. Mr Moss told me that I am to spend the next few days with the old mare and the manure distributor, news I accepted dubiously. I am not very smart at leading horses.

But he also told me I might have the weekend off as Charlie wrote that Penny is to be married and I have been asked to be bridesmaid.

The days go so quickly. I am out of breath after the slower tempo of Nunningham. I am up each morning at four-thirty, fetch the cows and have them tied in their stalls by five o'clock. One morning our little red heifer calved. Mr Moss marveled even as I did. When I heard the heifer lowing in the loose box I called him as he had asked me to do. The little fellow arrived very quickly, a deep-red, bull calf, and within ten minutes was struggling to find his feed. I looked in an hour or so later and the shaky little chap was standing, sucking away.

All day I felt that I had shared in a thing of wonder. Whenever I looked in on the little family I expected to hear someone say, "Take off thy shoes from off thy feet," for there seemed an aura of holiness about that freshly littered loose box and the proud little heifer with her first calf.

I learned to harness the mare and to hitch her up myself and to un-harness her when day is done. I learned by experience many months ago how to remove a horse collar. John had not told me that it must be turned upside down and it took time and patience on the part of old Snowball, for which I gave her some pilfered cow-cake, before I found out.

Mr Moss took me to market with him on Friday morning. On Saturday I was a busy girl as it was his weekend off and then, bright and early Sunday morning, Charlie arrived. Mr Moss wanted me to take the day off but, as I shall be leaving for Penny's wedding next week, I carried on. Charlie helped me, chuckling as I do, at old Mr Burke and poor Fred Poplett. We walked into the village and had tea there and later Mr Moss picked us up and drove Charlie to his train.

On Saturday Mr Moss drove me to the train and I went to Mr Young's to meet Charlie for Penny's wedding. Mrs Young had invited the wedding party to lunch and Mr Young drove the bride to

Penny's wedding, May 17, 1941. Col. Calder, who gave the bride away, me, Penny, Mickey, Mrs Young, and Charlie

the church. Later, with Penny and his bride, we all went to an Inn near Dorking for dinner. We talked in the garden after dinner on Sunday and I came back to Green Farm in the evening.

Here I may do my work as well as I can but no longer am I able to make it my whole life. Save for about twenty acres of swedes and kale, thirty of oats, and perhaps fifty of flax, which I have not yet seen, Green Farm is all pasture and, at present, the work is mostly indoors with the cows. Consequently, the days are more routine and less absorbing, and a more social life is entertained. And no job is too important to leave at a moment's notice if something more amusing turns up. However, if the boss lets work take second place, he is the boss, mine not to reason why.

We have been whitewashing cow stalls and painting them this week. When we mixed the whitewash and Mr Moss began on the walls, I asked, "How do we do the roof?"

"With a spray. I'll rig up the stirrup pump and it'll do the job."

"How about doing that first? We'll get the walls all mucked up with ladders.

"I suppose we should. Oh well, the stirrup pump is up at the house. It's too much bother."

My offer to fetch it was rejected and we had finished one side and nearly done the other when milking time intervened.

Next morning I collected the whitewash pail and brushes to go on with the job but with great glee Mr Moss opened a can of black paint and began with that.

"Hey, how about the roof?" I asked.

"Oh we'll do that later."

"I'll go get the spray, Mr Moss. It'll be a shame to spatter all the nice shiny black."

"Oh, it'll wash off."

Well, as I said before, mine not to reason why, so now the walls and stall divisions are all flat white and shiny black and the roof as yet untouched. Mr Moss purrs with delight and thinks it looks marvelous but I cannot help wondering when the roof and rafters will be done. And yet Mr Moss is so amusing and such good company that certainly I have no complaint. He let me do something which John would never have permitted, let loose two young calves which are tied all day in the building. I asked if I could let the little red one loose first. Walter would have said, "Women again. Leave the darn thing tied up," and meant it. Mr Moss just grinned and said, "Sure."

The poor little fellow, he has been tied up since birth. He is the lad I saw delivered about a fortnight ago. At first he was not quite sure what to do. Then he discovered that his legs worked and for about an hour he leaped and hopped and galloped up and down the stalls. I was alone with him most of the day and of course I have petted him since the hour he was born so he had no fear of me. He nudged me, chewed at my smock, and I think was quite happy when I tied him up again and he could flop down and sleep.

The next day I let Susan loose, which proved a different sort of affair. She is about three months old and much more lively than the little bull calf. She had one free day, but today I had to tie her up. She was altogether too smart, sticking her nose in the paint and skidding against the wet walls.

Those were days with calves. I had a spell with chickens too. The bulk of the hens range in the pasture, some distance away, but two stunted little pullets live in a coop near the cow stalls. Last fall Mr Moss bought a couple of hundred day-old chicks and put them in a foster mother. The man whose job I now have had let the lamp out and all but two chicks died. These two have been struggling along together, fed on layer's mash, poor little things, which is cruel as it forces them to lay before they are mature. Last week the bigger one came in to lay and has continued fairly regularly and so I have had orders to shut up both of them with the hens at night.

When I opened the hen house this morning they huddled miserably in the corner. I do not imagine that the old hens had been very hospitable and I had to coax them out. Later in the day I noticed the bigger chicken in her old haunts and went over to investigate the condition of the little one. She wasn't pecking around with the hens and again I found her huddled in a corner of the hen house. I left her there feeling that she must get used to it. At feeding time I collected the bigger one from the cow pens and took her up with the others where she must learn to feed. When I rooted out the little one she flew into an overgrown hedge and I could not reach her. I knew that that would not do. Mr Fox could reach her if I could not. Once again I collected the stronger pullet, put her down outside the hedge, called the little one, and finally she came. I left them contentedly together and came back to wash the milk pails. I shall have to feed those two alone to give them a chance to get on an even footing with the hens.

And not yet a year has gone since the first time I tried to catch a hen. Kath and Walter sat on a nearby roller, incapacitated with laughter. It took me half an hour and I was more winded than the hen.

Now, enough of Green Farm. That was the way I felt one day last week. After quite a little systematic planning, I borrowed a cycle, skipped tea, changed buses twice, and finally ran down Nunningham lane. I opened the back door, hung up my coat, Gyp thumped her tail but did not move, and I went into the dining room. Walter looked up, "What – well I never! How did you get here?" He had not moved at the sound of the door for he thought I was Kath, who was outside feeding her chickens. I had very little time there but I had proved that the trip could be done in an evening.

Milking as usual today, and tonight I helped Mrs Moss to alter a dress. A sewing-machine, even this little hand one, is an anachronism in the checkered light of these old diamond-paned windows, beside the carved oak seats which lead into the old open fireplace. We sewed till nearly dark, when I went out in a fine misty rain to shut up my chickens. I dropped in to say goodnight to William, the bull, who is a great tame animal like Ferdinand, and likes to have his head scratched, very unlike Grandma Marshall 's bull who rants and roars and lusts for blood.

I had a word with my calves and then climbed up on the gate and thought it all over. I like the easy-going atmosphere here, and the animals, and soon I shall have a place in the community. I have met Iris Wolfe several times and enjoy evenings in her little thatched cottage with other girls wearing the same uniform as mine. I have met the Wilmotts, who have the farm nearest the village, and Miss Ashton, who is the local Land Army secretary. She has a beautiful home and her farm and garden is the district showplace.

There will always be diversion here, but I am no longer consumed with interest in my work. At Nunningham the farm was well and properly run. I was never besieged with doubt or mistrust. I learned something from every hour spent with Walter or Old Ted and came in at night with a sense of achievement, weary and content to knit by

WLA Guard of Honour at the wedding of a Land Girl, June, 1941,
with me at the far left.

WLA Guard of Honour. Iris Wolfe far left, then me,
Kathleen Hodben far right.

the fire. Here the days are a happy-go-lucky, any-way-will-do sort of picnic. We spend hours, day after day, getting the cows out of the corn, or off the road, in preference to spending two or three days systematically mending fences and hedges. Everyone turns up at once at milking time and stands idle while I, or old Fred fetch the cows, and if we finish at five, or five-thirty or six, no one cares or notices.

At Nunningham work was timed to finish at five and, if something occurred which kept us late, the men were paid overtime.

Here there is evening activity, a social round Mr Moss always ready to drop his work and rush off somewhere. I enjoy the company of other Land Girls, evenings with the Wilmotts, a drink and a game of darts at the Yew Tree with Mr Moss, but in the depths of my heart I know I would rather hoe turnips all day with John, or trim hedges with Walter and Old Ted and share in Nunningham's integrity and endeavour and the slowly ripening fruit of Walter's labours.

June 13, 1941. Green Farm
Here follows the tale of a day on a tractor – a bloody-awful, slip-where-it-should-hold, hold-where-it-should-slip tractor disc-harrowing. For one thing, I can't steer the damn thing, which is my own fault. Secondly, I can't steer the damn thing which is its fault. Then I stalled it. Mr Moss came along then. I had cranked to the extent of my cranking ability. I admit I have not discovered the knack, as yet. It sputtered and died.

"Damn and blast the bloody thing." I was winded and ready to weep with disgust.

"Now you're talking English. Now I understand you." I had not known I had company. "What's your first name again, and goshsakes, everyone calls me Brian, you can, can't you?"

He swung the crank again a few times and when the engine was running I was left alone again.

Brian has never thought of all the things about which Walter warned me and I live in fear and trembling. The discs stick and I have visions of the tractor rearing and me with a broken back. They did stick and firmly so I went back for Brian and learned that there is a lever on the discs which straightens them. I had never seen a set of discs before this day.

Then the water filter on the tractor ran dry. Another thing of which I was ignorant. Walter's tractor is of more recent vintage than this one and has an oil filter. Perhaps it did not need immediate attention but I decided to take no chances. Two hundred pounds worth of tractor was my responsibility. I went back for water. Because she was cold on my return I had to start her on petrol. Then I could not understand why, after about two "wents" she stopped dead, clutching, giving her more air, letting her out, all no good, she blinkin' well stopped. Of course bright little Polly had forgotten to switch her onto paraffin and the petrol had run dry. I switched her over and, as she was still hot, she finally went. Then just as I got her going nicely, didn't I lose the back set of discs! I was the best part of twenty minutes backing straight to them and then could not hitch them on. It was long past tea time so there she lies.

Record of a Successful Day's Tractor Driving – At Last.

Filled her up myself today, fuel, oil, and water, greased her, and checked her over generally. Started her up and went out to the field. Hitched on the discs, adjusted them, probably Walter would not have approved but Brian had no complaint.

Disc-harrowed the field, not so well because it was my first time mapping out a field and I found myself constantly confronted with triangles at the end of a cant. Disced it again, worse than the first time, could not see my tracks and became very involved.

Drove discs back to the road and returned to field, successfully maneuvering through four gateways. Hitched on roller. Rolled field, much more satisfactory, could see where I was going. Learned one thing, how wide to make the cants. Found that by going too far the first time and rolling the headland down like a rock. Only two triangles finally, and corners getting much better, though still much room for improvement.

Got into a jam parking roller and had to do in a bit of kale to get out. Back to the roadside for discs. Harrowed field again, much better. Could see tracks after rolling. Finished 10:39 p.m. Very satisfactory day.

Just as I finished my washing this morning, Charlie arrived full of news and plans. He has a week's leave, beginning July first, and Brian agreed to our hopeful suggestion that he come to Green Farm. It is hay time and I would not suggest leaving, so it is all working out beautifully. Brian said that he thought that he could lay his hands on a barrel of beer and we have agreed to split the cost with him. I led Charlie down the worn stone steps to the cellar to show him the niche where I had long been assuring Brian that a barrel of beer belonged. The cellar is deep and whitewashed, with a sort of inverted flying buttresses supporting the ceiling. One whole wall contains niches, cut deep into the stone, rising to pointed Gothic arches. I have never seen a real wine-cellar, but I am sure that, besides being cool and restful, this must at some time, have been a mouth-watering spot.

The balance of Charlie's news was that Penny and Mic, whom I have not seen since their wedding day, wished to come with Charlie for their deferred honeymoon. Brian suggested that we bike over to Wilmotts' to see if they could put them up. We returned just at milking time and reported that Mrs Wilmott was delighted to have the opportunity to welcome a Canadian soldier and his bride. Charlie lit the boiler for the sterilizer and fed the chickens for me while Fred and Burke and I milked. After tea we went down to the Yew Tree with Brian till it was time for Charlie's train.

Hitler attacked Russia yesterday. Why, no one seems to know, but it may mean our salvation. Perhaps he looks upon Britain as his supreme traditional enemy and thinks to conquer all and save juicy little England to be crushed as a last tidbit. Ha, ha! The juicy little tidbit will have time to ripen now. Hitler will find that when he turns to us he reaps the whirlwind.

Last week, the twenty-third, I wore my good breeches to work and rushed through the afternoon milking. Brian let me leave a little early so that by five o'clock I was well on the way. It was on June twenty-third, just a year ago, that Dado and Alec first drove me down Nunningham lane.

As the bus schedule has changed with the double-daylight time I can no longer make the round trip in an evening, but by cycling all the way I was just able to manage it. I walked to the bottom brook meadows with Kath and talked to them all, Walter and Old Ted and John, in the hay field. I dwell on my visit with particular pleasure as I am annoyed and not a little indignant tonight.

Brian came in, late for dinner today, hung up his cap and began washing his hands.

"Well, I've arranged for four soldiers to help with the hay and the harvest. She," pointing his finger at me, "must help you." He jerked his thumb at his wife. "I couldn't get 'em else I promised to feed 'em."

I was about to refuse sharply. Land Girls are not required to be household servants, and at hay time too, forced to remain indoors at the loveliest time of the year. Had Brian asked me to help him out, had he said that there was no other way, but no, just a bald order and a few words of explanation as to how I was to clean out the empty cottage beyond the orchard so that the boys might sleep there. Brian held out the key to the cottage.

I took it and the broom and dustpan and went right out and I am glad I did. As I swept the situation straightened itself out. Mrs Moss is not strong, and suddenly to have four hungry men added to the household would mean a great deal of work. If I help to feed them, I am still carrying out my job. Nevertheless, I see that hay time for me will mostly consist of milking this year, for there will be no time for me to get down to the hay field save after tea.

The soldiers turned up after breakfast this morning and seem a nice crowd. I spent the morning pulling and washing spinach, pounds and pounds of it, and peeling spuds. After the dinner dishes I made sand wiches and bottles of tea and took them down to the hay field, driving the cows back to the cow stalls in time for milking.

Haying at Green Farm

I went back to the house and had tea with Mrs Moss and then drove the hay sweep all evening. Walter had never even let me try sweeping but Brian was quite satisfied with the results, and so, to my surprise, was I. And I did enjoy being in the midst of haying again, with all the familiar tackle. Driving the sweep meant that I came home clean and minus hay down my neck and in my socks. Certainly sweeping is the pick of hay time jobs.

Brian brought the boys in for a mug of beer, and we all trooped down to the cellar to draw off our own. It was something very special for all of us, the cool old cellar and the cask set up in its niche. I am a little disappointed though, for Charlie comes tomorrow, comes for a whole week, and he and Penny will find that, with these thirsty hay makers, the casks will soon run dry.

July 2, 1941. Green Farm
I was up at four-thirty as usual and milked till breakfast. After breakfast and the dishes I picked beans and prepared them and the endless potatoes and then Mrs Moss discovered that there were enough raspberries for tarts for dinner so I made them and a large jug of custard. Twelve o'clock seemed to come very soon and our five men trooped into the huge old kitchen. How they enjoy its shadowy coolness and the few little Canadian touches I add to make dinner seem like home, and how I enjoy their crazy teasing and familiar slang. Brian sits proudly at the head of the table and beams on his noisy family. Charlie will certainly find that our keg of beer is very short-lived.

Brian said that I might skip milking and go to the train to meet Charlie and the others, so I helped Mrs Moss with the dinner dishes and left. I did not take time to change and arrived in my old WLA overalls just as the train was due. The station was deserted and I sat on a bench in the sun, watching the curve of the track. The sun was warm and I stretched out comfortably, glad of the silence and the freedom from duty. The train was two hours late, and I slept two restful hours. We left Mic and Penny at the Wilmott's with plans to meet at the Yew Tree and reached the farm in time for tea.

I drove the sweep all evening and Charlie pitched at the stack. I brought in one extra large load and Brian said that that would be the last and he sent Charlie and me off for the evening.

Charlie demanded his white shirt, and while I washed my hands in the kitchen, he went up and changed into gray flannels which Mrs Young had lent him. It was the first time he had been out of khaki in eighteen months.

We found the Wilmotts at the Yew Tree, with Mic and Penny and Iris and two or three other Land Girls. Later Brian came down with Mrs Moss and the soldiers and we had time for one drink together before closing time.

We have been up at five and haying till nearly eleven for weeks now, it seems. Charlie's leave is over and poor Penny is again in hospital. They helped with the hay several evenings and then one day when it rained, Archie said that I might have the whole day off. We went into Lewes, shopped a little, saw Kath of Cleves house in Southover, climbed all over Lewes Castle, where Charlie took a picture of Mic and Penny in the stocks, and then we had lunch at the White Hart. It is a lovely old inn and I have grown to know it quite well during my year in East Sussex.

The following day was a sad one for me. Charlie went into Eastbourne with Mic and Penny. They swam in the sea and had dinner with Dado and Alec. I was to join them in the evening but by an unfortunate error I missed the bus. I telephoned them and then returned to Green Farm by the footpath. It was a lovely evening, and after walking through the churchyard and the wood behind it, through bracken over my head, I began to forget my disappointment. I skirted two clean, ripening wheat fields of Mr Wilmott's and crossing the bridge, followed the stream, intending to join Brian and the boys and carry on with the evening's haying. However, I found that they had just completed a stack and were about to repair to the local. They decided that they were too hot and thirsty even to wash so we all trooped down, direct from the field.

The first person I saw was Penny, sitting with Mic on a bench that circled an old willow tree.

"What have you done with Charlie?" he demanded.

"Charlie – but –"

"Look, when you telephoned, we came right back from Eastbourne. Mrs Moss said that you hadn't come home, so we thought you were here. When you weren't, Charlie set off to find you."

"He went by the road?"

"I don't know. He must have, he's biking. You stay here. He'll be back. What'll you have?"

"Oh thanks, Scotch please."

"Poor Charlie, it's miles by road," I said to Mic. "And then all the way back. Thank goodness he has a bike."

Penny came out of the door with a small Scotch.

"There," he said, "Consider yourself honoured. That is the last drop in the house and I had to do a lot of talking to get it."

I thanked him, put it down on the bench beside me and just at that moment Charlie came around the corner of the pub. I jumped up to meet him and over went the untouched, last drop of Scotch in the house. That was my day for being old John Lovell's "dam' ornery body" who "don't do nuthin' roight."

On Saturday Brian drove us to meet Alec and Dado at the Golden Cross, the big inn at the crossroads, and on Sunday Mic and Penny brought their lunch and we ours and we set off on cycles to explore the downs. I think I have mentioned seeing a dew pond before, but that day we came upon one unexpectedly and experienced the wonder all anew. Dew ponds are always perfectly round and to find them so far from any stream, on the top of the smooth green downs, they seem to be magic things, like the little red toadstools one comes upon in sunlit glades, or fairy rings in the grass.

It was a pleasant day but on the way home Penny came to grief. We were biking down a steep hill and, trying to pass Mic on a curve, he piled up against the stony wall of the opposite side. I was ahead, and when they did not all catch up with me I went back to see why. I found Mic and Charlie holding Penny between them.

"We're waiting for a car going our way, to ask for help."

"Damn a car going our way. Stop the first one that comes," I said and did. The driver dropped Penny at the cottage of a lady doctor in Alfriston who was not at home. We lowered him into a chair, where he sat with his head on his knees, unable to sit back or sit up in any comfort. We seemed so useless that I had to do something. I tried to get a shot of brandy from the inn next door. It was too early for opening time, somewhere about four, and the landlord refused to give it to me. I explained the urgency of the situation with some degree of heat, and demanded a gift of some spirit out of his private stock. He was most unhappy about the whole idea but finally I left with a tiny glass of Scotch and carried it through the sunlit village street, to the little cottage where Penny waited. It was many hours before the doctor came home and many telephone calls were put through before Charlie went off with Penny in an army vehicle to East Grinstead and Mic and I, very disconsolately, wheeled the four bikes home. It was a flat ending to a week's leave.

Since then I have been milking, preparing vegetables, packing teas and haying in the evenings.

Today is Sunday and Brian's day off. Old Mr Burke came with me to get the cows. We could find only half of them, which I brought in and began to milk. I had nearly finished when he arrived with the others and called me, his voice hoarse with panic. I ran out and the poor old man was in a dreadful state. "Get Mr Moss, quick!" he said. Then I saw Bluebell. She is an old cow with an enormous udder which, because she has just calved, was almost bursting. She had jumped a barbed wire fence and her swollen bag was torn terribly. The blood poured in a steady stream from one gash and was flowing from several others. Mr Burke clapped great handfuls of udder salve on the tears when I returned with Brian, and they decided that they did not need to send for the vet. Of course she had to be milked, and it was wonderful to see how gently Brian milked her and to hear old Mr Burke talking tenderly to her all the time to keep her from kicking. Brian carried on with the milking and we were only just finished when the lorry arrived for the milk.

Kath and Walter came over and took me for a drive in the evening, along high-banked twisting lanes, between fields of beautiful wheat, many of which have grown under Walter's supervision. This WAEC farming scheme is vast. I miss seeing the wheels turn as I did at Nunningham. Brian has little use for the Committee, although for his finest crop, the flax, he has followed their instructions to the letter.

We drove through Steyning and Bramber and in both places I wanted to linger. Steyning has an old Saxon church and I would like to wander along Bramber's winding street under the ruins of the castle. Walter said that we could stop on the way back but we called at his cousin's farm, a neat little place, in meticulous order, and it was dark when we returned. I seem to be fated more "to travel hopefully than to arrive."

Today we were to have finished the hay and to have had a farewell party with the soldiers. We finished the hay all right but no party. The soldiers were called back last night while I was out with Kath and Walter. Because they were gone I was spared my usual indoor work, but as another cow had calved and the weather looked threatening we have been working against time all day and seem busier than usual.

My hands are bothering me a lot these days. I have had twinges of rheumatism since early last winter and have been taking some type of iodine which the doctor advised but which has caused little improvement. My hands ached and were stiff at first, but now they really cause a good measure of difficulty. Two fingers on each hand snap shut, and I pry them open painfully and then they remain straight. I find myself less eager to join Brian in his pub crawls and much more ready for bed.

It is quiet tonight with the soldiers gone and only the three of us for tea. The hay is all in. It was an excellent crop and Brian makes light of the work and takes everything in his stride, but I do not feel the satisfaction I did at Nunningham. It is my second season haying in English fields and perhaps the facets are dulled with familiarity. The air has not seemed so fragrant, and Brian's haphazard, careless attitude detracts from the sense of sharing in a work of value. I take little pride in helping to build a rick which bulges, and on which the roof slopes drunkenly when it has stood a week or so. Brian says, "Oh well, we've got the hay." Perhaps my feelings are coloured by weariness. Brian has gone up to the Swan tonight and I am going to bed.

The two heifers which run with the herd jumped the fence again this morning. The others, of course, followed. By the time we collected them all and finished milking it was long past breakfast time. I had to come down to the cow stalls after, to feed the chickens and wash the pails and cooler, before I was free to find my way up the flax field. Brian had told me where they would be working, so I crossed the road in front of the house, climbing the steep bank and skirting a large hay field, soft and purply with red clover and scenting the air heavily. I must ask Brian why that field has not been cut, certainly any cows turned into it would have "five mouths." That is, they would trample down as much as they could eat. I found the path in the far corner and walked through the wood. I had never been over there before nor had I ever seen a field of flax.

There is a particular beauty in a field of silvery oats and in the golden ripple of a wheat field, but today I felt that never I had seen anything more lovely than this softly tossing, blue-flowered flax, bowing before the light breeze. It is so fragile and delicate, so essentially feminine. I thought of a dainty lady in dotted Swiss muslin, as I watched the slim stalks, their little balls of seed waving with every breath.

The men were pulling a path around the field, wide enough to allow the flax-puller, which is due tomorrow, to circle the field without damaging the crop. I stepped into place and found that flax pulls out of the ground very easily. One pulls enough for a sheaf, then makes a bond, as Old Ted showed me last year, ties up the sheaf and tosses it against the hedge. The object of the pulling is so that the whole length of the fibre may be utilized, which makes for superior linen. Linseed, which is much the same crop, though bred for seed, rather than for length of fibre, is cut with a binder like corn.

We have been shocking flax between milking times all week. The sheaves are delicate little things and seem to shock up nicely, tangling their sticky little heads together, but it is surprising to find next morning, how many shocks, or stooks have quietly leaned over flat. Brian does not bother to go around standing them up again, and perhaps he is right. We have had no rain and there is no sign of them growing.

Tonight I biked over to Pat's to return a borrowed flashlight. She is a Land Girl who lives at Rook's Corner. Her father was killed at Dunkirk and her mother bombed out of their home in London, so they have taken this little cottage together. It is a charming place, covered with flowers and truly rural from the outside, and, save for the cairns, tranquil and uncluttered when one enters. Pat and her mother have six cairns, and as they are so tiny, and curl up unobtrusively on chairs or in doorways, one seems almost certain to sit or step on one.

I have spent several peaceful and pleasant evenings with Pat and her mother, but tonight I scarcely arrived when a car drew up at the gate. It was Dado and Alec, who are growing used to chasing me around the countryside and to meeting my friends. We drove down with them to the Plume of Feathers, a charming little roadside inn, half hidden under three or four very old oak trees. The roof is part thatch and part tile, a recent repair job I imagine, and the walls of cream-coloured plaster show through the heavy branches and blossoms of climbing red roses. We had only descended the few steps from the road to the low doorway when we discovered that about four of the cairns had followed us. From then on, as Alec and Dado had brought their aristocratic Airedale bitch, there was more excitement than we had bargained for.

I had an exciting trip home too, steering my bike with one hand, and hanging on with the other to the handle of Alec's car door.

I biked into Lewes today between milking times. Mrs Moss had driven me yesterday afternoon, which was Saturday and, after a little shopping, we heard several whistles and were aware of a sense of activity in the High Street. A girl in the shop, where we happened to be, said that there was a mock gas attack to be staged that day, and that tear gas was to be used. Neither Mrs Moss nor I had our gas masks, and Mrs Moss became most upset, so we left and drove right back to Green Farm. I went to a whist drive with her in the evening but, though she seemed to find it very interesting, I still did not feel compensated for my lost day in Lewes.

After breakfast this morning I biked to the village to telephone Mrs Mullins, who now works full-time for the WAEC in Lewes. She assured me that I could lunch at the WLA Hostel there, so I spend a few hours with her and the few Land Girls who had not gone home for the weekend. I enjoy meeting other girls in uniform and feel part of a service with whose members I so seldom rub shoulders.

My hands were very sore again after milking and the muscles in my forearms very hard. What worries me most, I think, is the nausea I feel when milking and the consciousness of all my stomach muscles.

August 6, 1941. Green Farm
We have been carting flax the last few days and it is an easy crop to carry. The sheaves are light and Brian pitches up a whole shock at a time. I do not think Fred enjoys his job of stacking as they are all tangled sheaves. But no one cares very much. It is all due to go off to the flax factory almost immediately. I wonder that there is no way to cart it direct from the field and save the labour of stacking.

Brian had to go out after tea last night and I assured him that we could manage. The men could help me bring in the first load and while they are stacking I could bring in the second alone. I have done that more than once, drive up, pitch all the shocks onto the trailer and drive up again.

My intentions were good, my spirit more than willing, but I could not start the tractor. I cranked and cranked, old Fred fussed around with deep concern, and Mr Burke was disturbed and very upset. His silent sympathy was harder to bear than Fred's constant mutters of encouragement. They were terrified of the tractor but offered to swing her for my sake. I dared not let them try. That tractor kicks like two mules and I could not let two willing but innocent old men hurt themselves. Their relief at my refusal was almost audible. After nearly an hour of this I was shaking like a leaf. Finally they made me give up, their scorn not for me but directed at, "they machines." Two kind old men that they are, they hoed with me till dark.

But I knew better than they, knew that it was the driver too that was found wanting, and I cried bitterly till I slept.

Today has been one of those special days when everything goes smoothly and well. I awakened a little on the early side, which is a good beginning. It was a misty blustery morning, with fields and hedges blurred, and long searchlight fingers probing the sky. The cows were all together and I drove them in contentedly, with none of the usual frustrated feeling when, after counting again and again, they add up to only forty or forty-one. Brian turned up for milking and we sang lustily, rolling the full churns to the roadway and striding home for breakfast, chickens all fed and pails washed, before there was any sign of the milk lorry.

I told Brian my sad story of the night before and he found it amusing and the tractor started for me after breakfast on the fourth swing. I did hope that something was wrong with it, something beyond the scope of my meagre experience, but I was not given that consolation. We stacked the last of the flax in the morning and Brian began cutting a field of oats in the afternoon.

The cows were conveniently waiting at the gate, when I went for them this afternoon. Brian bought a little bull calf last week and presented him to Lady to rear. She was mooing impatiently just before I let them in. As old Fred said, "Hark at that sil-ly fool, bellerin' fer her calf and it ain't hern at all."

Brian's oat field is a poor sad thing, mates well with his binder. However, we caught up with him tonight, shocked up the corn he had cut this afternoon and, before he stopped, we were following the binder waiting for the sheaves to fall. On the way home I caught sight of a few plums glowing in the last of the sunset. Brian said the old tree seldom bore fruit so we picked them and took them in to supper.

I came in at tea time feeling quite ill. Brian had been out in the oat field all day and I had milked twenty-two cows. When he came in he asked how the milking had gone.

"Fine," I said, "but I milked Bessie last." Bessie is an old cow with great fleshy teats. I find her very tiring to milk. "And it's a good thing I did too, for I could not have milked another."

"Let's see those hands."

I held them out, with second and fourth fingers each curled tightly against the palm. Archie snapped the fingers open, I winced a little and could not bend them again.

"You change your clothes after breakfast tomorrow, and go in to see the doctor."

I shall be glad to go. The backache and muscular nausea I have had for sometime, but lately, to my surprise, often when I have been working alone, I have discovered myself to be crying. When I finish my work in the cow stalls too late to walk out to the hay field or corn-field before dinner, I would hoe for an hour or so in the kale near the house. My work was mechanical. I can hoe for whole days now and not suffer. I would time myself during the first row and determine to do the next one in two minutes less time. After hoeing about four rows, long ones, I would stop to roll a cigarette to find tears rolling down my face. It seems just plain stupid to me.

August 18, 1941. Eastbourne

Things happened so quickly that I have difficulty in keeping abreast. I went to the doctor. He told me that I was run down and full of rheumatism, that I must stop living in damp farmhouses, cut out milking completely, and give up the Land Army. I said that I was of no use to Brian if I did not milk and refused flatly. He said that no one should milk as many cows as I did, certainly not unless they had worked up gradually over a period of years. In addition, he said that I was not accustomed to such heavy work and such little sleep. I went off with a sedative of some sort and orders to return in a week.

Charlie came down on a forty-eight and came with me the second time. He and the doctor talked over my head as if I were a naughty child, and I was finally forced to agree to leave the Mosses as soon as a girl was found to replace me.

"Ever heard of the willing horse?" the doctor said, as we left. When I nodded, he said, "Well, remember it."

Charlie and I walked down to Mrs Ashton's that night and told her what the doctor had said, and the following night Brian and his mother went out, so I took a book and went to bed at six-thirty. About seven there was a knock at the door and Mrs Mullins and Miss Ashton came in with a new Land Girl. Bag and baggage she came and began milking next morning. I packed immediately and came to Eastbourne but I am leaving again for Nunningham in a day or two.

Walter telephoned that he had a new tractor and is short of a driver. Would I come and drive? I explained that it was not quite cricket for me to leave Moss' on doctor's orders and return to Nunningham to work. He explained that I would not need to work hard, no milking, someone would crank the tractor for me. All I would have to do would be to "sit on the bloody thing and steer." I agreed to go and called Charlie for his final opinion. His reply was, "After all they have done for us – there is no question about it. If the time has come when you can help, you go."

October 20, 1941. Sutton, Surrey

It must have been with great delight that Kath and Walter saw this year's harvest home and me on my way. I was irritable and bad-tempered. Walter was cautious as is his nature, and watched over my tractor-driving which made me more nervous. We had continuous rain, and while the wheat did not suffer, the oat is sorry stuff. We shocked it and it rained. We spread open the shock and it rained. We turned them and finally cut open the sheaves, and still it rained. In the end, the field which suffered the most was carted loose and stacked like hay. Walter remained even-tempered, which infuriated me even more. It was his harvest over which my heart was breaking, and he seemed to take it all in his stride. I saw the vision which we kept always before us, of saving by our labours, the shipping of food to England, saving the lives of the men of the Merchant Navy. I saw the long hours of ploughing in the cold and rain, the heat and dust of harrowing. I remembered the days when we methodically covered the cornfields, Walter and John pulling out every dock while I carted them to the hedge and burned them. I watched with excitement the young, green shoots coming through in their straight drills, claimed a share in England's pride of this, her greatest harvest, when the blue-green fields ripened and I felt the heavy silvery heads.

I was stiff and tired and sore and I had no courage to face the rain. Each night I felt that it must stop, that we could go down to the oat field to find the sheaves drying and the straw lifting in the wind. But each morning the rain fell from leaden skies and the corn was limper and blacker than the day before.

Walter said that I would never make a farmer, that one must take a longer view than one crop or one year. And besides the oats had not grown badly, and he would not be surprised if it threshed out fairly well. I walked down alone one wet evening and morosely watched the smoking stack, in the centre of which Old Ted had made a funnel. It infuriated and terrified me.

I wakened each morning wondering which part of me would not work when I tried to get out of bed, and wishing, as I am sure Kath and Walter wished too, that I could leave. I felt that I could not go until the corn was in, and yet I knew all the time, that working with such poor grace was worse than quitting.

SUTTON

February 2, 1942. Sutton, Surrey

For the first few weeks of my stay here I did little but sleep, sometimes for as long as sixteen hours. Charlie secured a sleeping-out pass and shared my rooms at Cheam. I met many of his friends with whom we would have dinner or drink in the evenings.

One morning I wakened early and telephoned Charlie at the office. Sergeant Peacock asked who was calling, and when I told him, he replied, "Oh no, it isn't. *She* never gets up till one o'clock."

And then Charlie and I found a little apartment and moved in. He left each morning before eight and returned each night to dinner. Mrs King lent me a few things which made our furnished flat a home: linen, pottery, a coffee table. I was able to invite her to luncheon and Charlie brought his friends home.

Our memories of these days will stand out clearly when we have a permanent home again, my meeting with Bob Durham, for instance, Charlie's great friend.* Initial introductions were brief.

"How do you do?"

"How do you do?"

"I imagine I shall see you at the dance tonight?"

---

* Bob later married my sister.

"Yes, I believe so."

"You don't mind dancing with a drunk, do you?"

"Not a bit. We'll see you later then?"

"Right, 'bye for now."

"'Bye."

Bob spoke more seriously than I knew. Towards the end of the dance he and Charlie lay at full length on the grass verge, happily reciting Omar Khayyam verse by verse to the stars.

Charlie and I were caught in a raid one night coming home from Egham. We changed trains safely at Twickenham and had a twenty minute wait at Wimbledon. Big guns were going off in all directions and we heard the occasional crump of a bomb in the distance. Trains pulled silently into the station with no light showing. Passengers alighted from dark compartments, doors slammed shut, and the trains slid off again – all efficient, undramatized, typical English cooperation. It was "business as usual" in a nightmare situation. A plane zoomed over our heads and crashed in flames on Wimbledon Common, the one open space where no damage could be done.

We waited well over forty minutes, knowing that trains would be late. Finally, on making enquiries, we learned that our train would not be coming through, "tho if we'opped it there was a bus to Morden in three minutes." We hopped it. I wonder if a Victoria Cross, or rather a George Cross, has ever been awarded to a bus driver who has safely guided his passengers through Stygian England in an air-raid. There were no headlights on and, of course, no lights in the bus. We travelled at what seemed a miraculous speed – perhaps fifteen miles an hour – in complete blackness. Suddenly the flare of fire from an oil bomb would blind us all, the driver would slow his pace, quicken it again as he grew used to the light, and then we would be past the glare and pushing through the dark again. We ran the two miles home after we left the bus with HE's (high explosives) and oil bombs dropping every few minutes. We dropped flat once or twice, then jumped up and ran on. Tiles clattered from the roofs and glass shattered in the road. I asked Charlie what caused the peculiar ping-ping which I heard everywhere. "Shrapnel," he shouted. "Guess I'd better put my tin hat on." I wondered if I should knock on a door and try to borrow a dishpan. We finally arrived at the house in Cheam to find the owners under the dining-room table with their dog.

The raids have been almost a daily routine. I was in one of the theatres when a notice flashed on the screen, stating that the warning had just been sounded and requesting those who wished to take shelter below to proceed in an orderly fashion. Nobody moved and the picture continued. Some little time later another notice was put on the screen.

"The all-clear has just sounded. It wasn't so bad after all, was it?"

The Japanese attacked Pearl Harbour on December seventh, and the next day the News Chronicle headline stated, "Japan at war with the U.S. and Britain." So now we feel that the States are actively with us.

The Youngs' invited us to spend Christmas with them. We spent a delightful family day, though it began with a slight accident. I was carrying a basket on my arm as we walked over on Christmas morning. In it were a few small gifts and a pint of milk. At the corner of Christ Church and Brighton Road Charlie offered to carry the basket and somehow we dropped the pint of milk. I wonder if the folks at home could understand the tragedy of it. A little crowd of people coming from church grouped about us.

"What a dreadful shame!"

"And on Christmas day, too!"

"A whole pint!"

February 16, 1942. Dene Dip, Petworth
Just before Valentine's Day the RMR's were transferred to Petworth Park, the home of Lord Leconsfield (where the famous Holbein portrait of Henry VIII hangs). Charlie found a room for me on the Milford Estate in one of several seventeenth-century stone cottages used to house the staff for the "Big House." I live with the carpenter and his wife, next door to the cook and close to the butler and the dairy and its staff. The walls of our cottage are four-foot thick solid stone.

February 20, 1942. Dene Dip, Petworth
I had written to Brian Moss for a reference. He replied, stating that I had done "general farm work, including tractor driving which she was very good at, and is an excellent milker. I found her willing and keen, honest and trustworthy." I have never received such a glowing recommendation – I bristle with pride!

I applied for a job in the Farmer's Weekly and used Archie's reference, but it was of no use. I received a most friendly but definite refusal. Too bad, too, for the farm was at Itchen Abbas. Though a most incomplete angler, I dreamed for a night or two of fishing in the Itchen and of growing to know Winchester.

March 9, 1942. Dene Dip
Just back from leave. We spent a few days in Eastbourne with Dado and Alec. They do find war time difficult. Dado feels the cold terribly. She is not the domestic type and misses her usual life of gaiety. She and Alec have lived in Paris many years and war-time England is a great contrast.

We fulfilled a commission for Charlie's mother on our final week-end and spent a delightful few days with her friends in Horn Church. One story conveys the ends to which they went to assure our comfort. Mrs Blakely showed me my room and the bathroom and explained that there was a certain utilitarian vessel available if I so desired.

"I had one," she said. "But it was cracked. I didn't know if you were a –" Here she smiled. "A big girl. And I feared it might not be safe, so I went into town and bought a new one."

By this time I was laughing too, for I could see what had happened. We leaned on the little brown newel-post, carved in the form of a monk, while she went on.

"Of course, I hadn't thought of wrapping paper." (Shops no longer supply wrapping paper.) So I had to come all the way home on the train with it under my arm."

March 12, 1942. Dene Dip
Last night Charlie was on duty and said that he would not be in until eleven. By ten o'clock we locked up, leaving a key outside in the appointed place for Charlie, and turned in. I had been in bed only a few minutes when, after hearing several planes go over, I heard a particularly heavy barrage. It was a peculiar sound. It seemed quite near, but there was no bombing, only a gigantic sputtering. I ignored it at first but soon curiosity got the better of comfort. Shutting my book, I blew out the candle and drew the blackout. My window faces south and on the extreme right great clouds of white light were rising, and there was a constant staccato of machine-gunfire.

This was too much to miss so I pulled on my clothes and sneaked out. Dene's Dip is really a narrow gorge. I climbed the steep rise behind the house. Through the woods and across the pheasant fields it was quite dark, with only a glimmer of the stars or searchlights above the tall beeches and sycamores. But once onto the common I could see the brilliance of the searchlights. They were no longer slender, groping fingers, but grouped five and ten together in a brilliant belt of light. There were ten or twelve of these and the southwestern sky flared with bursts of blinding, white light. I could not understand it at all. The light leapt and swirled and was reinforced just as it began to drift away, just as an oil bomb bursts and flares. But oil bombs are diabolically orange, with puffs of gaseous yellow cloud and spurting tongues of flame. This was dead white light.

I walked a mile or so along a path, the black humps of the downs* beneath me. I was nearing the main road and had not yet met Charlie. I could hear the tramp of soldiers' feet coming home form the "King's Arms." I did not wish to encounter these gay lads so I turned home.

As I crossed the common again the excitement died in the western sky and a little thrill went through me as I saw the slow-moving truck of a tiny light overhead. Jerry gives no signals, and when one hears that vast roar in the sky, it is reassuring to see a little winking light. Its signal is for its own formation or for the searchlights, but it seems to say, "It's all right. It's only me." Just one of the family, announcing itself at night.

Later, when Charlie got in, he told me that the brilliant lighting was part of a scheme by his regiment. He might have warned me.

April 20, 1942. Dene Dip
Charlie spent a week on an Aircraft Recognition Course and my boredom and impatience, the former because of inactive, simple life, the latter caused by no reply from the Land Army, mounted steadily.

On Charlie's scheme the boys set up their headquarters at a farm near Wisborough Green. It was a fruit farm and impressed Charlie deeply by its well-run appearance. It is a very beautiful old house. And to interest us even more, the owners were looking for a Land Girl. As there had been no reply from East Sussex, I decided to go over to interview Charlie's acquaintances. We planned to go on Sunday and I borrowed a neighbour's cycle for Charlie.

---

* "Downs," which are really "ups," comes from the Anglo-Saxon "dun" or hill, a use which survives in "sand-dunes."

Charlie with a tommy gun

The farm was all that Peter had depicted. The old house had settled with the years and we stooped to enter through the Tudor doorway, whose lintel was not five feet from the ground. The hall was
large with old chests and a suit of armour. We, complete strangers,
were invited to tea, accepted, and welcomed.

I felt an immediate respect for Mr Davis, as a man and as a farmer.
He led me through acres and acres of young apple trees, showed me a
pair of secateurs, and demonstrated the pruning which would be my
work. Clip, clip, clip in all winds and weathers, not for four hours a
day as with milking, but all day, every day. My forearm muscles were
still knotted and stiff. I knew I could not do it. Mr Davis amused me
by his horrified surprise when he looked over my papers. He seemed
most disturbed to find that I preferred agricultural work to some un-
defined post for which he seemed to feel I was qualified.

Here follows the substance of a letter received yesterday from
Mr R.H.B. Jesse, Exec. Officer, East Sussex War Agricultural Executive Committee:

A new tractor school is being started in a fortnight's time and your name
will be sent in if you so wish. You will then become a permanent driver
doing tractor work in various places. You may, if you prefer it, do Gang
Work, that is field work, hay making, harvesting, etc., living in one place
and cycling to work at farms in the vicinity.

We should propose you as a Gang Leader where you would get 42/6 and 4/ – extra as leader. It you decide for tractor work you would get 45/ – rising to 50/ and 55/ – as you become a first class driver in charge of other girls.

As luck would have it, Charlie was away on a scheme again when the news arrived. I was afraid to accept immediately, lest he consider permanent tractor work too heavy for a mere female, so I telephoned Walter Marshall and he gave me his full approval and good wishes.

I replied immediately that I most definitely wished to join the tractor school. I am not concerned about the extra five shillings but I am going to become a first class tractor driver or know the reason why. Not for nothing did that orange fiend of Walter's leer at me two long years ago. I left Nunningham without mastering it, but here is my opportunity. I shall hitch my tractor to a star.

I can see much in favour, and no disadvantages to this new work.

1 No milking, pruning, or otherwise automatic handwork, no hands-in-the-wet, no work at which I cannot wear mitts in winter.
2 I shall remain in East Sussex where my roots are. I prefer to remain a member of the East Sussex WLA.
3 I shall be working again within the Coastal Danger area, so that I may come and go to the areas where my friends live, and also, if the balloon goes up, I shall be on the spot.

So rejoice with me, for joy is abroad in the land.

TRACTOR SCHOOL

April 29, 1942. Tractor School, Cralle Place

I have been here twenty-four hours. We live in converted brooder houses, eleven other girls and myself. Instead of a foster-mother, warming fifty little chicks, in each room there is one Land Girl, one bed (one thin mattress on three-ply wood, no spring), one small plywood wardrobe, and one chair.

But I have learned to forage, like Caesar's men and the Canadians. I found that a few planks, scrounged from underneath the chicken-coop and arranged on a couple of saw-horses, also scrounged, make an excellent dressing table and desk combined. My books on the table, my sepia print of Tintern Abbey on the wall, and a big bowl of primroses in the honey-pot which Mrs Moss gave me, make me feel very much at home.

I was off to a flying start this morning. Mr Winters, our instructor, told me to hitch on to the roller and stood watching carefully while I did so. While he held up the draw bar I backed straight in, leaned back and dropped the pin in the hole. Mr Winters looked at me with awe.

"By gum," was all he said, and I was forced to confess that I had driven a tractor before. I swapped the roll for harrows, and as we have had no rain for weeks, I was enveloped in clouds of dust all day.

I called Nunningham at noon and asked if Fatty Cornford, the local carter, could bring over my working kit, which I had left at the farm. I expected him to come when he had a trip in this direction, but he made a special one and arrived just as I came in from work. He is a great friend of Walter's and we sat on the step and had a real old gossip. Fatty was glad to see his "little ol' de -ar," as he and old Dan call me, and I was delighted to talk to an old friend.

When he had gone I disrobed piecemeal on the doorstep, and whacked the dust out of my clothes on the outside wall. I gave my hair a good brushing and then washed, "up as far as possible, and down as far as possible. Poor possible," as the Welsh girls I met in Sutton used to say. As yet we have no bathroom facilities and may bathe, only on sufferance and advance notice, at the big house.

Two years ago tomorrow I sailed from New York to a British Port.

The girls change and rush off to the Pig and Whistle every night. I have not yet grown accustomed to unescorted pubbing, but I can see that I soon shall or else be dubbed a snob.

Last night, George, who is farm manager, asked me if the girls had gone off and left me alone. When I explained that I had not wished to go, that I had been busy unpacking, he said that if I were through and if I felt lonely, his wife would be glad to have me spend the evening with her. I walked up this evening to thank her. She is a plump, cheerful person, about my age and they have a practical, modern cottage.

Tomorrow night is pay night and George says that Mr Winters tries to make it Land Girl night at the Pig and Whistle. He and Mrs George go, and all the girls. I may as well give in gracefully and brush up on my dart game.

I was quite right about the Tractor School. It was a brooder house and has been beaver-boarded inside. Two bathrooms are to be built and another building to house dining and recreation halls.

Major Batten owns the farm and a guest house. The Cralle Place has been run with much sparkle and gaiety and the farm not at all. Recently the government stepped in and took over the farm, with George as manager, and the tractor school was installed on the grounds. Our poor and repeated ploughing will give the land a good workout and clean it well for future cultivations. All this information is gleaned from my visit with Mrs George. I enjoyed my evening and have come home early. I hope to be asleep before the girls come in from the pub.

As yet there is little love lost between us. They are all proud veterans of two weeks tractor driving and, of course, know all there is to know. Today one of the girls, who is self-appointed leader, undertook to show me why I could not start my tractor. The carburetor was flooding so I turned off the petrol.

"Don't turn that off," I was ordered.

I pointed out the flooding, so she proceeded to drain the carburetor, saying flatly, "You must drain off the paraffin."

"But it's not paraffin, it's petrol."

"Look, my dear girl," went on my instructor, proudly explaining that when I stopped last night I was running on paraffin and therefore the carburetor was filled with paraffin "Or," she continued sweetly, "could I, by some chance, be in error?"

"I'm more than sorry," I was delighted to reply, "but you are. Because I always switch over and let her run off on petrol."

By this time I had cranked her again and she went. My friend had not yet learned that little trick and was very irritated. The girls take great pleasure in talking among themselves about how simple it is to drive a tractor and how only an idiot could have any difficulty. Thank goodness I am not as green as they believe, or I should be crying myself to sleep. Mr Winters insisted that I not mention my previous experience.

May 2, 1942. Tractor School
At present we must eat in the house, in a tiny room allotted us by Mrs Batten, and we are considered an unavoidable and not even necessary evil. A Land Girl is a person who feels forced to intrude in the house, and who comes in muddy boots and with greasy fingernails to eat, bathe, or telephone.

Today I am alone. Everyone else has gone home for the weekend. For some odd reason I preferred to stay here. I am near Nunningham, and the knowledge that Kath and Walter are just over the hill, that Charlie is four or five hours away, and that Dado and Alec are within easy distance is all I need. I choose to stay here, to read a little, to mend, to explore and push in my roots.

When I went to the house for my lunch Mrs Batten showed concern lest I was cold "over there all alone." She immediately dug out a paraffin heater for me, told me to come over and fill it whenever I needed, and also contributed a beautiful green brocaded chair for my room.

"And now, come in and have a drink with us."

So I shared a Scotch or two with a gentleman in breeches and two girls in jodhpurs and then had lunch with them in the big dining room. Later I had a hot bath, washed my hair, and was presented with an electric dryer. I rather enjoy a weekend alone.

The weekend it began well. Saturday morning was one of brilliant sunshine and my tractor behaved beautifully. My ploughing is improving too. It is so glorious out there on the hill, little pink-breasted chaffinches, with blue caps and barred wings, diving, sweeping swallows, and tail-tipping magpies, all following the plough, picking up grubs on the newly turned earth. I found and gathered an enormous bouquet of foxglove on my way back at lunch time.

And I had a very satisfactory afternoon. I walked along the road to the little cottage which is the Post Office and general store.

"Have you any cigarette papers?" A routine question.

"Well, I can let you have one package."

"I suppose it is useless to ask for cigarette tobacco?"

"Well, you may have one ounce."

This was really deep in clover, so we talked a little and I explained how hungry we girls were at night. I said that we were able to have a bit of bread but that there was no jam or cheese to spare. By then a pot of honey had appeared on the counter and two little triangles of processed cheese, and finally some chocolate. I left feeling like an antique dealer who has made a genuine find.

I have been here about two weeks now, and with the addition of two or three embryonic tractor drivers, I am no longer the newcomer. I have little to offer to make me one of the group, but as we all have a meeting-point in our work, we get along well together.

We are all in different stages of proficiency. The newer girls cruise around on tractors to get used to driving. The next step is rolling, which initiates one into driving with an implement, gauging the turning space, and learning to drive straight and to measure out a field. Several stages follow, until one proud morning one hitches on a plough and proceeds to realize that the three levers which one must master each produce a multitude of results.

Last week I came in for a job I did not relish. Like each of the other girls, I had a two-furrow Cockshutt and was really beginning to get the knack of it, when one of the newer girls graduated into the ploughing contingent. We were one plough short, and much to my disgust, I was given a three-furrow International. I was not sure enough of myself with a two-furrow to carry on easily with a three, and in addition to my lack of skill, the plough proved to have something wrong with it.

We began at the front and adjusted the hitch differently but there was no improvement. We changed the set of the coulters, adjusted the tension of the axle on the furrow wheel, then on the land wheel. After four days of adjustment and experimentation we discovered that the trouble was in the set of the rear wheel. A morning's work, removing the wheel, trying on one from a new plough, taking both to the blacksmith, and finally resetting the repaired wheel, resulted in three identical furrows turning smoothly over the moldboards.

They say that it takes twenty years to make a plough man and I can well believe it. However I can now cut out well, set my plough with some method, plough comparatively straight and evenly, but I still make a dreadful mess of closing up. The tractors themselves are all 1942 Fordsons and run beautifully. These girls must experience ploughing, which requires full concentration, while at the same time they are nursing along an old worn-out tractor which is always most cussed at the critical moment. I had just such a problem on Brian Moss's old 1932 tractor, and I breathe deeply on these perfect WAEC machines. Certainly we have much to learn.

Evenings are always full. The girls still wend their ways nightly to the Pig and Whistle. Last Saturday was a red letter day for me. George asked me if I would care to go fishing with him and Mrs George. The old light of battle flickered in Polly's eyes. We had a singularly peaceful and lovely evening and I caught two small trout. We went back to the cottage and Mrs George fried them for supper. Long live the delicious memory of my first English trout, tiny, but oh so succulent.

On Sunday Kath and Walter came for me and I went back to Nunningham for tea, and felt wrapped in the soft warmth of homecoming, when everything smiles from its accustomed place. All my heart is there, the birth of my love for England and all that she means to me. My first thrilling hopes of helping come back to me when I turn the bend in the road and see the old gray house under the willows, against the rolling blue hills of the Sussex Weald. Gyp comes to meet me, barking joyously and Peter can hardly speak for excitement. "Auntie's come – Auntie's come," and he jumps up and down in glee. His is the only child's welcome which has ever been mine.

I talked over my ploughing problems with Walter, saw Kath's beautifully ordered garden, the raspberry canes all restaked, a bit of lawn forfeited to make room for currants, strawberries, and tomatoes. Where last year the moles had played merry hell with the lawns and I

Peter driving, John on the wagon

rolled and struggled so to obliterate their traces, there is now a level stretch of green. And for some reason the moles, this year, have given Nunningham a wide berth.

Charlie telephoned me while I was here. He is in this area on a scheme, here within reach of me but he cannot come to me.

June 3, 1942. Tractor School
There seems seldom a moment one can call one's own. Two weeks ago I went to Rottingdean with Pam, a tall, slender, cool-mannered, very precise member of our tractor school. Pam and I share the bathroom, fill our hot-water bottles at the house to make hot chocolate at

night (from powders I receive from home), walk and talk together, and have formed a strange temporary relationship based on mutual respect and transient common interests. She has overwhelmed me with invitations to go home with her for weekends. I have refused for some time, only because I have so enjoyed the spacious quiet of weekends here alone after the week's gregarious and routine living.

Last Saturday, however, I was scheduled to leave with Pam on the 2:15 bus. We parked our tractors at noon, and oil and grease to the eyebrows, rushed in pell-mell, to be first in the bathroom. As I was collecting my towels and soap I heard Charlie's voice in the hall of the brooder house. He had dodged his scheme and had four hours to spare. We let Pam take her bus and lazed away the afternoon talking in the sun. At five, Charlie went to camp and I went to Brighton. The only gift I could find for Pam's mother was one lonely lobster which lay in the window of a fish shop. I felt like an idiot when I arrived with it in my hand. I had had no wrapping paper, nor, of course, had the fishmonger.

We had the most luxurious baths that night, no queues, no hammering on the door. Pam went riding on the downs. I watched, relaxed, through the rain-washed windows and did not leave the blazing fire. And I realized that though I enjoy the rest and relaxation of weekends, I have become thoroughly absorbed in the boarding-school existence of the Tractor School, in learning how to use machine implements and in having the opportunity to practice. I enjoy too the impersonal companionship of my classmates, the clamour at meal times. We share and borrow and help one another. I swap my butter for Pam's sugar ration, I lend my iron to Rhoda and Lil and I borrow their bikes.

Pam and I found that our minds wandered back to the Chicken Coop, to Lil and Iris, who had not gone away for the weekend, to Doris, who had left to see her handsome fiancee, home on leave. We realized that we were anxious to return to our plough fields, to complete and improve upon the work which, when noon arrived on Saturday, we had left unfinished.

We returned on Sunday night, joined each mile or so by one or other of our girls who boarded the bus.

It was at the Long Man, where we all left the bus, that Pam and I received an invitation and made a new friend. We all went into the pub and were greeted joyfully by Mr Churchill, a remarkably handsome black and white cocker spaniel. Charlie and I had made his acquaintance the day before when we had taken the bus at the same spot.

His mistress, Clare Inman, introduced herself to us, and invited Pam and me to have supper with her. She made excellent waffles, she said, and would give us waffles and syrup. Two Canadian soldiers were in the pub and announced that they were coming too. Miss Inman seemed delighted. Pam and I exchanged glances. We were not too sure of this, but we had no reason to refuse the invitation. Once again I thought of the reserved cold-shouldering Englishman. I have not met him yet.

Our supper-party was delightful. We met at the Long Man on the following Wednesday and easily found Miss Inman's cottage. We drank beer from curious old mugs, in a shady, rose-filled garden. Clare Inman was an odd person; the house was neat and sparkling, every one of the polished brasses, which almost hid the fireplace, shone in the evening light, each boss and hollow on the deeply carved chests and benches was gleaming and dustless, but her little garden was wild. Tendrils of climbing roses caught at our clothes, sprays of blossom touched our cheeks. Tall, unpruned rose-trees, here and there on the lawn, left little space even for walking. Two girls in WLA uniform, two soldiers with Canada badges, whose names I have already forgotten, the lovely, long English twilight, the scent of many roses. It was a most unusual evening.

Clare called us in when the waffles were ready, and told us the story of the old carved chairs which were drawn up to the table. They were Italian milkmaids' chairs, three-legged, deeply carved, with high backs. Into each was beautifully carved the name of its onetime owner. Mine was Philomena, Pam's Lucia.

I have never eaten such waffles in my life. They had a delicate flake of golden crust on each side with an ambrosial substance between. The shame which Pam and I felt at the damage done to Clare's egg and syrup ration was more than equalized by her delight in our enjoyment.

The problem then was how to say goodnight to two Canadian soldiers without leading them to our lair. This proved fairly simple, as we had cycles while they had none. They insisted on riding us home, but by the time we had reached the Long Man, beered and waffled flesh could not stand the test and Pam and I dealt satisfactorily with the spirit.

She and I were to go to tea at Nunningham on Saturday and Charlie was to telephone me there in the evening. The day was a scorching one. I played truant in the morning, switched off my tractor and gone paddling in a cool spot where the river winds through the woods.

At lunch time Pam and I bathed and were moist and hot again by the time we dressed. We were languidly wheeling out the bikes when a telephone message came for me. It was Kath, "Bring your swim-suits and we'll try to manage a swim."

The heat seemed to recede immediately and, with so welcome a respite before us, we enjoyed the hot cycle ride. The way was a lovely one, the road climbing and twisting. Violets and primroses are gone, but the hedges are overhung with lilac and laburnum, and the red and white of May trees and rhododendron. I know many of the people we pass who greet us from roadside and cottage and the same gentle sense of homecoming steals over me as we turn down Nunningham lane.

Walter had to see someone at Pevensey and we took our tea and had a picnic on the beach. I swam back and forth beyond the shallow swell. How still the Channel is on a calm day, compared to the mighty breakers of the Atlantic on the American coast.

Charlie's call came through, just as we were unpacking the picnic baskets in the red-tiled kitchen.

"I have a week's leave, beginning Wednesday noon. Can you meet me in Sutton?"

"I imagine so." I had prepared for just such a contingency with Mr Winters.

"Right. Let's go to Cornwall."

As calmly and as simply as that the arrangements were made.

June 12, 1942. Cornwall

Mr Winters drove me to the train on Tuesday morning, teasing and scoffing, assuring me that he did not expect to see me back within the week. "You all say that, you women, but you'll go off with that fine hus-band of yours and forget all about your work." I swore by all the gods that I would be on the job again by seven the following Wednesday morning.

On my arrival in Sutton I took my good breeches to the cleaners, and because, in the WLA as in the soldiers army, clothes come in two sizes, too large and too small, I took my greatcoat, just issued, to a tailor to be fitted. Then I went to Mrs Young's. Charlie and I had dinner with them, and as before, when we turned out of their gate, his, "Aren't they the *nicest* people," was simultaneous with my, "They are the very nicest people." We walked over to where we had lived for the winter months and had a hilarious reunion with our friends. We heard the local gossip and they learned how we had fared. We could not stay more than an hour, but knew again the great pleasure of meeting old friends.

To Falmouth

The train was very crowded and it was a dreary day, so we spent most of the journey reading. After we had passed Exeter, Charlie remarked that the book he was reading reminded him of *Prester John*. We spent a few moments trying to remember who had written *Prester John*. I thought it was John Buchan but Charlie disagreed.

"Your wife is right," said a soft voice beside me. "It was John Buchan."

I then noticed the quiet little man who had been traveling with us. He stammered apologies and we introduced ourselves. And so we ended up going to stay at a tiny farm at Gurnard's Head instead of Falmouth. Foxglove grows everywhere here, bordering each stonewall and flourishing right to the cliff edge, taller and stronger than any I have seen in Sussex. We walked many miles exploring old tin mines, and high in the rain clouds we walked the seven miles to St Ives with no company save little mountain goats. Soaked to the skin we waited in the sunshine for the bus to take us back. I saw an old shed with a large sign: "Cornish Clotted Cream 1/3." There was a damp little man sheltering with us and I asked if the cream were still available.

"Reckon not," he said. "Least ways to buy it. But we has it. My missus allus has a old saucepan in the back o' the stove."

I was quite excited, hoping to learn how to make it, when a large woman loomed before us under a big umbrella.

"There you are!" she shrieked triumphantly. "I told you to come home directly!"

We gasped and withdrew. She put out a grasping hand and then she and our little man were gone.

"What price clotted cream," said Charlie, as our bus came along.

June 17, 1942. Tractor School

By the skin of my teeth I did arrive back in time to call Mr Winters' bluff. Charlie and I arrived in London with just time for each to catch his train. Mine left first from Victoria. Charlie stood at the window talking to me, worrying because we had not had time to check my train connections.

"Remember," he said, "If you are not able to make sure, get off at Eastbourne and spend the night with Alec and Dado."

The only other occupant of my compartment was a Canadian lieutenant colonel, whom we did not notice until he spoke. As the train pulled out, he said, "Don't worry about your wife, I'll see that she gets to her destination safely."

Charlie had just time to say, "Thank you, sir."

We had not left London's chimney pots behind before I realized that my companion had been very efficiently celebrating. He had reached that comfortable stage of inebriation where no end was worth any great expenditure of effort. Nevertheless I maintained a fairly regular shifting of my position from one side of the compartment to the other and evinced far more interest in the passing scene than was merited by suburban London.

I explained that it was imperative that I return on time and that if there was no train at Polegate I would spend the night in the Horse and Groom and go on first thing in the morning. He listened but did not agree. A car would be meeting him at Eastbourne. He would drive me wherever I wanted to go.

I tired of the argument quickly, and our conversation ranged over many subjects, punctuated by our feeble little game of tag.

As we neared Polegate, I prepared to leave the train, when to my distress it did not stop, did not even slow down. I reiterated my independence. I could spend the night with Charlie's relatives in Eastbourne.

But at Eastbourne station my companion carried my bags for me. I planned to hail the first taxi I saw and wish my young colonel goodnight. But there was no taxi. Instead, when we stepped out on Terminus Road, a station wagon pulled up at the curb, its driver at attention.

"Good evening, sir."

"Good evening. Take these bags." And to me, "Get in." He stood back and the young lance corporal opened the door.

I should have said, "Thanks very much, but I'll get a taxi." But I knew Eastbourne station. When there was no taxi, there was no taxi. The situation was one of relaxed politeness. To become stiff and suspicious seemed stupid. I went ahead into the station wagon. The driver was told to drive on to the mess. I protested and was told not to worry, just a quick one and then I would be driven home. It was his easy manner, his command of the situation, which were my undoing. I hesitated, like any youngster, to disturb the pleasant social tenor by refusing his offer. And what alternative had I? Take out my mad money? There was no taxi. Walk home?

We drew up at the officer's mess, a most imposing residence in Willingdon, and in company with a major or two and a full colonel I felt safer. That most definitely was the word. We all had a drink and I was taken to the garden to see the fishpond.

"There are sixty-seven goldfish in it," said my colonel, leaning on an urn. He proceeded to walk across the stepping stones.

"Come and see, there are a hundred and eighty goldfish." He walked across a few more stones.

"Look, three hundred and ten goldfish –"

No thank you, Mr Spider. That is one parlour I refuse to fall into. His companions were encouraging him and for a few moments I saw a sudden and satisfactory solution to my situation. But not so. He negotiated the stepping stones with satisfied pride and stepped ashore.

"Hurry," I said, "You promised to get me home by eleven," hoping that he would take my word for that promise.

"So I did," he said. "And so I will."

His driver had never heard of the crossroads to which I directed him. My conversation was strictly defensive.

"Excuse me, turn left here."

"Please, move over a little, I must watch the road."

"Just a minute, I think that was a wrong turn."

No doubt my lieutenant colonel thought that the drive would last forever and that he would succeed in wearing me down. But as we turned into the long lane of chestnuts which led to the house I thought with genuine panic of the last bit to come – the long dark walk through the woods, and across the paddock and the standing corn. Of course he would offer to carry my bags. Of course his driver would stand by discreetly, not daring to interfere. And here we were.

What now? In the inky blackness my amorous companion would feel that the devil must have his due.

As the station wagon stopped the back door of the house opened and Major Batten flashed a light on us.

"Good evening, Major Batten," I positively beamed on him. "This is Colonel Andrews who has kindly driven me home. Thank you so much Colonel Andrews. Oh I can carry those myself. Thank you again. Goodnight. Goodnight Major Batten." I grabbed my bags and ran. Phew!

Charlie said that I was a silly little fool, when he telephoned tonight. I was very nearly a sad little fool too.

The girls were amazed to see me this morning. They had gone to the bus to meet me last night and cannot understand how I got back. Nothing will make me satisfy their curiosity.

I have been back on the potato ridger today and I am very tired. Charlie and I walked some twenty miles the day before we left Cornwall. Percy Frampton left for London on Monday and we went into Penzance with him. When his train had gone we walked on to Marazion and Saint Michael's Mount. We took the bus to Constantine, seat of the ancient kings of Cornwall, and walked back to Helston, the "quaint old Cornish town" where one dances up and down the streets "all together in a floral dance." Then we walked on to Gweek, where a little old lady made tea for us and then went out to watch for the bus for us that we might rest till the last minute.

And then this morning Andy said, "Thank God you're back. I had to put two girls on the ridger while you were away." So I have my old job again. The ridger is bolted on the tractor, consequently to trip in or out one has to lift its whole weight. It took the strength of two of us to raise it, or to lift the lever out of the notch when it first arrived. Then I discovered that by putting one foot on the mudguard of the tractor and using my back as a fulchrum, I could do it myself. From then on the job was mine. I am proud of it too, for my ridges are straight.

And so, add together a week's leave, the stress of my drive home from Eastbourne, and a day's work, and I am ready for an early night.

Today I took the pneumatic tractor up to Tanyard Close, about five miles away, to pick up the fuel trailer and take it to Goosegreen Common, another five miles or so, where the girls are working now. I helped them take off their road bands, heavy wooden segments which must be bolted on to spade-lug tractors for road travel. I helped to set a couple of ploughs, more moral support than skill, and then brought the pneumatic back. By then it was noon. After lunch I hitched on a hay rake and clean raked the big hayfield down by the river. The hay lay silvered under the shimmering heat and I got hooked up in the corner between the gate and the river. If it had not been so cool there I would not have tarried, but the men were working near the stack in the far corner of the field. To fetch help meant a long hot walk for them as well as for me, and I knew that in time they would come my way.

And so, I was sitting under the willows, where the river eddies over smooth white pebbles, when I heard the sound of a car stopping and Lady de la Warr came through the five barred gate. As the sole representative of the Tractor School, to be found sitting in the shade, my tractor and hay rake at right angles, hooked onto the gate, I let the girls down badly. Lady de la Warr seemed to understand. I remember Walter saying that she was the most charming lady he had ever met. I fully agreed.

The hay wagon came back then with Andy and the boys and they helped me out of my troubles easily. I drove up to the stack, had my share of a round of beer, along with Traveler, the old cart-horse who empties a bottle with the best, and then drove "The Bastard" home.

One of the tractors.

"The Bastard" is my tractor, a genuine hybrid, a green 1941 tractor with an orange '38 fuel tank, and sometime ago, before I fell heir to her, affectionately christened and inscribed "The Bastard."

This morning I was detailed to cycle into town to the Food Office. Several new girls arrived yesterday and Mr Winters discovered that it saves time to send one of the old crowd to have ration arrangements made.

I was cycling carefully past a long Canadian convoy on a narrow lane when one truck crowded me over to the side of the road, and, over the grinding of brakes, I heard,

"Hey McGill! Where did you get that red coat?"

"It's mine," I shouted back. "Arts '35."

"Put it there, pal," and out came a long, brown arm. "Science '37."

We shook hands, there was a general cheer, and the convoy moved on.

I raked hay again this afternoon, much more satisfactorily than yesterday. I left the hay in long orderly rows and did not get hooked up in any gates. There were eleven men in the field, working with rakes under the hot sun, while I sailed gaily around with my big tractor rake.

When I came in at tea time I found two big baskets of strawberries from Percy Frampton. There were plenty for all, no cream and little sugar, but very delicious strawberries.

I heard muffled sobbing a little while ago from Lil's room. Poor Lil just returned from a weekend with her husband and feels upset and lonely. I know how she feels. When I first came over and thought, each time I said goodbye to Charlie, that it might be the last, I was desolate. Lil is a bride of a few months and is a nervous, jumpy little thing. She was soon cheered when we found some cocoa and biscuits in the kitchen and now she is squealing with delight over some foolishness of Rhoda's.

Mr Winters gave me permission to take Saturday morning off, as Alec had invited me to go with him for Speech Day at Brentwood School, in Essex, where Charlie's young cousins attend.

The trip made me realize that I am rapidly becoming one hundred percent country hick. We had to rush for the London train, ate a quick lunch near Victoria station, then took the tube to Liverpool Street, followed by the stuffy, smoky trip to Brentwood.

We were late. Lord Caldecote, Lord Chief Justice of England, was speaking but the hall was too crowded for us to get in and the boys hustled us off to see their studies and a cricket game. Here I hoped for a little rest, but no, we had to see the gymnasium, the swimming pool, be introduced to the head master, see model aeroplanes and then back to the cricket field for a glimpse of The School vs. Old Boys.

We missed the train back to Eastbourne and decided to fit in one quick drink at the Regent Palace. Alec met a young doctor there whom he knew. When he had shaken hands with me, he turned my hand over slowly and looked at the calluses.

"When the war is over," he said, "The men will all have soft hands, and the women – my God!"

We went back to Victoria by bus and managed to find an empty compartment. I took my shoes off and we both slept as far as Haywards Heath. At Lewes the compartment door opened and Charlie walked in! The gods smile upon us.

I enjoyed the visit to Brentwood. I was interested in everything I saw, and it was pleasant to feel well-dressed again, from top to toe. But, for one accustomed to the steady gait of farming life, the rush and excitement of London is almost too much. Dado's garden, Charlie beside me, desultory conversation under a June sun, a feeling of real companionship with Alec and Dado, these are much more my style these days.

Another glorious day hay making – warm sun, fragrant hay, everyone laughing and singing, brown legs, hair gleaming in the sun, my tractor purring like a kitten.

I found a clump of beautiful poppies growing on an ash-heap today, large brilliant rose-coloured petals and cool frosted-green leaves. They are dropping already but are a lovely colour against my open windows. Beyond them is a blue softly waving oatfield, just breaking into head, and then the shadowy curves of the Weald Hills, fold upon gracious fold of blue.

The river winds below the oat fields and then flows through the woods to border the fields where we have been haying. Such a tiny thing to call a river. I went wading today with Pam and Doris, just where the stream leaves the shadows of the wood. I found a deep pool, threw my clothes on the bank, and, while Monica screamed in embarrassment, had a real swim. The pool was about four feet deep, crystal clear, and it was wonderful to be free from hayseeds.

July 7, 1942. Tractor School
I mowed my first hayfield today. Now I have done nearly every phase of hay making. Perhaps someday I shall build a stack.

A kind gentleman, a friend of Walter Marshall's, did us the honour of recognizing us as tractor drivers, and offered the job of mowing his hayfield to the tractor school. No one has shown such faith in us before.

Mr Winters gave me all manner of instructions and I consider that I did quite a fair job, because the mower was not functioning properly and I had to circle in an unorthodox way, instead of backing and lifting the bed on corners.

BROOMLYE

July 7, 1942. Broomlye

I am growing accustomed to this now you're here, now you're not sort of life. Two weeks ago Grace went off to a job at Withyham, a little later Betty left for somewhere near here – and how we missed her. Betty is pink and white, comfortably cushioned, happy as these long sunny days, and loved by us all. After Betty's arrival at the Tractor School no one had any need of an alarm clock. We were wakened each morning half an hour earlier than necessary by the full volume of her lovely contralto voice. Strains of, "I've Got Sixpence," or, "Good Old Sussex by the Sea," filled the Chicken Coop every morning and Betty was never told to pipe down, nor did she ever receive bangs on the wall or well-aimed boots. It may be seen how infectious were her high spirits, how lovely her laughter, and how highly esteemed was our Betty. We all overslept twice after she had gone.

Then Mr Winters reported that he had found a niche for me. I was to be lent, by the ESWAEC (East Sussex War Agricultural Executive Committee), to a private farmer for harvest time and I just heard the news when Charlie arrived on a forty-eight. We slept down at Mrs George's and Charlie showed me on an ordinance map just where my new farm is.

Many times I have traveled hopefully to a new home, to Nunning-ham, Southwater, Green Farm, and then to the Chicken Coop, to new customs, new work, new friends. And always, till now, with an underlying tremor of fear, fear caused by my inexperience, by the need I felt for patience and understanding on the part of my employer. But these doubts and fears have gone and I travel confidently now.

Here at Broomlye I think all should go well. I see little of Mr Botting, who owns the farm, and less of his wife or his home. He is a gruff Sussex countryman, who bellows out orders, has a dreadful temper, but knows what he wants and farms well.

We are in the heart of the downs and I find peace in the beauty around me. The rustling fields slope on all sides of the farm, stiff with ripening wheat. When we turned the last bend of the road, on the night of my arrival, the yellow evening sun shone through the tops of a long avenue of elms which lead to a solidly built low stone house. A lamp-lit window was shining through deep sycamore shade and spreading its beam across an irregularly shaped pond, in which the long facade of the house was mirrored.

Mr Botting met us at the door and introduced us to his wife. We glimpsed heavy mahogany and horsehair and then Mr Winters came with us to introduce me to Mr and Mrs Staplehurst, with whom I am to live.

Their cottage is the tiniest bit of a place, two rooms downstairs and two up, a perfectly adequate little home. The scullery is about eight feet square with whitewashed walls and a stone floor. The stone doorstep is worn so that quite an inch of light shows under the heavy iron-hinged door. I am glad that I am not to be here for the winter months. One corner is completely filled by a huge oven and its whitewashed receding chimney. Between the big oven and the copper is a little duck's back grate. There is no sink, only a hollowed-out stone slab which catches splashes from the wash basin. One empties the basin into a bucket, which, in turn, is emptied into the open ditch that runs between the cottage and the road. The other downstairs room is a run of the mill kitchen, tables, chairs, sideboard, couch, a little kitchener stove, and an organ with two vividly coloured prints, "The Angelus," and, "The Gleaners," above it.

Mrs Staplehurst told me that the rent for the cottage is 6/6 a week: "It's when people have to pay fifteen shillings ($15.00 a month), that's when they have no rest. It's awful ain't it, all that money! Yer life ain't yer own."

My bedroom is a comfortable little room, full of furniture, but with heavy rough hewn beams and a view of a little copse in the hollow and the smooth green downs. My first surreptitious move towards comfort was to put the feather bed underneath the mattress and to remake the bed. Even at that, sleep does not come easily after the plywood beds at the tractor school.

Mrs Staplehurst is an able housewife whose god is cleanliness. She shines, her small house shines, and she intends to do her best with me. Whenever I return, she opens the back door to greet me with a jug of hot water in her hand.

"I've worked for the gentry," she told me. "I knows 'ow to do for a lady."

Again and again I have told her my name, but "Lady" I remain.

"Ain't it wunnerful, Lady, when you gits 'ome yer times yer own." Or again, "I'm allus busy. Ain't it wunnerful. Lady, 'ow fast the days go?" Every little conversation with me ends with, "Thank ye-ow," and a little curtsey. She takes great pride in caring for me. Each day there are fresh flowers on my dressing table, and just now she has gone upstairs, and I know that she is turning down my bed and wrapping my pajamas in a hot bottle, which I cannot convince her is unnecessary in July.

It was some time ago that I first heard the story of the Wiltshire Moonrakers, of how a happy party were returning in high fettle from some roadside inn and saw, when crossing a bridge, the reflection of the full moon in the still water. One version has it that they thought it was a large silver coin, another that it was a great round cheese. Whichever it is, Wiltshire folk are smiled upon as simple folk who try to rake the moon's shining reflection from the river bed.

I saw Mr Botting for a few moments today and I asked him if his people had come from Wiltshire. He shrugged, mumbled, "Happen they did," and went off. I see him working the other tractor or driving off to town in his old Morris, but never do we exchange more than one or two words.

On my first morning he jerked a finger at me, "You go plough the ten acre."

"Which field is it?" I asked.

"Over the hill, behind your cottage."

"Where is the plough, Mr Botting?"

"Behind the barn. Take the International."

I though of Southwater and decided that if I could find a small cow shed in the blackout, I could find a plough and a ten acre field in broad daylight.

I saw him about eleven o'clock that same morning, standing in a corner of the field. He watched me for a few moments and then went away. I have not seen him since, except when I have finished a field and he appears to give me further directions. My work must be satisfactory for there is no complaint, but I wish he would make some remark.

The binder has been hauled out and I have seen him walking around the oat fields, so I think that soon harvesting will begin.

Betty found me tonight. She is working a mile or two away, for two young brothers. She finds them unreliable, careless masters and made me aware that my comfortable cottage and stolidly efficient master were much to be thankful for. She arrived very late, having lost her way over the downs, so I walked part way home with her and hope to see her again. But with harvesting due for each of us, we shall have little time for visiting.

Will, the cowman, helped me this morning while we harrowed a field which had a crop of maple peas. I drove the tractor and Will cleared off the harrows. He went back at noon and I had my lunch in the shade of the little copse. Such blissful peace, high noon, and the sound of the tractor stopped. At first there seems only silence, then a pigeon coos, and the sound of rustling corn emerges and occasionally, the sudden enormous roar of hedge-hopping planes.

I ploughed and sang all afternoon till I broke a share, which was worn out anyway. That field is so stiff I really should use a new one daily. I had to go back to the cow stalls to borrow Will's knife. I have lost mine and a sorry thing it was anyway. Will said, "Humph, what kind of a tractor driver do you expect to be without a knife, I'd like to know." However, he lent me his, and I cut the peg and went on ploughing till tea time.

When I started her up after tea, petrol was pouring out of the float chamber. A whack, which often fixes it, did not work, so I had to go down to the house for Mr Botting.

His only remark as we walked back was, "Corn-cutting Monday, if the weather holds. Oats. In the chalk pit field."

When we took out the float it was full of petrol, which a float should not be. He tried to fix it and it came apart at the seam. I laughed, he frowned, and I went back to the yard and brought the float from the other tractor. When I had started her up, he spoke again, "I'm taking the Missus to the Agricultural Demonstration at Plumpton, on Saturday. Reckon we've room for you. Knock off at nine. You've had enough today."

I tried to say thank you but he stalked off.

Plumpton! The girls from the Tractor School would be there, Kath and Walter perhaps, Brian Moss. As soon as I put the tractor under cover I telephoned Pam at the Tractor School and we planned the weekend.

August 15, 1942. Broomlye
"Alive and well," seems all I have time to say, these days. We work from seven in the morning till ten at night in the fields and my initial pride at driving the binder has become second nature. Mr Botting did not seem the least bit perturbed when I said that I had never driven one before. I had driven it down to the cornfield, expecting to carry on shocking while he drove. He merely nodded while I explained, gave no instructions, no advice, told Will to get up on the binder and said, "Go on."

I started in bottom gear, very gingerly, watched how the corn was laid at the bottom of the knife, and soon was sailing around merrily, in second gear, turning on the corners and leaving clean fields with no stalk of standing corn. It is an easy job. Walter had given me the impression that one required special skill and more than special intelligence. One does not. One needs care and patience, with which I am poorly supplied, but which I managed to spread out thriftily.

I am not nearly so tired this year. Driving the binder is easier work than shocking or pitching sheaves. I love driving it. I love beginning a new field or watching the last swath fall, "swarf," as Sussex men say, and I love all the round and round between. Towards the end there is much excitement. There are still a few rabbits and these fields are full of young pheasants. Yesterday as we neared the end of a field a beautiful cock pheasant flew out right in front of me, and there were several whirrs as the hen pheasants went up and then went back in a hurry to the little speckled chicks that kept starting up and dropping back, like little beige streaks. I cannot become accustomed to mowing down their homes, yet I know that the corn must be cut. Over the golden corn I catch glimpses of the rounded slopes of the downs, of silhouettes of trees on the ridge, the sudden flash of poppies, the scornful purple of thistles before we mow them down and, too, the clear blue of scabius, almost as tall as the corn – Mr Botting's tall, thick, heavy-headed corn. Nunningham is still my love, and I shall always take Walter's word against anyone's, but nevertheless, I must admit that nowhere have I seen such wheat and oats as here at Broomlye this year.

Charlie is still in Wales and writes of constant rain, and a small village with twenty-two pubs! Here the sun shines as if the skies must always be blue and tomorrow we begin carting. The last sheaf was cut this afternoon and I hauled up the binder tonight. No more greasing her eight-three nipples, morning, noon, and night, no more covering her with a sheet and packing her with sheaves, lest the dew shrink the canvases.

We have a gang of Canadian soldiers harvesting and they have been a disturbed and restless crew the last few days, because planes have been roaring over constantly and we have all felt that there was something in the wind. But tonight, when a Home Guard officer stopped by the rick yard to speak to Mr Botting and brought the news that the Canadians have raided Dieppe, those boys were fighting mad. Like Charlie, they are First Division lads, and have been in England for three years. When they heard the few available details, that the raid had been made up mostly of Canadian Second Division, they voiced their resentment bitterly. Ricky, one lean, tawny-headed youngster, had tears of rage in his eyes.

"If we're no good, we'll bloody well quit," he shouted, banging his fists against a half-built stack.

They went glumly off to the pub and I drove the tractor home, knowing that the day would come when they would all go, and secretly, though I dared not say so to them, glad that Charlie was safe in Wales.

Friday night it rained heavily and there was no carting Saturday morning. By noon, however, the sun was shining and when I came home I nearly fell over our long tin bath, which was out on the back bricks. Mrs Staplehurst told me that Mr Staplehurst, who worked on a neighbouring farm, would not be home until late so I could have my bath outside in the sun.

"I'll watch," she said, "and won't let nobody go round the back." I thought that this was a wonderful idea, but I shall never understand the mixture of her make-up. Cleanliness is next to godliness, modesty apparently nowhere.

The good little soul has to carry every drop of water which we use in the house from a pond some distance down the road. Nevertheless, a bath full of hot water and a pail full of cold are religiously provided for each of us every Saturday.

Tonight I have been trying to translate a leaflet, several of which we found in the cornfields a few days ago. They are in French and are, "Distribués par vos amis de la RAF." We think that they must either have been jettisoned by one of our planes, or possibly been blown back across the channel. If they had been dropped from a great height it could happen.

September 7, 1942. Broomlye
We were carting on Saturday afternoon when Charlie arrived. He had tea with us in the rick yard and when we finished the stack about eight o'clock we all went to the "Bull." Because of Charlie's arrival, and because the harvest is nearly all in, "as near as makes no matter," as Will said, we celebrated with a pint or so of the landlord's "old and dark," and with some qualms, I was persuaded by Will to be led home over the downs.

The night was dark and misty and I could feel no path underfoot on the smooth downland turf. We were all "fou and unco happy" and I expected, any moment, to see Tam O'Shanter's "witches and warlocks in a dance." The gorse tore at my unaccustomed skirt and Charlie talked happily of nights on wet Welsh hills. I thought that we had been hours when Will said, "Yonder's the road, turn right and your cottage is just a step." I felt sure that we should turn left, but Will was right and Mrs Staplehurst had not gone to bed. She loves to fuss over

Charlie and the fire was blazing brightly and cocoa was waiting for us, with bread and cheese on the table.

September 13, 1942. The George Hotel, Crawley
Charlie has a week's leave, or will have beginning tomorrow, and I am here for a night or two. On Monday Charlie and I leave for Oxford. The Army Educational Services have arranged with English universities for special summer tours for the forces.

Charlie enrolled at Oxford for this coming week and is to live in New College as a student.

Charlie is stationed in Tilgate Forest, just near Crawley, and the bar of the old George last night was full of familiar faces. The George is an old coaching inn and the halfway stage of the coaches which traveled from London to Brighton. The Gallows, which stretches across Crawley High Street, dates from the fifteenth century, and the inn sign, Saint George and his

Charlie at Oxford

white horse, which swings from it, bangs and creaks under our bedroom window. The dining room, a spacious lofty hall, was built over the old stables.

Mic, and Penny who has a sleeping-out pass, have a room which looks like a small vaulted chapel, in "The Priory."

"The Priory," now a typical English tearoom, is still dark with old beams and carved vaulting of what, in the twelfth century, was the Prior's House. We all had tea there and now Charlie has gone back to camp. I take much pleasure in these leisured hours after the rush of harvest, and intend to read this evening, by the open fire in the George's private lounge.

CAMBER CASTLE FARM

September 23, 1942. Rye, Sussex
I returned to Broomlye, late on Monday night, thinking less of the week to come than of the week that had passed. It was all wrong and most inconsiderate of us but when Dr Cam, whose sister I know in Canada, learned that Charlie was to stay in New College and insisted that I stay with them, I accepted with mixed humility and excitement.

Dr Cam is a very famous professor at Cambridge and her name is steeped in Oxford history. When I met Dr Jones of Jesus College he asked me where I was staying and replied, "Not *the* Helen Cam! I should consider it the greatest honour to sit at the feet of Dr Helen Cam." I was impressed.

I reported this at dinner and was met with – silence. Obviously this was no more than Helen's due.

Later we went to the Bodlian and looked down on the tiny garden where nearly a hundred years ago Charles Dodgson told the stories which became *Alice's Adventures in Wonderland*.

Rhodes House was opened that night to the members of the Overseas Forces and we attended a dance there. One of the Polish officers whom we had seen on a bus the day before bowed and asked me to dance. By some fortunate chance they played, "The Blue Danube." A dance became a very different thing with a partner such as mine. His steps grew longer and longer. I had never known I could dance with such glorious lightness. The floor fell away and we were dancing on air, dancing on, alone, long after the music had stopped.

Later my partner brought his friends to me and I presented Charlie to him, but the spell was broken. This rigidly formal young officer with whom we smiled and bowed and shared refreshments could not have been the person with whom I had danced as I had never danced before. We could not speak Polish; he knew no English. The flowing communion of motion we had shared fell apart and we each joined companions of our own tongue.

Dr Cam took us on a tour of the old wall of Oxford. We saw Magdalen and New College and Christ Church, walked along the Broadwalk, by the Isis, heard the story of the bells of Tom Tower at Christ Church and had tea at the home of Sir Charles Peers.

There Charlie had a most interesting afternoon for, as we stood talking in a little study, Charlie remarked upon a small fragment of early stained glass. When Sir Charles asked him, in surprise, how he knew that it was so old, Charlie replied that he recognized by the yellow colour that it was glass stained by a lost art. (Charlie's father is a well-known artist who works in stained-glass.) After examining an early French missal, with beautiful illuminations, Sir Charles told us that he had, given into his care for safe-keeping during the war, several carefully crated sections of stained-glass windows from Westminster Abbey. The oldest of these and the most precious, he took from its case to show Charlie.

Sir Charles and his Lady live as simple a life as do I, in my little English cottages. They have several evacuated families living with them, mothers and children, and we all had tea together in the big basement kitchen. Sir Charles led me off later to show me the old Elizabethan linen fold carvings on the pantry doors. I smiled as I heard Charlie ask where I was and heard someone reply, "She's in the butler's pantry, with Sir Charles."

We saw Noel Coward's "Blithe Spirit" in London, sitting beside a sailor and a girl in WAAF uniform. I enjoyed it more than any play I have ever seen. We, soldier and Land Girl, sailor and WAAF, never having seen each other before or since, all laughed heartily together. "Even an ectoplasmic manifestation has some right to the milk of human kindness —" It was delectable entertainment.

London's night life is over very early in war time. The play began at six and we were both in before ten. We called Percy Frampton, who was most distressed because we had missed our visit to his home in strawberry time. He arranged to meet us at three the following day.

The next morning Charlie said, "I bet that no one would ever believe that a Canadian soldier and a girl spent the night in the Regent Palace, each in his own twin bed."

Frampton's house is a great barn of a place, most of which has been closed up for years. It has a minute central heating system, which looks most inadequate, and two bathrooms, one for guests and one for Percy's mother, who, to our great surprise, is a tiny, blue-eyed little lady, as Irish as Paddy's pig.

We saw acres and acres of fruit trees, cabbages planted mathematically on the square to facilitate cultivation, which made a deep impression on me, and several fields of as yet unharvested barley, which Percy says are of malting quality.

Percy is a most peculiar mixture, a graduate of Wye Agricultural College, studious, slightly anemic-looking, "a real old woman," as Charlie says, and yet strangely naive and full of quick enthusiasms. When we first met, Charlie and I liked and felt at ease with him immediately.

Thinking of these things, of how one finds time to do many things in a week but that the week is too short for them to be assimilated, I walked under the high stars and decided that I was suffering from aesthetic indigestion.

But there was no time for dwelling any further on our leave. When I pushed open the cottage door I saw my candle lit, waiting for me on the edge of the copper chimney, with a note beside it.

"Report to WAC Offices, Rye, Monday morning."

And so here I am in Rye.

And what a different situation this is, a landlady who lives my kind of life, thinks my kind of thoughts, who is friend and companion, rather than a subject of interest. I live in a little modern home, electric light, bathroom with a modern little family, Mr And Mrs Skipage and their daughter June, age ten. Mrs Skipage mourns her son, Bill, as dead, although he is with the forces, and actually still in England.

And is Mrs Skipage a good cook! Her filleted plaice, fresh from the sea, are succulent morsels and she makes macaroni and cheese just as Mother makes it.

I work for the WAEC, whom I consider the best of employers, and of all small towns in Sussex I could have chosen none better than Rye. As yet I have seen but a glimpse of it for I have been working on my marshland Castle Farm, ploughing, and I look up to Rye, like an old feudal castle. I must hurry if I am to see more of it, for Jerry smashed up quite a bit of the town yesterday.

I am full of impressions, of the blue green of the sea, and the unbelievable colours of the Pevensey marshes when I came past by train on Monday, of the twisted little cobbled streets of Rye, of Camber Castle, around which I work all day, the sun setting between Rye and Winchelsea tonight, and the long, silver strips of my furrows in the moonlight.

Pam, who is working here in Rye, is ill with jaundice. Tonight I am going to see her and on Friday I return to the Tractor School to spend the weekend with Mr and Mrs George.

My first day in Rye was a lively one. Mr Syer, for whom I am to work, gave me a sketchy map of the town and I set out to find the food and registration offices and the government office, where I was given a special pass allowing me to work in the immediate coastal area.

I called for Mr Syer at noon, as he was to show me the way to the farm. We crossed the river, the Tillingham, and turned towards the coast.

"That little garage," said Mr Syer, his head turned, as he listened to the sound of approaching planes, "is where you'll have any necessary repairs done to your tractor. I'll take you in now and let you meet everyone."

As he spoke we heard bombs falling on the south cliff edge of Rye. Mr Syer jumped out of his side of the car and ran around into the garage. I heard machine-gunning and saw the black and white crosses under the planes as they flew over my head, and I decided that I had better get under cover too.

The street was filled with glass and smoke as I ran across it, and as I slid into place beside the men on the floor of the garage, we heard a sudden heavy thump just behind the building. The two garage men looked at each other. That we each thought it was a time bomb was obvious. No one dared move lest he disturb the mechanism. Half suffocated with plaster dust, I lay still, feeling very annoyed. There was no escape from this, we were not ten feet from it. I thought, "If it is going to go off, why the devil doesn't it hurry up and go off." But nothing happened. Five minutes and still nothing happened. Someone got up, tip-toed carefully out of the garage. One by one we followed and peeked cautiously around the back corner, expecting to see some monstrous swastika'd missile. Each drew a breath of relief. There is too much realism for self-consciousness in this sort of thing. There on the quay, bricks spattered over to the edge, where the masts of the fishing vessels were just showing, lay the chimney of the garage. It had been blown off by the blast of the bombs that had fallen across the river.

We went back into town then, to make sure that Mrs Syer was safe. Mr Syer felt that this was the occasion to broach a very special bottle of old whiskey. We just managed to get down to the farm before tea time.

I find Rye a little like Petworth, which I loved and where Charlie and I visited in April. It is a town in which one is easily lost, and I have not yet sorted out which is the bomb damage of last Tuesday and which of the week before. I know that the Mermaid Inn has suffered and the houses in Traders' Passage. The cinema is completely flat. All that remains of it is a clean, tiled floor and a few long serpentines of tickets which have not been cleared away.

Men repairing cottages at Southundercliff, which had been damaged in the first raid, were killed in the second.

Ypres Tower, the twelfth-century watch tower, built in the reign of King Stephen, which looks towards Calais, was damaged, as was the more modern house of a doctor or dentist adjoining it, and the Gun Gardens below. Senseless destruction to a little storybook town, wanton raids which create no terror at all, only grief and labour and determination. The whole stupid malice of it all makes my blood boil.

Today has alternated between drizzly fog and gusts of cold, driving rain and now I am tingling before the warmth of a new-made fire.

I was ploughing in my field before eight this morning, with the steady fine rain making it hard to see. By dinnertime I had finished the headland and brought my tractor back across the railway tracks, for whose gates I have been entrusted with a key by the military. Camber Castle Farm is in the double danger area so we have to check in with a sentry on going to work and check out every night when returning home.

I had to go home for lunch because I was wet through. My mackintosh has had its day and from two green uniform sweaters my shirt and underwear were dripping with green dye. My overalls were wet to the hips and covered with mud. Again, praises be for my good-natured landlady. In this modern kitchen there is little room for muddy boots and wet clothes, but Mrs Skipage copes cheerfully with all the trouble I cause.

My afternoon was spent mowing thistles. Castle Farm consists of 1025 derelict acres, rank marsh-grass and thistles, stocked with a few lame and mangy sheep, abandoned by the dispossessed owner. It lies between the channel and the coastal road and stretches from Rye to Winchelsea, a thousand lonely acres, with a ruined sixteenth-century castle in the centre and a once proud farmhouse at the Winchelsea end. The house is now uninhabitable, a crumbling structure of old stone and tumble down thatch.

Castle Farm is managed by Mr Syer for the Agricultural Committee and is staffed by two old men and a boy, with Doris, who arrived today, and me, as tractor drivers. Mr Syer, a quiet-spoken, gentle-mannered person, is also sweet and kind. If we work an hour or two overtime each night we may have the weekend off. Last weekend Charlie met me at George's and this week I am going to Nunningham.

Camber Castle

Fortunately part of the old Camber Farmhouse is still watertight. The rain was pelting down when I checked in this morning. We must sign in each morning and out again at night with soldiers in a sentry box at the gate. I cycled as far as the RAF post at the Castle and found shelter there. I found that the rest of the farm staff had done the same. As one after the other we all turned up, we and our wet clothes were crowding out the RAF boys, so in their old lorry, they transferred us all to the farmhouse. We have lit a fire and I am now comfortably settled on a couple of planks, an old rat-trap and some sacks of wool.

Mr Syer has driven up and told us to stay here until the weather clears, and then he told us about the legend of an underground tunnel from the Castle to Rye. To substantiate it, he said that he had been ploughing in front of the Castle, in direct line with Rye and had ploughed up a lot of bricks and shaped stones, which did not conform with the subsoil and pebbles, but that he had been unable to discover any tunnel entrance inside the Castle.

Every day when we drive past, there is a whir of wings, and thousands of jackdaws are disturbed, to circle and settle again. I wonder if I shall ever have time to explore the old towers and crumbling walls, or to search in the half-filled in moat, for an entrance to the tunnel.

October 11, 1942. Crawley, Sussex

After a maddening series of crossing and contradicting letters and wires Charlie finally remained in Crawley and I came up for the weekend. Several times I felt that he would arrive in Rye as I was journeying to Crawley.

My train got in at 10:31 p.m. Verna and Benjie, with Bob and Charlie, waited for me at the George till closing time and then they met the train singing, "Waltzing Matilda," which, they explained, seemed to them to be a good welcoming song. Bob apologized for them all, saying that although they had done their best, they had been unable to arrange for a brass band, for which omission I was silently grateful.

We all went to Horsham on Saturday, but it was early closing day, and Verna, who is very pregnant, did not, as she said, "Feel up to searching for Horsham stone or Shelley's house." So we had dinner at the Black Horse and returned to the George at Crawley, where we met Kay and Jeff Scott, who are also prospective parents. Charlie, I noticed, could no more cope with the proud young fathers-to-be than I could with the young mothers, and we withdrew from the conversation.

I thought affectionately of my tractor and was glad that I did not have to adjust myself to a pseudo-home life in this little colony.

I have been mowing thistles all day today on the Pett Level end of the farm. When I covered the tractor at tea time and cycled to the gate at the Winchelsea end of the farm, an unusual number of soldiers were grouped around the sentry-box. I mounted my bike after shutting the gate and was about to call out my number and say goodnight, when one of them called,

"Hey, you can't come through there."

"What on earth do you mean?" I said.

"You can't come through that gate, we have orders to let no one pass."

"Look, I've been working there all day and I'm going home. There is my pass. What goes on anyway?"

"There are six unexploded bombs in there. Didn't you hear them?"

"No, I didn't. You can't hear bombs over tractors on rainy days, even when they do explode. Now, let me pass. Your orders are to let no one in, you stupid idiots, not to let no one out. Goodnight."

So – six unexploded bombs on Castle Farm. This should be interesting. I did hear planes several times, but no bumps. However, if they did not explode I certainly could not hear them with the tractor running. I wonder how near they fell to where I was working.

November 1, 1942. Rye

I found out the next morning. The bombs fell right around and behind the old house. We were not allowed on the farm. Doris and I went with Mr Syer to the Police Station on Watchbell Street and were told that we could not go to work. We were forbidden to go. We were furious and Mr Syer bestowed on us an unwished for holiday.

Today I went back to the Winchelsea gate. I got past the sentry with little difficulty and though I was met with a rush at the house, I managed to ask questions of the bomb disposal squad, who were bursting with information, to make them forget to send me away. A large red-lettered poster, "DANGER. UNEXPLODED BOMB," was tacked up on my tractor shed. It was some hours before I talked the men into submission and drove away with my tractor.

Doris's tractor is at the Rye end of the farm. We shall get a fuel trailer from the WAC depot and carry on down there till the BDS (Bomb Disposal Squad) disposes of Jerry's garbage. Six unexploded bombs on a derelict farm. That was smart work!

The days are never the same. The day before yesterday there was no Rye nor Winchelsea, rising above their level marshes. A curtain of drifting fog hung before them. We lit our little fires, dozens of them, for we are raking and burning the thistles I have mowed these past two months, and the mist glowed with little lights. Where the old willows stand crookedly, after years of wind, we could see only cobwebby suggestions of their branches, and the three great corn ricks on the ridge, which are our only landmarks, were vague shadows. Cycling to work was like pushing my bike through black angora, with the drops of fog spattering off my front wheel, like a tiny golden fountain under the dimmed headlight. But yesterday the sun shone warmly and Rye was a fairy castle. Her church tower and highest buildings glinted in the sunlight, while all the net houses and buildings below, on the Tillingham and the Rother, were lost in radiant swirls of dispersing mist.

This morning the moon was high and clear as I cycled past the wan and ghostly windmill, swathed in the silvery land mist which always lies in the valley. Ahead Castle Farm was dark and flat, under the cold green strip of dawn between the horizon and woolly gray cloud.

Doris and I cracked black ice on the frozen dike, filled our tractor radiators in silence and numbly and mechanically started the engines and went to work. It was a long time before there was any warmth in the sun.

We worked today, a cold, sunny Sunday, carting linseed. I was driving towards Rye, with the boys from the RAF post pitching onto the wagon, when someone shouted at me to turn off the tractor. I stopped and tried to see a reason for shutting off the engine. One of the airmen walked up and calmly turned it off, pointing towards Rye.

Faintly and clearly, in the soft hush after the tractor's deafening noise, came the joyous sound of church bells. Our victory in Africa has been confirmed. England's church bells which have been silent since Hitler entered Holland and Belgium, were ringing out the victory.

We listened until they died away and then went back to work.

November has been a month of rainy days, long hours of work, and frequent "hit and run" raids. Planes swing in over us, spit a few machine-gun bullets down on us, as they curve in a quick arc, drop a bomb or machine-gun Rye, and then streak out to sea again.

Gert and Daisy, the two patrol planes who regularly pass back and forth over our heads, always seem to have disappeared east beyond Camber or west of Fairlight whenever Jerry pops over. As they return, always just too late, we yell frantically, "They've gone that way, out over Winchelsea," or Doris moans hopelessly that they will never catch the swine, and we go on with our work.

Night comes early now and I come home bone weary, want, and, *deum laude*, get my tea immediately. Then I feel that I ought to bathe and change but I move to a comfortable chair and sit. Sometimes I summon up sufficient energy to write or sew, but if not, I feel my conscience assuaged by the knowledge that Walter, after a full day's work, is sitting in his big chair, reading and dozing, too.

I used to deplore his absorption in farming, to the exclusion of all else, to feel that it was wrong for him to have so few outside interests. I chafed because, tea time long past, he ploughed or sowed or mowed till it was too dark to see.

How could we have teased and badgered him so! Tonight I could cry from sheer weariness. The girls try to include me in their evening activities, but I have learned, at first grudgingly, by Walter's example, and now conclusively, by experience, that the change and recreation which I had felt to be so necessary, the outside interests which Walter seemed to be missing, are not worth the candle. Tonight I am one hundred percent Land Girl, and I know that nothing can re-create more surely than the knowledge of that last bit ploughed. That there is no greater peace than that of the satisfaction brought by an aching back and callused hands and work well done.

Today I live again. Today, with the only two others on this farm who derive any pleasure from mere work, I was carting litter. As there is a colossal amount of it from the dikes whose banks we cleared, it was decided to build a stack. The stuff is rubbish really, cocked up and resembling very coarse hay, and so I asked to be allowed to build the stack. If I do not succeed it will do little harm. But oh, the joy of it!

It is rising, so far, straight and firm. I can hear John's old Dad yapping, and see old Snowball strain as Ted leads her off to pull up the grab. Being on a stack has long lost its first thrill, the magic I knew on the first huge haystack, when the sweep came in with its great loads and my heart was warm. I learned where to put the pitches for the stacker and how to receive a great prongful from the wagon. I saw the far valleys from my vantage and sensed the fragrance of the sweet hay and, though sweaty and dusty, felt cleansed and purged as I had never been before, there in the almost tangible sunset and the soft June evenings.

Now, though a warm sun gleams dully though November mists, and as I look over flat marshland with its winding innumerable dikes, instead of to the rolling, blue hills of the Sussex Weald, I feel again the same ecstasy, the joy in working, in learning something new.

Before my Land Army days, any farming scene had been meaningless, as I was completely ignorant of the science of it. But later, during those first days at Nunningham, not only did I enjoy the beauty of it, but my delight was because of my understanding, because of my useful participation in the work.

In the intervening months, I have been on many stacks, on several farms, and the excitement has worn away. Simply to be on a stack is not enough. To build one is my ambition. And so today I live and learn again. It is my stack. No one has laid a single pitch of hay save me. We have about two-thirds to go, but so far I have looked on it and it is good. If it is a failure, I promise to confess.

Last Sunday I walked to Winchelsea with Mrs Skipage and June. We went up Udimore Road and turned towards the coast down Dumb Woman's Lane and came back by the lower road. Just past the Bridge Inn we saw a herd of the loveliest little black bullocks. They were short-legged and sturdy, long-horned, with silky, heavy coats. I had never seen such beauties and seriously contemplated telephoning Walter to see if he could enlighten me as to the breed.

Therefore, it was with great pleasure this morning that I had to stop my tractor to let them pass, and to learn that they are Welsh cattle, "the little black cattle of Wales." And I shall see them often, for they are to graze on Camber Castle Farm.

December 30, 1942. Rye
The day is bitter cold, ground frozen hard, and a biting wind driving intermittent gusts of fine snow. But luck has been with us. Yesterday was cold but not freezing, and we were working at the far end of Pett Level where there is no shelter. We ate our lunches standing as there is no dry spot on these marshlands. But today the ground is frozen too hard for fieldwork and Doris and I are going around the farm collecting implements and putting them under cover, "in the dry," were our orders.

That sounds simple, but not for Doris and me. We hitch a trailer on a tractor and a plough behind that, to save two trips, or a plough to the tractor and a hay rake behind it. Two implements behind the tractor make gates difficult to negotiate. Then when we get them to the yard, we have to back them into the sheds. Doris and I can each draw a plough much better than we can coax one in reverse.

I have been saying a special thank you all morning for my warm ski-boots and my heavy leather jacket, both of which have just arrived from Canada. And, as I have said, luck was with us, for dinner time came just as we had arrived back at the house. We lit a fire and dragged some sacks of wool into this room, which is used as a store for hoes and swaps and prongs. Poor old house. Between us and the soldiers who are billeted here periodically, the place is being gradually burned up for firewood. Charlie is off on a course somewhere. I have not heard from him since he left me at Nunningham on Boxing Day. We had a busy holiday, saw all our friends, spending a day or two with Alec and Dado in Eastbourne, Christmas Day with the Youngs in Sutton, and Boxing Day at Nunningham.

The best part of Christmas was milking six cows at Nunningham. I had feared that I was completely out of practice, but six cows is fair enough.

January 2, 1942. Rye
Mr Winters, who is here in Rye with the Agricultural Depot, suggested that all the Land Girls, about thirty of us, from Rye district, meet at the Queen's Head and go from there to the dance at the George on New Year's Eve.

Some of the Welsh boys are still stationed here, and listening to their voices, mingled with the North Country speech of the boys from the Durham Light Infantry, was the most enjoyable part of the evening for me.

I danced with a soldier from Yorkshire who spoke with a burr and had a chuckle in each word. There was Pam, dancing with Sussex-born George, who was saying, "Come on, duck," while my Yorkshire partner was begging, "'Tis New Year's Eve, luv, gi' us kiss." I dodged that kiss for some little time, but when midnight came, when the music stopped and the radio broadcast the chimes of Big Ben, I stood happily, on tip-toe, and as always on New Year's Eve at home, was kissed by my partner as the clock struck twelve.

But in Rye, no one kissed anyone else.

I blushed, was teased and scolded and we all joined hands for, "Auld Lang Syne," and then, "God Save the King," and by quarter past twelve we were all out of the inn, singing, four abreast, all the way home.

Mrs Skipage, kind and thoughtful as she always is, had left the kettle on the hob and cocoa and biscuits by the fire. I sat on the fender for an hour, in the peaceful solitude, writing to wish Charlie a Happy New Year, and then undressed by the fire.

At eight o'clock next morning I was down at Castle Farm in the rain. But New Year's Day, contrary to Sussex custom, was to be a holiday after all. The rain pelted past us in great gusts and by eleven o'clock we were all sent home for the day.

Doris came to Mrs Skipage's with me and, warm and comfortable, we ate our sandwiches beside the fire, instead of crouched to leeward of our tractors. After lunch I stretched out on the hearth rug and slept till three o'clock, wakening to find that Pam had joined the party and was doing jig-saw puzzles with Doris.

My pen poked its finger at me from the top of the piano, and my mending wriggled and squirmed on the table under the window, but I turned my back on them and built myself a beautiful picture of, "The Tower and Tower Bridge in Winter."

And we had bread and cheese for tea, instead of turkey and plum pudding, on January first, nineteen forty-three.

Just my luck to be home in bed with a sore throat and to miss all the fun. Pam came in at tea time to tell me.

Two tractors were working on the Pett Level piece when a Jerry swooped down to machine-gun them. He came so low that he hit the wires and crashed into a ditch just behind the Castle Farm buildings. One of the soldiers found his head in the ditch.

Pam was one of the tractor drivers, and has gone off in a rage to the local newspaper office because some stupid reporter printed a tale about her crawling in agony for help.

Young George Allen told me his experience with that Focke-Wulfe 190. He had been up in the tractor-shed, trying to start my tractor, when he saw it coming right for him. He lay flat, a most unhappy lad. Jerry dropped a thousand-pound bomb as he crashed, which did not go off. There was another explosion a second or two later. The engine had gone on another hundred feet. The pilot was caught in a tree and fell into a dike. George helped to fish the body out.

The bomb detonating squad is on the job again and we are not supposed to go near the plane or the bomb. But one of the guards pried off the little aluminum factory plate from the engine for me, and Doris has a real souvenir, the "Bosch" nameplate from the magneto, which is identical with those on our tractors.

This is a superstitious country. Old Ted refused to let me pick gorse, worried about magpies, and even Kath did not like white lilac in the house. Doris will walk half a mile across the marshes for me rather than pick up a dropped glove. Mrs Skipage refuses to let me cross the threshold if I forget something and come back for it. I should say that she has immediate bad luck, for there is seldom a day on which I don't forget something and she goes up to my room and searches diligently.

As my sore throat refused to improve, and Charlie did not arrive for the weekend, though we had expected and watched for him all day Saturday, Mrs Skipage is convinced that there will be a third unfortunate occurrence.

And, though I cannot compare my small troubles with the sad news which we have heard tonight, Mrs Skipage assures me that she, "Just knew something else would happen." Today Winchelsea, our neighbouring "quaint little old-fashioned town," was raided by those hit-and-run swine. Bombs fell in a little "street that winds up-hill and down," killing one person, injuring about a dozen others, and damaging a great many of the houses. Mrs Skipage had gone out and June and I crawled into our "safe spot" – under the dining room table – till we heard the all-clear after the Winchelsea raid.

I wonder how often fetishes and mascots bring luck, how often jinxes and gremlins prove their existence. Though my future may be less interesting, less coloured by the vicarious thrills of hope and fear that superstitious folk seem to welcome, I shall continue in my matter of fact way, walking under ladders, not changing underwear which happens to be donned in reverse.

And yet, shall I ever refrain from wishing on the evening star, though I place no faith in the wish, or repeating, when I see a flight of birds:

One for sorrow, two for joy,
Three for a girl, four for a boy,
Five for silver, six for gold –
Seven for a secret that's never been told.

February 19, 1943. Rye

When I left for Crawley, ten days ago, I thought I should be lonesome for the raids which have made life on Camber Farm an exhilarating experience.

There were few days in January when Jerry did not dash across, leaving a few bombs or spraying anyone in sight on Castle Farm with machine-gun bullets. There was a heavy raid all along the South Coast on the evening of the 17th and again we heard machine-gunfire when a convoy was attacked on the channel.

Three big corn stacks stand on a ridge just near the channel edge of the farm. I was working near them when I saw the warning rocket go up at Rye Harbour. I yelled, "Duck!" to Jill, the old girl who was working with me. She was about to ask why, when two Jerrys came between the corn ricks and flew on towards Rye. We were flat on our faces and those planes were so low that as they rushed past, our sweaters and shirts were pulled up around our shoulders. They had flown about ten feet from the ground, not above, but between those corn ricks.

Jill and I were brushing each other off and tucking in our shirts when we heard Doris wailing, "Look at me." And she ran towards us from where she had been working in a far corner of the field.

"Doris," I said, trying not to laugh, "Whatever has happened?"

"Didn't you see them? Didn't you see the swine? I was scared to death, I jumped into the dike."

Poor Doris. The dikes had been our air-raid shelters in the autumn, when we could crouch under their dry banks. Doris, in her terror, had forgotten that February fill-dike is upon us and the dike's full to the brim.

She seems doomed to suffer for all of us during these raids. One morning when we were swapping thistles, she caught sight of a raider swooping in and was shrieking her choicest swearwords at him, when he let loose a burst of machine-gunfire. One of the men knocked Doris down flat and lay on her, but not for long. Before the plane was out of sight, while I was still watching the little runnels the bullets had left in the sand, Doris was up screaming and sobbing. A bullet had gone through her hair and she clutched a little tangled curl in her hand.

From that time on, she refused to work alone. Even in the tiniest field our noisy team of tractors worked together. That we secured permission to do so has proved satisfactory for a different reason. The fields at the southeast corner of the farm, which had come under the plough, are very sandy. Seldom a day passed but Doris or I needed the help of the other to get out of a bad spot. There is a large stone-crushing plant, known as the "Beachworks," on that boundary of the farm and we became quite friendly with those members of its staff whom we approached to borrow tow-chains and planks for digging-out purposes. One man told us that during one of the raids, while we were probably lying face down in the mud, he had been up on second-story level on an elevator or crane, and had looked down on the tops of German planes as they sneaked in between the buildings of the beach works. The reason for the low-altitude flying is that planes coming in almost at ground level can escape under the radar screening and also they are come and gone before gunners on the defense batteries can aim their fire.

We had several anti-aircraft guns on Castle Farm and while their crews derived great amusement from swivelling the long barrels of their Bofors to keep our tractors in their sights, never once, to my knowledge, were they able to fire at a raiding plane.

By the end of January, Castle Farm was a dripping bog from one end to the other. It rained regularly and day after day, according to regulations, we came to work and were told to go home again. I decided that this was a stupid situation, and asked Mr Syer if I might take a week off without pay, if I left him a telephone number and promised to return at a minute's notice. And so it was that I spent a week at The George, in Crawley.

At first, I did miss the sound of the Rye siren, and the stimulation of life on the alert. But on the ninth day, I was wakened by the heavy shudder of the whole George Inn. Four bombs fell in quick succession. I heard the staccato of machine-gunning, and my nose twitched with the acrid smell of gunpowder. I looked at Charlie's bed. The sensible thing was to crawl underneath it, but the show seemed to be over. I

Charlie and I in uniform, Rye. I had these posh breeches made for me in Lewes, WLA breeches being a tragic cross between plus fours and pyjamas.

went to the window and drew the blackout. The old George gallows sign was still swinging, but I could not see across the street. Clouds of dust and rubble filled the air and drifted in through the window.

At breakfast, when I asked the waitress if she had had any trouble, for I knew that she walked to and from the inn each day, she said, "No, but they got the Post Office."

I waited to hear no more. The house in which Verna and Benjie lived adjoined the Post Office. I could not get though High Street at all, which was waist high with the debris of crumbled buildings, but I climbed around by a back street and met Bob.

"Verna? How is she? Is she safe?"

"I don't know. I've just come, too. Open the door."

"I can't. It's jammed. Be careful."

I was picking out enough of the broken glass to climb through a window. We found the house empty and Verna's room open to the four winds.

"She's been hurt, look, they've taken her, bedding and all," I said, as we turned to leave.

"I can't wait. I'm driving the Colonel." Bob ran ahead of me. "I left him high and dry. Find Verna, then go and tell Benjie."

I picked my way over the broken glass and splintered boards. The old lady next door had swept off her doorstep and walk and was down on her knees polishing the brass doorknob.

After having searched the town, I found Verna safe and sound, waiting for me at the George. When I remarked upon her appearance, made-up face, every hair in place, she returned shortly, "Jerry's not going to stop me from dressing properly."

Completely unperturbed, and her baby due in a month, she told me what had happened as we walked back to clear her rooms as well as we could and make arrangements to have the front boarded up.

She had been astoundingly lucky, first because she had been in bed when the bombs fell. The blast picked her up and dropped her down again on the bed, so that she was spared any jarring. And secondly, the French doors, and windows and frames all went out instead of in, which saved her from serious damage.

When we returned to the George we were told of the damage sustained by the inn, and that the wing where the permanent guests had their rooms was damaged. The situation was explained simply, and as the older residents had more need of my room than I, I took a three o'clock train and returned to Rye just in time to hear a stick of bombs which was dropped about six o'clock. Because I had taken a short-cut from the station, I was lucky again and just passed the danger area when they fell. It was fortunate that the Syers are not at home. I called in as I passed but there is no one there and all their windows were blown in.

I never cease to be thankful that my tractor is inanimate. Things may go wrong, breakage occurs, but machinery is not willfully perverse or antagonistic. I have fuel and oil and grease in plenty, and treat her intelligently. She is obedient, pleasing to run, and good company.

All this week I have been ploughing again, quickly and well, completely by myself, in this far corner of the farm, seeing no one save on my pilgrimages for fuel, every second day. The fog has held me closely. I followed my furrows, seeing no world beyond the dim edges of my field, bounded on the south by wind smoothed dunes. I have never been near sand-dunes before and I could imagine that the sea was only a matter of yards, instead of knowing, as I could see when the fog lifted, that it was half a mile away, beyond the ugly sprawling cranes and derricks of the Beach Works.

Charlie is coming for the weekend. I hope that we shall have time to come down here. I would like him to understand the spell of this lovely marshland, to see the browns and golds of furrows and sand and to hear the little rustles in the tussocks of withered grass.

But Charlie said that wandering around in fog was not his idea of celebrating and celebrate we had to. For he had brought down four new sets of sergeant's stripes for me to sew on to his tunic and greatcoat. He said that this was the night to find the little sailor's pub of which I had spoken. Pam and a Welsh soldier joined us and we descended the steps from Ypres Tower. Pam had told me about the old salt atmosphere and we hoped to find parrots and old seamen in navy blue sweaters and gold earrings. But there proved to be no atmosphere, no parrots, no sailors – only the inevitable soldiers and smoke.

March 5, 1943. Rye
Charlie met me at Nunningham for the weekend. He was concerned about me and the bombs and machine gunning and Percy had been pressing me to come, so after tea we decided that I should go to Kent.

Walter knows the WLA rules and says that I am perfectly free to go. So we telephoned Percy and I shall go in April.

While I was still feeling very much a traitor to Sussex and a little sorry that my bridges were burned, Charlie said, "I have leave the end of March. I have made inquiries and we can go to Ireland if you like."

"Make your plans," I said, "and let me know in time to meet you."

Kath and Walter are accustomed to these sudden decisions. It was to Nunningham that Charlie telephoned about our first leave to Scotland. Our Cornish holiday was planned at Nunningham too. I think that if Charlie said, "How about Greenland on my next leave?" Walter would look at Kath and say, "Put another log on the fire, there's a good girl."

Charlie and I on "Old Meg" in Londonderry

SWANLEY

April 8, 1943. Swanley

I live in Number 8, Swanley Cottages, which is one of a row of old peeling stucco dwellings, strung out, door by alternating window, like a row of town factory homes, but oddly enough isolated in the centre of an orchard, two miles from a main road. Like the cottage at Broomlye, it contains four tiny rooms, but lacks the peaceful rural privacy of that little house.

Mrs Holden, my landlady, is a small-boned, active little woman of sharp tongue and curious eye, with thin white hair screwed into a tight knob at the back of her head. Her husband, long and lean and cowed, is the local snob, or shoe mender, and as far as his trade goes, is very much his own mater. He is home early and leaves late. In these days of short supply, the mood of the repair man, like the traditional plumber, cannot be gainsaid.

I must withhold judgment until a later date, for I have mislaid my rose-coloured glasses and still my cold hangs on.

Unfortunately, like Southwater this farm is situated in the heart of beautiful country which one cannot see. I have been ploughing all week on a large flat stretch of land, in the midst of orchard. Beyond the trees there is rolling land and distant hills, but here I am shut in on a vast block, some hundred acres, of flat fields.

There is no response in me to flatlands or to these orderly plantations. The fields are all square, the trees in rows. It is excellent farming but not soul-satisfying.

This morning Percy said plaintively, "I know you've loved cows and dairy farming, but I think that if you'll give fruit-farming a chance you'll find it an interesting and absorbing study."

He is right. I have been brooding on the gentle Sussex scene, hills and fields, little copses and woods. But that is because I have had a rotten job this week. The soil is stiff clay, full of flints and aching for rain. When the plough draws easily, as on Nunningham's sandy soil or Castle Farm's silt, I relax and enjoy my work, but when the tractor strains and nearly stalls, when the plough rides out of the dry concrete soil, I am tense and strain with my tractor. When Percy stood watching my exasperated struggles I said, "Look here, there are three elements which may be at fault, the driver, the plough, and the soil. If it's the driver, nothing would delight me more than for you to give the job to someone who can do better. If it's the plough, I'll see to it that I fix it and enjoy it, but if it's the soil, for Pete's sake let's pack up and wait for rain." Percy said that the soil was so hard that no one could do a good job of it, but he did not give me orders to work elsewhere.

To add to the difficulties caused by the state of the ground, a carload of sheep's trotters, with stinking gobs of flesh and fur on the bones, a wartime substitute for artificial manure, mostly phosphates, has been spread on the fields for me to plough in. I suffered less, up on the tractor, than the men who unloaded the smelly things from the dung carts and then scattered them in little heaps. Abner, a good-natured ne'er-do-well, rode home with me on the tractor the first night of the job.

"Don't they stink, them things? I lost me breakfus' this mornin', I couldn't eat no dinner, and I ain't goin' to be able to eat no tea, I know I ain't."

Two parcels arrived from home yesterday and there has been great excitement in No. 8. Mr and Mrs Holden have never had parcels from Canada before, and were overcome when they found Klim and cheese, dried fruit and butter added to their larder.

Charlie arrived just after lunch today so we had a party. Neighbours came in to play darts. Mrs Holden produced a bottle or two of brown ale and there were Canadian sardines and butter and cheese, and a two-pound box of chocolates which everyone seemed afraid to eat.

Everywhere the trees have stolen into bloom. I have driven through bright aisles of blossom to and from work each day and promised myself that I would find time to "loaf and invite my soul." But each day it has been dark as I finally filled up my tractor for the next morning and backed her into the shed.

I had just taken off my greasy overalls and changed into clean clothes when Charlie arrived. We had the whole afternoon to spend and lay in the orchard under soft puffs of blossom and the still, blue sky. I filled him full of my meagre learning, of which are pear and which plum or cherry blossom; how each have their own grub or parasite, a few of which – Apple Capsid, aphis, and Apple Sorefly – I have learned to recognize, and the treatment and time to apply it for each. Certain washes must not be used after the setting of the blossom, lest they harm the bees, some are poisonous when sprayed on the fruit.

I have learned only some of the varieties of apple and these I recognize more by their position in the orchard than by characteristics of wood and blossom. Charlie soon tired of my sketchy knowledge, and we looked through Housman's "Shropshire Lad" which I bought last week in Tunbridge Wells.

Loveliest of trees, the cherry now,
Is hung with bloom upon the bough.

The sun was warm and the faint scent of apple-blossom very sweet. We lay quietly, smoking and talking, sensing the transient beauty, while the full blossom stirred above us, tracing elusive patterns on the sky.

These months and years have dulled the dread of Charlie's departure from England. Thumbing through the pages of Housman, as the sun sank lower, I felt the afternoon grow chilly, knowing that one day he must say,

Square your shoulders, lift your pack,
Leave your friends and go.

May 1, 1943. Swanley
Last night Percy took me out towards Canterbury, seeking a farm where a certain old-fashioned variety of apple grows. This variety, which has good apple quality save colour, Percy plans to cross with a certain well coloured one of less flavour and fineness of texture.

We drove right into the orchard, acres and acres of blossom at its prime, and sought out the special old trees. He chose his blossoms carefully, those advanced sufficiently for pollen to be formed but not open enough to have been already fertilized. I was fascinated by the whole process, though I understood little.

Percy explained that he would remove the pollen carefully and, after removing the stamens from the other variety with which the cross is to be carried out so that there is no possibility of self-fertilization, paint that pollen carefully onto the remaining pistils. He would then tie little cellophane bags over the artificially pollenized blossoms to prevent any other possible fertilization.

When the apple develops he will plant seeds from it. Buds from the little plant will then be grafted or budded onto suitable stock, which should bear fruit in 1945. Percy stressed that chance plays a large part and that there are many factors which cannot be controlled, but that possibly in ten years he may have sufficiently positive results to place before an Agricultural Research Bureau and establish his new variety.

His conversation is full of botanical and scientific terms, and he races on, paying me the compliment of assuming that I follow him. He leaps from entomology to spraying formulae, and then to specific plans for grubbing out the plums which are on the cross, to leave the apples on the square, to simplify cultivating and spraying operations. His expositions are constantly interrupted as I get left behind.

"Pendiculous, is that a botanical term? Why not just pendulous?"

"Why do stones form in some plums and not in others?"

"Excuse me again, you said that a tree may have too many blossoms. Why?"

Or just, "Oh, Percy, I'm sorry to interrupt, but look at that swan drifting just beyond the Green Wheel, and the dark pines against the flax to complete the picture. Forgive, please do go on."

On the way back we turned a sudden corner. A deep valley lay beyond, filled with a green tangle of white leaf and young sycamore leaves. Percy stopped the car and raised one finger. A nightingale was pouring out its lovely joyous song, "In full-throated ease." It ceased almost immediately and did not sing again. I have wondered since if I really heard that, "Sweet remembered ecstasy."

Charlie has come and gone. It was late on Saturday when he came in, unexpectedly. I was mounting specimens of pests which I have collected for Percy to identify. It was a cold rainy weekend and we remained indoors until today, when about six the sun came through and I walked to the station with Charlie. The weekend has gone so terribly quickly, and I am not looking forward to tomorrow.

I have two jobs to perform before I can begin work. A new type of exhaust pipe has arrived for my tractor, to allow me to work in the fruit trees, and also new breasts for my plough. I have now reached the stage of proficiency where I can make the necessary alterations myself, but I am still sufficiently feminine to wish for, and to refuse, any offers of help.

Mr Holden has just come in prophesying frost and I felt a shiver of horror. Not frost, in Kent, in blossom time! A mild frost would not matter but a heavy one would be disastrous both to the farmer and to England's vitamins.

I crossed a corner of Swanley this morning on my way to work, walking quietly between the gray boles of the sycamores. A blackbird was bursting with melody and I heard the soft call of a cuckoo, and then, at first a few single notes, tentatively, almost shyly, then rippling little trills and again, liquid, magical, I heard the exquisite golden song of a nightingale. Listening, I turned to lean against a mossy stump. Four little spotted fawns, huddling in the striated shadow, peered at me with curious eyes. The nightingale ceased to sing, the rapturous notes faded to a slender thread of melody and were lost against the far purr-whirring of the wood-pigeons, and still the little fawns, timid, inquisitive, watched me.

But my watch ticked on, I had to move. The fawns, in a twinkling, disappeared in the cool vaults of the woodland, and mortal, though truant awhile to mortal things, I trudged on to work.

The British have broken through to Tunis. The fighting is over in North Africa. Von Arnim has surrendered and the Eighth Army boys will soon be home, after three years. And too, perhaps the Second Front, for which we so hope, and which I so dread, will be opened.

My days are full and uneventful. I have little time and little to report.

I cycled into town last week. I received a letter from the Labour Office, asking why I had not registered for National Service. This omission has rested lightly on my shoulders since 1941, when I was at Green Farm. My age group had come up at that time, but as we were busy harvesting I had neglected to register, feeling secure in the fact that I was already in services. However, in the transfer from Sussex to Kent, the registration offices must have caught up with me and I was requested to present myself at the Labour Office.

The girl at the desk looked over my papers with some irritation, and stated, as I knew, that I should have registered in 1941. Just then she came to my passport.

"Why, you're a Canadian," she said. "You're exempt from registration." She dismissed me with an impatient nod.

Why I, who eat as much food, wear as many clothes, help crowd the transportation system of Britain as much as any Englishman should have the freedom to live a parasitical life just because I am a Canadian is beyond me. However it is gratifying to realize that I am working, fulfilling Cousin Lilian's trust in me, and am working freely and completely voluntarily.

We had heavy rain on Monday. I was pulling out old apples trees with the aid of three men and my trusty tractor until noon, when the rain grew too much for us and we all tried to find indoor jobs.

I am a spoiled wench, always have been in this Land Army. Just as Walter used to take me with him on rainy days, so Percy took me to see an old gentleman some distance away who has a vast series of greenhouses. We walked through many of them when Percy asked if we might see the oranges.

First, however, we walked out through the cold spring rain to another greenhouse, where the old gentleman opened the door. Strange heavy perfume crept to envelop me, heady, exotic.

"Go on in," Percy said, "Walk down and look back."

The scent came from two lemon trees, heavy vine-like branches arching overhead, fruit and blossom, pale gold and waxen white, hanging together. I stepped beyond the cold English rain into a luxuriant paradise and was bewitched by the spell of smooth yellow lemons against their dark leaves and the damp tropical scent of their blossoms.

We saw oranges in the next greenhouse, but they were temporal earthly things, bulbous and blatant, like Christmas tree ornaments. Here was round firm fruit but no enchanted green mansions. On the following day the weather cleared and I have been discing all week, cleaning and aerating the soil between the little pyramid apple trees.

Percy's mother has been ill. I have scarcely seen her since my arrival but on Friday night as I passed the house she asked me in to have a bath. Such is the height of hospitality, and I met Charlie at the station feeling fresh and fragrant as a princess.

June 9, 1943. Swanley
Percy took Val, another Land Girl, and me to a strawberry demonstration last night. We had difficulty finding the farm and arrived late and there was no one is sight. We set out behind the house through the farmyard and hop gardens, and then climbed a stile into a cherry orchard where shiny Blackheart cherries hung ripe on the boughs. Val and I walked under the trees, enjoying the picture they made, great heavy clusters hanging under the leaves, some red, some black. Quite honestly, we had no thought in our minds of the cherries as edible fruit, till we saw Percy reach up and break off a cluster. We then proceeded to pick and eat as fast as we could without slowing our progress through the orchard.

We found the crowd eventually and, on the edge of a well-littered strawberry field, listened to the three men from the East Malling Research Station. Each spoke on his own phase of strawberry growing, pests, virus, runner-beds, varieties. I can now recognize three varieties of strawberries, though I can identify only one, Royal Sovereign, by its fruit alone.

Later we all went through a splendid young plum plantation to hear a discourse on currents and gooseberries. As we trooped through a gap in the hedge an old gentleman behind me caught his foot in a root and tripped, ejaculating a heartfelt "damn." I turned and, after picking up his hat, helped him up. He was a fine-looking old gentleman, in good tweeds, with a cane and white side whiskers. His manner was gentle and courtly as he thanked me, and said how fortunate he was to have fallen where the ground was so soft and where there was a charming lady to help him up. He told me that he was eighty-five, yet he had scrambled to his feet as nimbly as a kitten.

We walked back to the car, much impressed by the natural beauty of the farm and by its groomed and careful husbandry. The bush fruit, currents, gooseberries, and raspberries were cultivated and hoed clean of any blade of grass. Ours, too, have been disced and braked both ways but they are not so clean about the individual plants.

Percy really has too much on his hands, and cannot obtain the labour to cope with it. There are many hundreds of acres at Swanley but there are not the cottages to house the required personnel.

At Nunningham, Walter has pasture for his cattle and the remaining fields mainly in corn, but Percy grows every fruit and vegetable in common use in England. Walter has one main crop to harvest and a regular sequence of labour. Here there is no cycle of daily work, broken only by the rush of hay time followed by the lull before the frenzy of harvest. Instead, gangs pick lettuce and radishes and strawberries while I plough for cauliflower and Christmas cabbage. There are peas to be picked and beans to be staked while the orchards are being sprayed and tomatoes and cucumbers transplanted from the greenhouses. Percy has dozens of men and women to set to their various jobs. I would not want his headache for worlds. Today he will find that the cabbages have been seriously attacked by green-fly while the clutch has gone on the Case and the magneto on the Allis-Chalmers has cracked up. Big Cliff's lorry (which takes the produce to Covent Garden) has had a breakdown and someone shut the greenhouse doors and the seedlings were scorched badly. Val sprayed the tomatoes with too strong a solution of Pyrethex and the result is heartbreaking. Tomorrow it will be rooks in the peas, or trouble with the John Deere or my new plough shares will not have arrived.

June 13, 1943. Seaford, Sussex
Verna and Benjie have a little flat here and Charlie and I are spending the weekend with them.

Just before I left, the postman presented me with a large, official-looking letter which informed me that an overseas unit of the RCAF, WD (Royal Canadian Air Force, Women's Division) was being formed in England, and inviting me, with offers of high salary and smartly designed uniforms, to join the ranks. I dropped the forms in the fire, not remotely interested. A Land Gal I be, and a Land Gal I stays.

Charlie, when I told him, was quite indifferent and has gone off to the Seven Sisters with Penny.

July 1, 1943. Swanley
A week ago I met Charlie at Mrs Young's in Sutton, and last week, when he came down here, we took a picnic tea and went with Percy to a farm near Chilham, where Percy had business to transact.

The farm is on a high ridge, with winding hedges and sloping fields dropping in to the shadow of the woods. There are brooks and the little flowers which seem to shun Swanley. The houses are timbered and crooked with mellow tile showing through the trees. Charlie has leave again, and we hoped that we might find a spot here, where we would feel called upon to visit no one, nor make any pilgrimage, save possibly one, to Canterbury.

Percy told Val and I that we might help ourselves to any strawberries that remain, and so tonight we are comfortably settled in the straw, leaning against an old stack, periodically foraging in the strawberry field beside us.

Old Abner passed a while ago, saying "Ain't you gals got no home to go to?" He and his fellow country folk cannot understand that we are very happy, enjoying the peace, the sunset, and the last of the Royal Sovereigns.

We returned from leave last week, a restful leave in Alfriston, an old Sussex village with three old inns, the famous Star, the George, and the Smuggler's Inn. We slept early and rose late, walked along the winding Cuckmere, stood on the bridge in the sun, walked over to the Plough and Harrow at Litlington, and went into tiny Lullington Church.

We spent a day in Lewes and Alec and Dado came to dinner with us at the George.

The last two of Charlie's nine days we spent at Nunningham when Charlie returned to Seaford and I journeyed into Kent.

I have been picking apples all day today, which is not quite as pleasant a job as it sounds. The apples are perfectly beautiful, hanging in tight red clusters, and in the morning when they are all sparkling with dew it seems that there can be no lovelier sight.

But there is not time to drink in their beauty. There are mountainous walls of bushel boxes to be filled. That sparkling dew soaks one's feet and ankles and wild oat seeds prickle on one's socks. Dew-pearled cobwebs hang on every bough and between each tree, and one's face and hands and arms grow sticky with them. There are numberless little bugs and spiders which get down one's neck, harmless but irritating, while one's arms and clothes get black from trees sprayed with arsenate of lead.

We seem to be in for England's annual week of summer, and the weather has been decidedly hot. There is no breath of air in the orchards and as the trees are pruned down tight they afford no shade. Apple-picking, perched up on a ladder under the burning sun, is very hot work.

Tomorrow, however, I shall be grading early transparents. These are a fragile, easily bruised apple and will be graded in the orchards to save them from unnecessary loading and unloading.

Early transparents are a pale translucent green, ripening to a creamy yellow with a faint touch of pink, and after working with Gladstones, which have brilliant crimson cheeks, they will be cool and lovely to handle.

Charlie telephoned last night and I met him at Victoria today. I arrived early and sat in front of the platforms 1–7 notice board to wait for him. A Canadian soldier was sitting at the other end of the bench, when a painfully thin chap in civilian clothes came and sat between us. His tale poured out immediately.

He was a merchant seaman whose ship had been torpedoed just off Halifax, Nova Scotia. He had been badly wounded, rescued, taken to Halifax, and just returned to England. He was a poor colour, shaking from head to foot, and talked like a tired child. He hailed from Jamaica, knew no one in London, "Well, there were some people I did know, but I was so little then, and now –" He looked wondering and spoke wistfully, "They wouldn't know me now, because you see, I've – grown up."

Here the Canadian soldier walked away. The little sailor went on. He told me about the sinking of his ship and how his nerves had been affected, then, "You know America? This suit comes from America. It's different. It – it has a zipper." I said, "Has it?" and wondered what next. The Canadian returned just then with two cups of tea. I refused mine and suggested that he give it to the sailor. The essential male was piqued, but he managed to come through fairly well, saying that he could only carry two at once. Our poor merchant sailor could hardly drink his. He put the cup on the floor and when he tried to pick it up his hand shook so that he could hardly hold it. He needed medical treatment and should not have been wandering alone in London.

Charlie arrived at eleven-thirty. We walked up through the park, past Buckingham Palace and along the Mall into Trafalgar Square. After looking lingeringly at the Berkeley and the Ritz we had lunch in a rotten little restaurant.

Later we saw an exhibition marked "Free" and went in. It proved exceptionally interesting, and showed the extent and diversity of equipment required by an army in the field. One section showed the personal equipment of the individual soldier, another all types of rations, of portable ovens and bakeries, mobile laundries, mobile dental and medical clinics. There was an amazing variety of lorries, tanks, guns, and trenches, machine-gun nests, and an incredible range and variety of radio equipment and wireless sets. There were maps and relief maps of past battles, photographic histories of victories and retreats, wall space about a hundred feet long devoted to El Alamein, showing how supplies were brought up and the wounded taken away. It was a stupendous demonstration, incredibly well done, and held in a block of bombed-out houses so that it was doubly effective because of the fragments of walls and the varying levels, mostly well below the street, and all open to the clear July sky. Wherever one looked there were jagged walls, hung with camouflage nets, and Union Jacks and with great ack-ack guns manned, pointing skyward.

We had not nearly enough time to see it all before we had to part for our different trains.

August 24, 1943. Swanley
Just back again from Seaford. Yesterday was Charlie's birthday, but it seems that there is little he wants as a birthday gift. We toured Seaford's limited shopping district together on Saturday afternoon, with no success. All he wants is half a dozen pairs of leather bootlaces.

We sat by the sea, Sunday morning, at Seaford, and then took the bus over the downs through East Dean and Friston to spend the rest of the day with Alec and Dado.

Swanley is lovely now. Its thousands of apple trees are heavy with fruit. I have been carting from the orchards to the grading sheds. Val and I work together, driving up and down the lanes between the trees, loading the boxes of fruit on to a low trailer and then stacking them near the main roadway. Then I hitch on a colossal trailer, load it up and go on the long trip to the grading sheds. My trailer holds about three tons and I make about three of these trips each day. The work goes with a swing and I enjoy it, but my muscles are not yet accustomed to the constant lifting and I am very stiff. The plums are in little trays and are easiest to shift, but the apples are in bushel boxes which weigh fifty pounds, while a bushel of pears weighs seventy.

September 3, 1943. Swanley

I am still fruit carting all day, a job which is easy and hard alternatively. Helping to load is heavy work and then the drive to the sheds is a holiday, save for Hold Tight Hill, where I acquire one more gray hair each trip. The hill is steep and my load towers behind the tractor. For a few moments each trip I lose faith in my governor and I fear lest the trailer overtake the tractor.

The second hour of double daylight saving time is off now and night closes in early, bringing sad thoughts of winter close on one's heels. Fortunately Val lives in one of these cottages or I should see a fairly complete hibernation. With Mrs Holden's chatty ways there can be no peace, which I miss most after my peaceful haven at Rye.

Val dropped in tonight with the news that the Canadians have landed on the toe of Italy. Is this the Second Front?

The cable came last night telling of Mother's illness. I walked through the orchards and across the wheat fields of a neighbouring farm. Mother has seldom been ill. A cable gives such little detail. One corner of the field is yellow with charlock, a square patch where a stack once stood. Mother never thought of herself. Always she gives, of her time, her home, herself. If her heart is failing she has little energy left from which to draw. I pulled the charlock in even rows till I had cleared the patch. At the cottage Mrs Holden would be waiting to fuss and worry over me. I could not go back there. I walked on, over the wheat field and the stile, and then taking the road, went to a movie in the village. It was too cold to work any longer in the dark. I can count on one hand the number of movies I have seen in England. When I came home Mr and Mrs Holden were asleep.

When I was ploughing this morning Percy passed with his car full of Land Girls. They are working now in so distant a corner of the farm that he must drive them back and forth each day. He stopped the car to give me some new plough shares and said, "How did you enjoy the show last night?"

I was in no mood to play. Under pain of offending Mrs Holden's sensitive ego, I had wrested for myself a few hours of solitude, and now Percy was determined to prove to me that there was no escape. He loves to feel that nothing eludes him on the farm and he waited for me to express amazement at his efficient espionage. I could not explain about Mother then. I replied, "Very well, thank you," put my tractor in gear and let in the clutch.

Nevertheless, I am curious to learn how he heard so quickly. The night was dark and I did not meet a soul either way.

The days go by. I carted fruit all morning and Val and I went shopping in the afternoon and knitted together in the evening.

Slept in. Val and I cycled to the village to mail letters, had a drink in the pub, dinner, knitted, tea and bed.

September 27, 1943
Carted fruit all day. Knitted in the evening.

September 28, 1943
Carted oats from thresher to granary.

September 29, 1943
Carted fruit.

September 30, 1943
Carted fruit.

October 1, 1943
Carting fruit. The Case tractor broke down, my humble Fordson to the rescue.

October 2, 1943
Carting fruit – Charlie arrived.

October 3, 1943
Charlie gone.

October 4–10, 1943
Carting fruit.

October 11, 1943
Carting fruit. Counting fruit trees. It does not change.

October 16, 1943. Swanley
Still I cart the endless apples. Charlie was down two weeks ago and I have not heard from him since, do not know if he is still in England.

Percy came down tonight to see if I was still alive. I have not seen him for over a week as I have not gone to Swanley. With my cold I did not have the energy to cycle the long, dark miles.

I took the beastly, prickly burrs off the chestnuts which Reg and I had gathered only to find that most of them are wormy. Grace, another Land Girl who has been working with me, says that she knows where we can find good ones.

I am waiting now for my bath water to heat. For some time after my arrival here I went to some lengths to avoid having a bath at No. 8, but who am I, to be so particular. And so, my Saturday afternoons are employed mainly in getting clean.

Dinner is over a little after one, and then we light the copper in one of the common wash-houses behind the cottages. Mrs Holden has to go to the village for the meat in the mornings, so the copper cannot be lighted earlier. Since there are no longer any rural deliveries because of the meat shortage, and of course no ice, the meat must be fetched from butchers, and as late as possible. Therefore, the copper is not hot till nearly three. While it heats I manicure my nails to the best of my ability. Then I carry in the hot water. I like to do this myself, because Mrs Holden insists on using a slop pail for the job, which, though rinsed, is still faintly redolent of its baser use.

The bath is in a sort of scullery which leads from the kitchen. Mrs Holden magnificently lords the possession of a bathroom over her neighbours. I do not mean to be unkind. The cottage has no cupboards and certainly some spot is necessary for overflow, and overflow there most definitely is.

Several jars of this year's preserves stand in one corner, near a pile of clothing waiting to be mended or washed. I have never approached near enough to find out. There are two little oil stoves in the opposite corner, mops and carpet sweepers, old shoes, trays of onions, apples or whatever fruit is in season, excess china in the form of old-fashioned comports, huge vases, and spoutless teapots. Piles of music, a small store of canned goods, all these give the appearance of having been shoved in hastily, though unmoved in the six months that I have been here, with no shelf or method of arrangement whatever.

Till a moment ago all has been peaceful in No. 8, save for the usual clamour next door, clearly audible through the walls. I have been mending and listening to the Brains Trust on the radio. But Mr Holden, who was sawing wood outside, has come in and soon my tranquillity will end. He sits by the fire, an angular uneasy old man, with his long stocking feet on the fender and his teeth out. The latter, I know, are in an old handleless cup in the kitchen. Mrs Holden is asleep on the sofa, stolidly asleep.

Old Jake looked at her helplessly for some time, wanting his supper but not daring to disturb her. Nor has he done so. He has taken his old leather knife and is sitting now, holding a thick slice of bread with a hunk of cheese on it, between his thumb and the palm of his hand, with an onion curled in his little finger. With the other hand he pares off a piece of each and somehow conveys all to his mouth on the murderous looking knife.

By the fire, Witzy, the poor decrepit yellow cat, lies wheezing and I, another sight to see, sit just behind her, in greasy corduroys with a shrunken pair of Charlie's old socks over my golf stockings. My hands have had a good wash but still palms and nails are grimed with dirt. A neighbour's pup has had his way with my slippers, so that they look sadly the worse for wear but quite in keeping.

The table is littered with the family's usual residue, Jake's collar and tie, a half empty tin of evaporated milk, a bowl of chrysanthemums, Mrs Holden's knitting, the lamp, an apple, the bread board, and some un-ironed washing. The room is tiny and filled with furniture. A heavy sofa, a piano, a sideboard, and an elaborate Dutch dresser give one barely room to walk around the table.

Mrs Holden has awakened and I cannot compete with her steady barrage.

Later ...

The Holdens have gone to bed, and there is no sound save the kettle's whistling and a tap dripping. Even Witzy has crept under the stove and sleeps deep. This is a rare occasion. Usually Mrs Holden outsits me, nor can I turn in early, hoping to read, for then she comes into my room and, perching on the foot of my bed with friendly sociability, talks till I fall asleep.

Tonight I hate to follow them, to leave the silence and the fire, and yet I must, very shortly, for I had a long day today after a long day in London yesterday.

For some time I had been planning to go, as I was determined to send Mother a special gift for Christmas. Yesterday morning it was raining heavily and as we went in to breakfast, I asked the foreman if he thought the weather would clear.

"No, my gal," he said, "I can't say as it will. You got work to do on your machine, I reckon? Changin oil or somethin'?"

"Well, not the oil, Mr Stapley, but I suppose I could find something. However, do you suppose that I could have the day off to go up to London instead?"

"Up to London, is it? Sure, you go ahead. And what do you want, young Reg?"

Young Reg, who lives near us, has been working with me all week. He told me that never, in all his fourteen years, had he been to London and I promised that I would take him the next time I went. I looked at him then and grinned. He grinned back.

"Mr Stapley, if Reg's mother says he can come with me, may he have the day off, too?"

Mr Stapley's face straightened. He took out his cigarette papers, and began to roll a cigarette. There was no sound from Reg, standing beside me, looking down at the ground.

"Get along, the two o' ye," Mr Stapley jerked his head towards the cottages. "Mind ye look after her, young Reg." But young Reg was streaking off to seek his mother's permission.

"He's a good lad," I said and Mr Stapley agreed with me as we walked home to breakfast.

Reg sat with his eyes glued to the streaming windows, all the way to London. He remarked on the bomb damage but was more impressed by the height of the buildings. In his mature common-sense way, he said, "I don't suppose that they'd seem high beside a real skyscraper."

It was a most satisfying day, young Reg mostly silent but absorbing everything. He was greatly interested in a Barrage Balloon. The RAF boys explained details to him and he walked, enchanted, round and round it. I derived more pleasure from Liberty's where I bought a few gifts. And from seeing Big Ben and Buckingham Palace again, crossing Blackfriar's Bridge to find the new Women's Hostel on Stamford Street. The Abbey and Buckingham Palace did not impress Reg, so we fulfilled his one wish – to travel by underground very briefly to Mme Tussaud's, and then train home. Judging from conversations on the farm this morning, I think young Reg had a happy day.

November 10, 1943. Swanley

Yesterday we carted the last bushel box of apples out of the orchard and I have been ploughing all day. I feel efficient and happy again. I was told to plough the barley field. I took down the tractor and plough at seven o'clock. It was dark then but by the time I had greased tractor and plough there was enough light to see. I paced and cut out the headland and cut out the first cant. I finished that just after dinner, completed a second and cut out a third. Then I scraped the mud off my plough, greased it, came home, and filled up my tractor for morning. No one has been near me. I needed no help. It is pleasing to know that the foreman shares my confidence. And to think that there was a time when I was always in hedges and ditches! No longer do I have any dealings with them. I trip in, trip out, all day long, with little trouble, unless some actual breakage occurs, such as losing a share, which may happen to anyone.

Charlie and I have been anxious to see "For Whom the Bell Tolls," and being a sergeant has its advantages. Charlie can now more or less count on being free on Sunday afternoons, and he promised to try to get tickets for the show, which is now showing in London.

Val and I, after securing beds in the hostel on Stamford Street, went up to London on Saturday.

We slept very comfortably, for one shilling and nine pence, one and six without bath. American school children made the knitted Afghan and patchwork quilt, which cover the bed. I am sorry that I did not record the name of the American school which made mine to write a thank you note. Val called me just as I was emerging from mine and when I came into the hall I found her sitting at the foot of the stairs with Charlie.

He had been unable to secure seats for "For Whom the Bell Tolls" and, as we did not relish the idea of standing in the long queue on the chance of getting in, we spent the morning in Petticoat Lane. There, on a Sunday, one is reputed to be able to purchase anything from a hairpin to a motor car. And that I do not doubt. We saw bobby pins, elastic, cups and saucers and sheets and tablecloths, all of which have vanished from provincial shops. I bought two cans of soup and an adjustable spanner and Val bought material for a dressing gown.

After a good lunch at the hostel, we went into the lounge and, with London still full of uninviting fog, three country hicks that we are, worn out by city life, we sat, peacefully, half asleep by the fire, till train time.

December 6, 1943. Swanley
I returned from Nunningham, still the loveliest spot in England to me. Charlie arrived by motor bike for an hour this afternoon, and I found an airgraph, with better news of Mother, waiting for me here. Ten by the clock and all's well.

My newest job is spraying, an easy job and a filthy one. Percy took me to Maidstone some time ago when he went to see about buying this new machine, which I now drive, but it was not until I began to work with it that I understood the masterly job it performs.

Last week the power drive for my tractor was installed and now each morning I hitch on my tractor, remembering to connect the power drive to the trailer, and draw the washing machine to a large stand pump. There we fill it with 400 gallons of water and 18 buckets of tar oil winter wash.

Two men work with me, and as I drive up and down the rows, between the trees, they walk behind, directing the spray, force pumped by power-drive from the tractor, through thirty-foot lengths of hose pipe.

The long, fine spray envelopes us all, and in time, the men assure me, turns one's skin a pale yellow. I have the easiest part of the job, to drive up until their hoses are taut, watch as they work up to the machine, and then drive along again. As the spraying must be done while the buds are dormant, it is a winter job and a cold one. I wear all the warm clothes I have, with my mack over my leather coat and a long smock, supplied to all the spraying gangs, over all. And though spraying is a cold job, it is a change for me to work in company with others, and infinitely preferable to sorting beets and potatoes, or pulling parsnips, which are the other jobs of the moment at Swanley.

January 5, 1944. Swanley
I had my share of traveling in December, and well I did. Charlie and I spent the weekend of the twentieth in Sutton, with the Youngs. I returned on Sunday night and worked each day on the spraying machine till Christmas Eve, when I went to Seaford.

The Sergeant's Mess played host to a gay party that night. Dado and Alec were waiting up for us when we arrived, late, to spend Christmas with them. We spent a merry day, made perfect by the receipt of a wire from home saying that Mother would be up for an hour or so on Christmas day. After a flying visit to Nunningham on Boxing Day I returned to Swanley and my spraying machine.

On New Year's Eve I was to return to Seaford again and made every preparation possible at noon to facilitate a quick departure at five o'clock. I remember quite clearly looking at my watch at three fifteen, as I sat on the tractor seat, the air filled with pale green vapour from the spray we were using.

My next memory is of a strange cottage, strange faces and consciousness that ebbed and flowed. It was seven o'clock then. Sometime after four the men had looked up to see why their spray had ceased. They did not see me on the tractor and walked forward to see where I had gone. No one will ever know how, or why, but my long coat must have caught in the universal gear of the power drive. I had been pulled down against the connecting-rod, jammed the gears, and stalled the tractor. My face, they tell me, was black. I have a long burn across the back of my neck, where my clothes were drawn tight. The boys cut me loose and carried me to the nearest cottage. Percy was sent for and he called Charlie immediately. By the time the doctor had strapped up my broken ribs and had gone, Charlie was beside me.

A day or two later, I discovered methods of getting out of bed and dressing myself. Mrs Holden was terrified. I think that she expected me to fall to pieces before her. But the doctor says that I may do whatever I can and when I can move less painfully I am to have my shoulder X-rayed. The arm is quite useless, but I can use the hand normally.

All the girls come in to see me each day, Percy drops in on his way home. Even old Abner came to see me. Mrs Holden finds flowers for my tray and uses her best china. Now that I have been assured that my back is unharmed and that the accident was not due to carelessness, I admit that rest is what I need, which I would never otherwise confess.

Charlie met me at Nunningham for the weekend. I showed them all that I can travel safely. Friday night Jerry paid us a visit and dropped the only bombs I have heard since our last night in London. Walter made us all sleep in the shelter, which seemed stupid, but which meant that we could talk longer into the night.

Charlie made a sailboat for Peter, and in spite of the cold they spent most of the daylight hours sailing it on the pond.

Sunday Walter came in from the barn, saying, "Have you finished that sock, come on, girl. I want to wear them today." I had given him one golf stocking, with a Fair Isle cuff, for Christmas. It was the unfinished mate to which Walter referred. So, while we discussed Charlie's next leave around the wood fire, I cast off the toe and presented the sock.

Kath said that Walter needed a holiday and after many long arguments he agreed that he could get away to come with us to Canterbury. Charlie's leave begins on the first of February and we had actually pinned Walter down to details when he remembered that he had obtained a license to kill a pig on February second. To both him and Kath that was an unchangeable agreement. Finally they convinced us that it had to be done, and that Kath would be busy all week salting and curing. Charlie's disappointment was as deep as mine.

Throughout January the days have been made interesting solely by progressive discoveries which lessen my dependence on Mrs Holden. I found very quickly that by tying a scarf to the foot of the bed I could turn or pull myself into a sitting position. By rolling onto my stomach, I could get out of bed and so get up alone. It was some time before I dared to carry my kettle of washing water, but even before my venturous trip to Nunningham, I discovered that I could ride my bicycle. The shoulder, when X-rayed, proved to be broken, but presented little difficulty. Once I had evolved a system of mounting and dismounting, I could ride with one hand very satisfactorily. I met my charming doctor one morning, while cycling through the village, and after receiving a sharp scolding for my foolhardiness, I persuaded him to allow me to continue riding. It was necessary for the preservation of my sanity, I explained, that I expand my horizon beyond the limits of the Swanley orchards. I promised to dismount and walk whenever the mud or the ruts offered any chance of a fall. He said, "You're a tough one, all right," and dismissed me with a hearty slap on my painful back. I nearly fell flat on my face.

I was then able to cycle to Percy's for an occasional evening and to travel back and forth on my weekly visit to the clinic without bothering him for transportation.

For so long I had lived in grease-smelling clothes and with hands broken nailed and ingrained with dirt. I cannot express the comfort it was to wash and have my hands stay clean, to watch them becoming trim and well-groomed again, and to wear light shoes and fragrant silk.

I tire with annoying rapidity, however, and though I am determined to return to work after our week in Canterbury, the sound of cold winds and rain does not help to bolster my courage.

February 17, 1944. Swanley
Charlie and I went to Canterbury, each in a sadly unreceptive mood. We both had heavy colds and walking tired me quickly. Charlie was filled with concern for me and his constant worry added to my mental and physical inertia. To go anywhere meant to summon forth my depleted energies and then to contend with Charlie's solicitous objections.

To remain indoors was little comfort either. Our inn was draughty and cold and our room a refrigeration chamber, with windows so warped by bomb-blast that, open or shut, they afforded the same protection.

We did enjoy two leisurely walks around Canterbury Cathedral, but after two attempts to prove worthy pilgrims, one after a venture through the main door where a verger showed us many treasured vestments, and a second attempt to explore, we were forced to give up. The grip of thirteen centuries emanates from those stones and after paying brief honour to the tomb of Thomas à Beckett I returned, shivering, to bed.

Charlie's leave ended on a Tuesday and I went back to work on Wednesday morning. The ground was frozen hard, which meant no tractor work. I cut cabbages all day with the women. Cutting cabbage is to be compared with pulling parsnips. By eight-thirty or nine o'clock one's gloves or mitts are too wet to be of any value. By ten o'clock the pain of one's cold hands is excruciating. But, as my fellow workers told me, after that stage one doesn't feel them any more. This proved to be the truth, and with numbed, fumbling fingers one continues to cut the cabbage stalk, shake out the icy water and slivery ice, and pack them into enormous sacks. Dinner time comes, one begins to thaw out and feel fairly alive, when the cycle begins again. I was tired that first night but I had expected to be.

The following day I was cutting cabbages again, cold and miserable, doggedly determined to prove myself as hardy as the other women, telling myself that this cold weather could not last forever, nor could the cabbages, when suddenly I fainted.

I remember the excited hubbub of voices, someone carrying me home, and then the drugging warmth of my own bed. Charlie came down on Sunday and immediately resolved to take me back with him. I told him that the other girls were tired too, that it was my duty to carry on, I was now trained, and sufficiently experienced to be of value. Charlie's only reply to this is unprintable.

He took my cycle and went over to Swanley. He told Percy what he planned to do and telephoned the Land Army from there. I later wrote them, enclosing a letter from the doctor, who had grinned at Charlie, saying, "These women, you can't tell 'em anything. They have to find out for themselves." The doctor had not approved of my early return to work, but had eventually given me permission to do so.

Charlie went back to Seaford with the intention of looking for rooms and coming back for me as soon as he finds them.

March 15, 1944. Seaford

Charlie is still adamant. He refuses stubbornly to listen when I suggest returning to work. And although I can carry on very well for normal needs of life, I am forced to agree that I am stiff and sore. I cannot turn in bed, when lying flat, nor can I lift anything, even a teapot, at arms length. I worry myself lest I am to suffer any permanent disability. I feel that I must return to work shortly, then I move in a certain way and suffer acute pain and grudgingly admit that Charlie is right. I know that I can no longer paddle a canoe or play tennis.

May 2, 1944. Swanley

I came back to Swanley on Saturday. Mrs Holden gave me a royal welcome and even poor old Jake seemed to brighten and announced his pleasure at my return. My possessions, most of which I had left behind, gave me a real sense of homecoming.

I worked all day yesterday spraying fruit trees, the identical job on which I was hurt, and I have been studiously careful. Walter wasted no words concerning where the blame lay for my accident.

"You know who's responsible for that accident, don't you?" he said. "You are, my girl. You should refuse to drive any tractor with a power take-off unless there is a guard on it."

I came back intending to do just that. However, Percy is ill. I have not seen him at all and I decided to carry on carefully till I do, and then I shall insist on having the proper guard installed. The power-drive which was put on my tractor was the only one I had ever seen, and I was unaware that guards were mandatory for them.

The blossom is almost out and the orchards are breathtakingly beautiful. We are spraying with a mixture of nicotine and arsenate of lead, the former to kill capsid, the latter caterpillar. As the leaf is the diet of these parasites, this mixture must be sprayed after the tree is in leaf and the work must be completed before the blossom opens or the bees, which are necessary for fertilization, will be poisoned.

I was weary after my first day's work and had flopped on the sofa, unwashed, my tea awaiting me on the table, when Charlie knocked at the door. He is so near to me now that he had cycled over for the evening. Val came in, and two or three other girls. Alec, a fellow

tractor driver came to welcome me home and several of the neighbours dropped in to say "hello."

This morning I was to work in an old orchard near Swanley. I
cycled through the shadowy blossom in a chill gray dawn. By the
time I had filled my tractor the men arrived and were weighing out
the proper proportions of nicotine and lead. We all had a cigarette
while the four hundred gallons of water were being pumped into the
machine, and then went back into the little orchard, the original
nucleus of the farm. It is overgrown with old gnarled trees and
infinitely more beautiful than the younger scrupulously neat
plantations.

First we sprayed the Bramleys, large spreading trees with a pale
blossom, just beginning to open. Here and there was an odd Bismarck, a snowy white cloud, full out, blossom less lovely upon close
observation, because it lacks the Bramley's shell-pink tints, but nevertheless beautiful in its fleecy profusion of bloom.

We worked down to an aisle of pears. The pear blossom is almost
over, and fluttering down through the early morning sunlight, sometimes against the sparkling green of pear leaves, sometimes against
the sky growing steadily more blue, the breeze was blowing the petals
like a lovely gentle fall of snow and pushing them in little drifts along
the tractor ruts and against the tree trunks.

And then we finished the rows of Bramleys and were into the Lord
Derby's, rows and rows of dark boughs, covered at intervals of only an
inch or two with dewy, half open clusters of crimson and white
bloom. The buds are deep crimson, but when they open the petals are
white inside, deeply streaked with pink. I think that they are the loveliest of the apple blossom.

I drove up and down the rows. The spray leaped high over the
boughs and the sun threw shimmering rainbows through it.

At tea time, when I was putting away my tractor, Mr Stapley called
out, "They want the cultivator down near your place. You'd best drive
your tractor home and take it down." So I left my cycle in the shed
and drove back through the miles of blossom, dusky and purple in the
valleys and shining and white on the hills.

Perhaps I was too happy on those first days of May, too content to be
back on the job and to be working in the enchanted aisles of blossom.

At any rate, on the third morning, a chilly May morning, the more chill because of the promise of sunshine when the mists dispersed. I cranked my tractor for several minutes before she went, and out of breath, but satisfied, I climbed up onto the seat to wait for the gear oil to warm up. I knew from experience that nothing would persuade her to slip quietly into gear except to let the engine run for five minutes. But I also had never overcome the sense of incompetence which a gang of men, eyeing "that girl on the tractor," gives to me.

That morning my mates waited accusingly and grudgingly. It was cold and a Land Girl was sitting, seemingly at ease, while they stamped their feet, rubbed their hands together and yearned for the work which in warmer weather they would have been in no hurry to begin. Just then I saw Alec come into the yard. I knew that he could no more put the tractor into gear than I could, but I thought that if he tried and failed the men would realize that the waiting was necessary. I called him over.

"See if you can get her in gear for me, will you?" He stepped up, jamming her into first one position and then another, forcing out a raucous pre-stripping bedlam, so that my heart bled for the old girl.

"Don't force her into gear," I shouted, "or you'll stall the tractor," at which point she stalled. I walked to the front to swing her, catching Alec's eye as I went.

"O.K.?" I asked, with the customary implication. "Is she out of gear?"

"O.K." Alec assented. I swung, the tractor leaped, so did I, but too late. I was free, but the front wheel was spinning through my ankle, mercifully pinned against a buffer row of fruit crates, piled against the stone wall of the shed.

Alec was frantically trying to get the tractor out of gear.

"Switch the engine off!" I yelled.

"I can't get her out of gear!" screamed Alec.

"Never mind the gear, shut the bloody thing off!"

He was in a complete panic. I was furious and reaching round managed to ground the magneto and the tractor ceased to leap through my foot.

Willing helpers pushed it back and carried me to a nearby work-bench. I felt my ankle gingerly after a few minutes. It was tender but felt normal to my fingers. I tried my weight on it and succeeded in walking to the tractor. As the damaged foot was not the one I needed for clutch and brake I decided that I could get over the hit-with-a-hammer feeling just as well at work as sitting in a shed. Someone started up the tractor for me and I backed out into the yard when, in a second, sky and ground slid snugly into reverse.

The ankle was broken all right. X-rays, a cast up to my knee, and an uncomfortable three days followed before I discovered that crutches are a less clumsy form of ambulation than they look.

June 2, 1944. Swanley

It was some time later, after many visits and much kindness from all my acquaintances, that I met Percy one morning in the village. During his solicitous calls I had felt my part one of the welcoming invalid, but I had not forgotten that Walter had said the previous accident had been no one's fault but mine.

I tackled Percy directly. Did he intend to have the proper guard installed? Did he realize that he was legally liable? What would he do were someone to be killed? Mine was not the only power-drive on the farm.

Percy said flippantly that he was not aware that any guard was necessary. His attitude was one of, "You talk and get yourself involved. I'll keep quiet and give no evidence." That suited me. I explained my position clearly and pointed out that I intended to see that his duty was carried out. His look changed from one of tolerant amusement to one of thunderous rage, but he kept silent. I hopped off and he drove away.

Shortly afterwards I learned that another Land Girl was injured by a fall and we met in the hospital X-ray Department. We aired our views on the sad status of the Land Army.

The Women's Land Army, not recognized as a regular government service does not receive full medical services, such as free X-rays. We considered our work to be as faithfully carried out as that of the WRNS (Women's Royal Naval Service), ATS (Auxiliary Territorial Service), and the WAAF's (Women's Auxiliary Air Force) and were burning with the injustice of unequal treatment.

We decided to write to the Land Army and agreed that individual letters would be of more value than a joint one.

Val, and many of the other Land Girls, had only their Land Army pay which, when they paid for their board, laundry, and cigarettes, left them little over. I had Charlie's army check in addition, and could afford my small medical bills. Nevertheless I felt that the principle was wrong, and that the great majority of girls who suffered expenses caused by accidents at work could ill afford it and should not have to bear it.

I wrote that night and explained that as two members, each with a fair term of service, June and I were proud to be a part of the Land Army, that we did understand that Land Girls, a scattered group, could not expect many of the social events shared by the other services, that we did not complain about cycling miles for hot baths or because we lived isolated existences with complete immersion in our work as our only joy. But I did feel that we were unjustly treated in that we did not receive medical treatment as did the other services, and I hoped that some crusade could be organized so that the Land Army could benefit from a similar security. I concluded by confessing my entire enjoyment in, and dedication to my work, and I repeated my desire to see some publicity on and interest shown in the subject of which I wrote.

I received a letter in reply stating that I was not in the Land Army and that as far as records showed I had not been a member since February, and that if I wished to rejoin my application would be considered, otherwise would I please return my uniform.

Val was with me when I read the letter. I was crushed, but she exploded.

"Not in the Land Army! So you didn't break your ankle either I suppose. Consider your application, will they? What cheek! Come on, show that to Perc."

We found him working in his laboratory. I explained about the preceding correspondence and produced the letter.

He looked steadily at our tight lips, and then threw back his head and roared with laughter – funniest thing he had ever seen, had never known I had a temper. "Go on, to see you so furious is most interesting."

We left. I had not forgiven him his unfair hearing of my power-drive complaint but I had felt that, as I was his employee, loyalty on both sides demanded getting to the bottom of the Land Army ultimatum.

I spoke to the local Land Army secretary and she said "I see nothing to take umbrage about. What are you going to do?"

Charlie came over for the weekend. He and Val and I talked day and night. We ascertained facts. A new Land Army ruling stated that anyone on sick leave for more than two weeks was automatically struck off strength, and that, upon presentation of a medical certificate of fitness, must rejoin.

I said that I'd be damned if I'd rejoin. I had not been informed of this stupid rule. Checks for the rental of my Land Army cycle had been accepted and receipted throughout the period I was away. I had been hurt at work. My employer knew, and was willing, that I should return to my job as soon as I was fit. And I had done so.

But the fact that Percy had not offered to follow up the muddle and did not attempt to inquire whether I intended to carry on nor offer to investigate, was a bitter pill to swallow.

Finally I decided to write to Mrs Mullins, to tell her the whole story and ask if I might rejoin the Land Army in Sussex.

June 6, 1944. Swanley
Today has been the most unhappy day I have ever known. All day the roar of planes sounded overhead. All day there has been glorious news on the radio. D-Day has come. Our armies have landed on the coasts of France, their landings have been successful and the immensity of the undertaking is too mighty to comprehend.

All day I have been listening to reports on the radio, feeling a heavy shame and unable to see any road that will not bring more shame. I had hoped to be a Land Girl for the duration and to feel satisfaction in the job I had done. But the Land Army opened the door for me, and Percy stood back and watched me walk through. Had anyone held out a hand to me, had anyone said, "Wait," I would have grasped the hand eagerly. Have my years of service meant nothing?

June 18, 1944. Sutton, Surrey
We had a most peculiar air-raid during my last night at Swanley. The guns wakened me in the early hours of the morning and I wakened sufficiently to get out of bed and take the jug out of my wash basin

and put it on the floor. I have learned to do that automatically as the house shakes with the barrage. Then I went back to sleep again. Later the gunfire wakened me again. I heard a plane diving straight for the house and thought, in local terminology "Blimy, this is it."

Just then the engine cut out completely, there was a deafening explosion, and then silence.

"That's damn queer," I thought, listened for a moment to the excited voices of the neighbours out on the lane, and went back to sleep.

Next morning the girl at the station informed me that Maidstone had been shelled during the night. That sounded impossible. Maidstone must be thirty miles inland and to date Dover and Folkestone have borne most of the shelling.

When I told Mr Young of this report, he said, "Rubbish."

On the following day I went back to the hospital, hoping to have the cast removed from my leg. It had been on over six weeks. My spirits rose high as the doctor said, "Take it off? Yes, I think we can." But were dashed to the ground as he continued, "But we'll put another one on."

That night we had several alerts and again the most anomalous air activity. Siren, silence, sudden diving drone of engine, silence, bang, no more. Where did the planes go? I remained at my top-story window and watched the dazzling display of fireworks over unfortunate London. Mr Young joined me and we marveled as we watched. All the conventions of a self-respecting raid were defied.

The papers, next morning, gave us a little information, and we learned that rocket planes, not bombs, had caused the explosions we had heard. Charlie arrived for the night and was able to clarify things a little. He had seen dozens of rockets and comforted us by explaining that the danger period was after the motor had stopped.

No one seemed to sleep that night but Charlie and me. Mrs Young was frightened into prowling most of the night and rushed into our room immediately after one colossal explosion which had blown Charlie and me right out of bed. Charlie is like the Rock of Gibraltar. We talked for a while and when he said, "It's gone now, we should get some sleep again." Mrs Young went to bed and I grew sleepy immediately.

We found in the morning that the French doors in the morning room had burst outward and that the garage doors were blown off. I spent nearly an hour sweeping up fallen plaster.

A friend of Mrs Young's in disheveled wvs (Women's Voluntary Service) uniform brought us the news that the loud bump we had heard was a flying bomb which had come down just around the corner, killing a woman and two children. She had been on duty since just after the rocket landed and had fallen through a damaged floor when carrying a kettle of hot water to help others injured in nearby houses.

Mrs Young made me take old Cookie, who is stone deaf and will not take shelter when we warn her, to see the extent of the damage. Four houses have been completely demolished, and in all directions those nearby were badly damaged. Up and down the road, on both sides, each house has a neat little pile of broken glass in the gutter.

All day the sirens sounded at half hour intervals. In the afternoon the clouds parted and as the sun came out brilliantly we rushed out, just in time to see our bombers going over, one formation after another, about 60 in each. There were several hundred of them, sparkling little silver specks in the sky, headed straight for France. We cheered and wished them luck. Old Cookie stood on tip-toe, thrilled with their glory as we were, and stretched her arm out, fingers parted in the "V" sign.

Then the siren went. We heard the roar of a rocket, and then we saw it – our first flying bomb. It was a slim, stream-lined, half-size edition of a fighter plane, belching out a trail of rosy, mauve fire. A Mosquito appeared on its tail, the big guns opened up and we bolted for cover from the shrapnel and heard the rocket explode a few minutes later.

When we came out we felt strangely exhilarated. We were up to date. We had seen a flying bomb. And this led to another new experience, moving beds into a subterranean shelter. Most of the spare bedding is on the top floor. Every time we were at the top a rocket came over. Mrs Young and Cookie flew down to the shelter and I hobbled after them.

How splendid these people are! They discuss the situation quietly and decide upon the wisest move. Then they do the job and forget about it.

June 28, 1944. Eastbourne
The cast is off my leg at last. What a joy it is to have a bath without one leg sticking out. I am to have a final X-ray in two weeks and then back to work. Mrs Mullins wrote when I was in Sutton, very kindly.

Sussex has welcomed me home and there is a job waiting for me in Hastings, as soon as I have medical permission to go.

Charlie was here for the weekend and he thinks that it may be his last. He promised that when he is to go he will send me a postcard. The message will mean nothing, but when I see a postcard I shall know that he is leaving England.

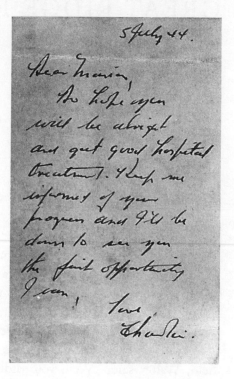

Eastbourne is a deserted town. Each successive trial, first the invasion scare in 1940, then the hit-and-run raids, and now these diabolical Doodlebugs, has seen its evacuation, until now only the most essential workers remain. All of these have suffered strain and fatigue, all are weary, but all display the bright courage which has belittled so fiendish a weapon as these flying bombs.

July 6, 1944. Eastbourne

Today Churchill published some facts about Doodlebugs:

2754 have been sent over.

2752 people have been killed.

And this afternoon my postcard came from Charlie so that I know he is no longer in England.

GREAT RIDGE FARM

July 12, 1944. Eastbourne

Walter drove me to Hastings this morning where he showed me the farm on which I am to work. It is a WAEC farm, and in Walter's district so that, indirectly, I shall be working under him. He assures me that I shall like the farm manager, Alec Crisford, an experienced, capable-looking man, with a twinkle in his eye.

As we closed the five-barred gate and walked across the sugar-beet field, Walter said, "Well, you said that you wanted a farm with a view." He spread out his arms as if to include the whole panorama. "This is the best we could do."

I held my breath as I looked at Great Ridge Farm. Walter said that I would like it. He had said that I would be happy here, but he had not told me that it was so beautiful, that there was such a sound integrity to it, that it embodied all that Sussex has come to mean to me.

Wheat fields sloped beyond the sugar-beet to deep valleys filled with dark strips of woodland. On the left, a large almond-shaped wood covered ninety acres of rising ground, while to the right, clear and shining in the morning sunlight, far below the heights of Great Ridge Farm, the channel curved inland, and Winchelsea and Rye were plainly visible in the distance.

I came back to Eastbourne for my final check-up at the hospital. The doctor said that I should wait another two weeks, but agreed that, as I shall be tractor driving and not using the foot, I may begin on Monday.

My first order from Mr Crisford was a gentle suggestion that I start up the tractor and get an old trailer out of the shed. That presented no problem. Mr Crisford leaned against a gate, talking to Harold while I checked oil, fuel and water. Then I started up the tractor and backing into the yard hitched on the trailer which was in a shed at right angles to the gate. I swung out in a large circle to allow the trailer to follow straight behind the tractor, and came through the gate with an even inch and a half on each side. Mr Crisford spoke to me as man to man.

"You'll do," he said, "Follow me." We went down to where a hay baler was set up beside a haystack. I met the other Land Girls and learned how a hay baler works.

My first letter from Charlie since he sailed for France was on the kitchen table when I came in tonight. "Nothing has been at all uncomfortable since coming over," he wrote. "One might imagine that we were all on a big training scheme, using live ammo. As for duck boards and silt trenches, I have yet to use them. Don't think that I have no intention of doing so, for when the time comes I will not be backward ... Had a good bath today, Canadian Mobile Bath and Laundries, had my laundry washed and dried this afternoon ... We had an interesting but uneventful crossing. Everything had to be lashed down as you can imagine, but we each had bunks to sleep in. As we approached the beach, we could see the mighty spectacle of our sea-power and there is much that we could not see. Due to being the last vehicle to go aboard we were the first off and I found myself leading the convoy out on to the beach and on inland. One simply drove, and accepted the pointers and directing of the MP's. Quite simple and effective."

Everything in the garden is lovely tonight. I am back at work again, Charlie is safe so far and I am happy and weary and content.

Still the corn is not ripe to cut. We hoed sugar-beet all day and I was pleased to find that I haven't lost my prowess. I have not hoed since I left Green Farm in 1941.

Walter came along about eleven, and suggested that I go to Nunningham for the weekend. I had to confess that my financial situation would not stand the trip. Walter pulled out a roll of bills and peeled off two pounds. He turned to the men, and said, "I know her well. She'll pay me back directly. She's a very wise girl, has money in the bank, but doesn't like to draw it out. I like to help her not to."

Kath is taking Peter to a safer area, and Walter and Fatty Cornford intend to keep house together. I wish I could see them. Walter does not know how to boil a kettle.

August 8, 1944. Great Ridge Farm
Returning to Sussex has been like coming home. I enjoy listening to Alec Crisford and Harold. I like the way one can leave one's coat on the fence post and find it still there at lunch time. I like the way the workers pull together and help each other and I like the long line of hills and the waves of ripe corn.

I live in a warm, red brick cottage, modern in that it has electric light, a bathroom, and picture windows, overlooking a terraced garden. At the bottom of the garden where the roses bloom and blue delphinium is a low stone wall. Beyond it the wheat rustles crisply.

I have a long rectangular room, with sloping roof and gable windows which Mrs Morris has made my own by removing all her possessions, save several little bowls on the handsome desk, the window-sills, and my dressing table, which she keeps filled with flowers.

Still each day I pull and twist wires as we bale hay and still the Doodlebugs come over and we crane our necks and watch. Today three came in quick succession. The first two came undeviated, but after the third came three Typhoons. Alec shut off the engine of the baling machine and we stood on the bales to watch the chase. When they had gone beyond sight we heard the explosion and a little later saw only two planes return. I wonder how many times I have watched a plane dive out of formation or watched the explosion of a bomb or a Doodlebug and turned back, chastened and helpless, to my work. I thought today of a young airforce officer who stood in front of me in a bus queue one night last winter. Our planes were thundering over, the mighty thousand bomber raids, and my spine was tingling with pride of them. I looked up and felt every fibre of me wishing them luck, when I heard a girl behind me say shrilly, "Hark at their row. Same thing every night. I can't get any sleep. Damn them anyway."

I stiffened, too stunned to speak, and I saw the young airman step out of the queue. His endocrines functioned more quickly than mine.

"The men flying those planes are my friends," he said in a low voice. "They are going over for you. Some of them will not come back. Try to remember that when you lie awake."

Alec delights in proving the efficiency of his balers. He puts enormous pitches of hay into the baler. The faster he feeds it, the faster the rammer packs the hay and Nancy and I must move nimbly with our wires. If we do not fasten them before the bale reaches the required weight, the entire oblong of straw is shot out loose and must be fed through again. At times Alec has sped up his pitching to the best of his ability, but neither Nancy nor I fumble. Laughing, as he grows out of breath, he will stop to wipe the sweat out of his eyes and be forced to admit that we are on top of our job. We all stop then, move back from the hay to have a cigarette and then return to work at a steady pace.

As we walked home tonight, well aware of the excitement his words would cause, Alec said casually, "If you'd like to put in a bit of overtime tonight, come back to the yard and we'll take the binder down to the forty acres."

"The forty acres, that's the big field on the hill. Can we, I mean is it – oh Alec – can we really begin harvesting tomorrow?"

"Reckon so, in about half and hour then?"

"Oh yes." I wonder if he knew how my heart sang as I darted off, scrambling down the uneven trail through the woods, over the stile and on around the wheat field to the rose-covered doorway of the cottage.

Mrs Morris was as excited as I. Soon she knew, the binder would be whirring below the cottage and all the ploughing and seeding, the progress of which she had watched in all directions about her home, would be brought to completion.

Each morning I join Hal and Alec Crisford as we meet at the gap in the hedge. Single file we walked around the wheat field, stopping only occasionally when we heard the barrage from the guns along the coast and our eyes followed the progress of a Doodlebug up the long valley.

Alec and Hal uncover the binder while I wield my grease-gun. One by one we discard coats and jackets and, as the sun dries the heavily dewed straw, we are away. Alec rides the binder with me and never have I had such a mate. Last year at Swanley I cut one or two fields of corn. The old man with me was continually falling asleep. I was terrified all day lest he fall off the binder and, in addition, I had to stop at each rise or fall in the ground and waken him to change the tilt of the floor of the cutting table or to raise or lower the height of the sweep as the crop varied. But Alec and I work as parts of our machines. When he raps for me because the string is low I know immediately and pop in a new ball of binder twine. If I point to an obstacle in the way of the knife Alec jumps down and removes it, sometimes motioning me not to stop. And there are many such obstacles. A Doodlebug came down in the woods. Its long, battered fuselage, ravaged by souvenir hunters, lies upended in a deep gully, but hundreds of twisted fragments of metal are scatted throughout the cornfields.

We stopped this afternoon when we saw a dull sliver gleam in the standing corn. We drew out a bundle, bigger than my head, of strips of silver paper, bunched together, like a tangled ball of wool. Alec and I have seen many such strips of metallic paper, usually of half inch width, which Jerry uses to confuse our radio location instruments. But these strips were much narrower, perhaps only a quarter of an inch in width, and neither of us had seen more than a yard or two of it before. We mused over it a moment or two, it was pretty stuff to be a weapon of war, and then we were away again, the binder shooting clean, full sheaves onto the stubble.

Alec would be patient and encouraging were I unsure of my work as I was in 1942. But no longer am I unsure. No longer are there stops caused by inattention, and the corn is standing tall, so that there are no bits laid by wind or rain. I am confident and capable now and the days are full of joy. I sing my head off on the tractor and Alec whistles on the binder from breakfast time till noon, and then on till tea time and dark.

The August sun sinks in the rosy, cloudless west and in the lovely hush when the tractor has stopped, we cover the binder and say goodnight. Alec walks up towards the yard, pleased with a good day's work and our progress. I turn back through the sheaves which the girls have stooked. The hills are dark now and I can just pick out the oast houses and the weathered roofs of the little village in the valley. Hundreds of acres of corn lie before me, soft and silvery now in the twilight, corn which I, no longer the weaker link, no longer the humble apprentice, help to harvest.

Charlie's last letter crinkles in my pocket and my heart is filled with gladness as I open the garden gate.

Mrs Morris and I walked down to the little pub in West Field a few nights ago and I brought home two quarts of beer to take out to the harvest field. We all had drinks, the bottle was capped and placed in the hedge, and we were unable to find it again. This happened to both bottles and caused much amusement.

This morning I met Alec and Hal again at the gap in the hedge. "Here she is," Alec grinned at Hal. "Here's the best tractor driver I've ever had, only she's always losing her beer." That beer never did turn up, but Alec's words will not be tossed away so lightly.

At lunch time, nine o'clock, I saw the bright flash of the red postal van on the road, and asked if I might go to see if there was a letter from Charlie. I returned to the corn field, sat down beside Nancy, and leaning against a corn shock, opened my letter.

"Hello dear," wrote Charlie, "I am sitting in a corn field, under blue Normandy skies."

Alec told me, when I asked him, that ten to twelve acres a day was considered a good day's work with a binder. All day as we worked, round and round, with no let or hindrance, stopping only to roll a cigarette occasionally, Alec's eyes twinkled whenever I looked at him. Tonight I swung around, clipping off the last little feathery stand in the field. I drove the tractor to the corner of the field and as we changed over the draw bar to get the binder through the gateway I said, "Well Alec, we did it."

"Did what?" Alec, flat on his back, fixing a block under the axle, was deliberately dense.

"Cut ten to twelve acres a day. We did a twenty-two acre field in two days."

"Yes we did, my girl, we've done a good day's work."

The wire was waiting for me when I came in tonight. Charlie was wounded last Saturday. All week I have been cutting corn in the glorious sunshine and all that time Charlie was wounded and I did not know. Shrapnel, left shoulder, the wire said, letter follows. How long must I wait for the letter? My little bowl of roses is gleaming before me as I write, luminous in the radiance of the fiery western sky, which, cloudless, presages another day of sunshine, just as if nothing had happened at all.

We worked all day yesterday and when we were covering the binder I showed Alec the wire I had received. He understood that I did not want to talk. A little later as we said goodnight I knew that he had told the others.

This morning the mail van passed near us and the postman brought me a letter. Charlie had written himself, in pencil, but firmly and normally. He said that he was, "Pushing along on the road back to England," and that he would see me soon.

When I came in at tea time Mrs Morris was coming up the crazy path with her shopping basket. She waved cheerily and said, "What would you like more than anything else?"

I looked at her stupidly. It was a Saturday, there could be no more mail. She could not produce Charlie safe and well.

"Come on," she said, putting her basket down on the table, "What would you like?"

I had no answer.

"There is no mail delivery on Saturday afternoon. But if there is any post they will give it to you at the General Post Office. I didn't tell you I was going in case there was nothing, but –"

She handed me a plain postcard on which was stamped, "Have arrived in the United Kingdom."

August 21, 1944. Basingstoke
Sunday and Monday we cut the home fields and on Tuesday noon we began the steep field below the cottage. I worked in sight of the cottage all morning and knew that if a wire or telephone call came Mrs Morris would come out to the harvest field for me.

I went into the house, cool after the summer sun, for dinner. I had just washed my hands and Mrs Morris had passed my plate to me, when there was a knock on the door.

The telegram said, "In Basingstoke Neurological Hospital." Neurological? What did it mean? Head wounds? Neuroses? Would I find Charlie as I had known him? Whoa, I must be sensible.

"What are you going to do? Do you want to wire him? Are you going up tonight?"

"No, I don't think I could get across tonight. I should have to spend the night in London."

I tried to eat my dinner, then, "It's no use. I must go right now."

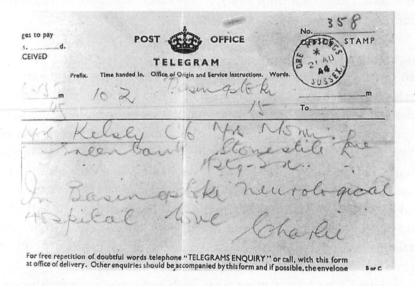

Mrs Morris packed my bag for me while I washed and changed. At Hastings Station I telephoned to Dado. She asked if my train came through Eastbourne and said that she would be there.

We arrived in Basingstoke just after nine o'clock. The taxi driver warned me that Charlie might be gone.

"They bring 'em in and shoot 'em off somewheres else. Have you got any place to stay?"

Of course we had not. He turned off the main road, up a small street, and left us sitting in the car while he disappeared in the blackout. A moment later he came back, a lady with him.

"Your man is in the hospital? You want somewhere to stay?"

"Yes but –"

"You go along to see him. Come back here. It's only one room, with a double bed, but you can stay as long as you like. I hope your man is all right."

Tears were smarting in my eyes as I thanked her. These English people, first Dado, dropping everything to come with me, then the taxi driver, gruff, friendly, and now this kindly soul, offering me, a complete stranger, a home for as long as I needed it.

At the D. & A. office the clerk told me that I might see Charlie. Dado waited while he led me to the ward.

Charlie was in the first bed, pale, thin, watching me as I came in the door. He did not smile or move. He raised his hand, as if to ward me off, and, very faintly, said, "Hello."

September 8, 1944. Basingstoke

In the days that followed I learned many things. Charlie is paralyzed from the waist down. Shrapnel entered his back, just below the shoulder and a fragment continuing down is lodged just near his third lumbar vertebra. I have learned that the skin of the paralyzed area is hyper-sensitive which is why he warned me not to touch him on the night I arrived. Each movement of the bed clothes, each footstep in the ward, brings tears of pain to his eyes. He can feel the vibration of an approaching plane long before it can be heard and groans with the distress it causes him. I have learned to sit quietly beside him, not talking at all, rubbing his legs often, comforting where I can and not showing the ache I feel.

I write letters for the other boys, fetch and carry for them all, peel peaches and nectarines which I can buy for them in the estate gardens.

I stayed for four days when I first came. Then the doctor spoke to me, told me how dangerously ill Charlie is, and said that I should make immediate arrangements for my passage home. As soon as Charlie was told that he is to be sent home very soon, I went back to Hastings.

August 23rd, and Charlie's birthday

Before I left I went into a little shop in Basingstoke to buy pajamas for Charlie. I could not decide between a pair of pleasing blue and one in a drab shade but much better quality.

The owner of the shop began wrapping the two pairs.

"You take them both up to the hospital and let your husband choose."

"Shall I pay you for the more expensive pair?"

"I don't think we need bother with that."

"But I am leaving Basingstoke, I won't be back for a few days."

"Well, you take the pajamas. I shall see you when you return."

From there I went to the Venture Inn. I bought a few things there and was given some little cakes, fresh out of the oven, "For you and for your husband." But I had only a note which they were unable to change so early in the morning. I was a complete stranger. Again there was no hesitation.

"Pay me another time."

"But I am going away."

"No matter, when you come back, any time."

In Sackville House, when I was explaining my desire to return to Canada to the soldier at the desk, someone called, "Hi, there," and came running to meet me. It was Bill Dawson, whom I had known back home. He introduced me to a Major who told me to let him know the minute Charlie left and he would see that I caught the first boat home.

At Great Ridge I packed all my things and took them to Nunningham. Walter promised to tell Mrs Mullins that we were going home and I returned to Basingstoke.

September 16, 1944. Eastbourne

Charlie has been gone for two weeks. I stayed at the hospital with him while he was prepared for the journey. At two o'clock in the morning he received a shot of morphine and a hundred thousand units of penicillin and labels informative of the dosage were pinned to his pajamas.

When his early breakfast was brought in about four o'clock I said good-bye to him. I could not have been certain of a dry-eyed good-bye had I waited to see that stretcher pushed into the dark vault of the ambulance.

Since then, I have been waiting with Alec and Dado until my own date of departure arrived.

I have seen all Charlie's relatives and I stayed a few days at Nunningham. Everywhere, at Mr and Mrs George's, at Great Ridge, at Nunningham, are friends we have known and loved. Everywhere the golden harvest is almost home but Charlie and I cannot see the job through. He did not want to leave England any more than I do.

Both Lady de la Warr and Mrs Mullins have written me letters which gave me a lump in my throat. Mrs Mullins said that when I go I take with me "a splendid record of work well done and the affection of many friends."

September. 28, 1944. v92, Liverpool*
All these days since Charlie left I could not know how he was. Two weeks he had been gone and two weeks more would pass before I would be able to know – two weeks at sea, not knowing how he had stood the trip, not knowing what I should see on the faces of those who would meet me.

And then, this morning, as Alec brought down my bags, the taxi arrived. We were opening the door to go when the telephone rang. It was a cable from home. "Charlie arrived safe and well."

At Eastbourne station we watched as my train came into sight at the end of the track.

"X marks the spot," said Alec seriously, drawing a mark on the station platform with his umbrella. "You shall return."

Return, I thought, return to this kindly England, this valiant

Land that freemen till
That sober suited freedom chose,
The land, where girt with friends or foes
A man may speak the thing he will.

"Yes, Alec," I answered, promising, "Charlie will live and we shall return."

---

* *v92* was the old *Mauretania*.

Alec, me, Dado, and Charlie in Eastbourne, 1949

My log of where I slept in England

EPILOGUE

Marion

I met Charlie while I was still in high school. I had been invited by my life-long friend Phoebe (our mothers had gone to convent together in the 1880s) to meet the friend of her young man. Those were more formal days, long velvet dresses and pearls, tea by the fire, music. Charlie sang "Ombra mai fu" to the tune of Handel's *Largo*, I had a canoe, he'd built a boat. Though we'd never met he knew all my friends, friends from my Longueuil childhood, Bark Lake in the Laurentians, family friends. We walked many miles that winter and later through Westmount and Murray parks and the lovely upper-level streets of Westmount. Those were depression days. We were engaged for five years, during which I graduated from McGill, worked a year in an insurance firm, and spent a year in a Grenfell Hospital in Labrador. When Charlie's advancement and salary increase were confirmed in his insurance office, we married in 1937. Two years followed of happy ups and financial downs with Doc, our lovely English springer spaniel, which we, thanks to youthful energy and a lot of fun, managed to weather.

The came the war years, followed by a return to Canada, paraplegia, and two years in the DVA (Department of Veterans Affairs) Hospital at Ste-Anne de Bellevue. During those war years, I'd gone from 30 s. weekly (subsistence pay) to 45 s. as a First Class Tractor

Driver (which was wealth), and Charlie had spent more and more of his leaves on my farms. Both for him, born in England, and for me who grew more and more to love, "this blessed plot, this earth, this realm, this England" – the idea became established that we would settle in England to study and obtain degrees, possibly in Animal Husbandry, and ultimately to purchase land of our own.

But Hitler presented us with the unknown and a hospital life which absorbed all our energies. Eventually, Charlie learned to use a wheelchair and to walk on crutches. Our beloved Dr Gingras said that Charlie was his worst patient and his best rehabilitated paraplegic. For several years, till medically, physically, and financially our lives were anchored here, our minds were not free for major change.

We adapted to the demands and restrictions of Charlie's disability. Our major objective became to use Charlie's talents and what physical abilities remained. And so, here he carried on.

In 1953 the Rehabilitation Society under whose aegis Charlie had organized a training workshop for civilian disabled closed down completely to reorganize and expand. Charlie was offered a job at an undreamed of salary but totally beyond his physical capabilities. The time had come for us to say goodbye to the big city. George Whalley, whom Charlie and I had met on May 5, 1945, VE Day, when two very ill vets shared an ambulance home, came with us. The word had been, "The war is over and anyone with a home to go to may go home for the weekend." Charlie and George worked in their training workshop and he and his wife, an English war-bride, became our fast friends.

And so Goose Haven, with seven acres by the sea, electricity, plumbing, a fireplace, and two cottages became our home in Nova Scotia. We rented the two cottages, whose tenants gave us many interesting and good friends for over a quarter of a century. Charlie worked for the Paraplegic Association, made a survey of all the disabled people in the Maritimes and established the K. & W. (Kelsey-Whalley) Bookbinding Business, which at its height employed over fifty disabled people. Those were the days when Charlie's dream of a local Liverpool airport worked out, a large investment in oyster cultivation was ahead of its time and did not, and he became involved in the County Council and the Historical Society, and we managed three fairy-tale freighter trips, the first to the Far East, then the Mediterranean, and to Scotland and Norway.

About then, paraplegia took over and forced him to give up his crutches and to withdraw from every interest beyond the house. He persuaded me to leave Goose Haven and to build a log house closer to town and closer to the sea. I am still in the process of being converted, but my roots are taking hold. Good thing too, as our trips for the past five years have solely been ambulance trips to Halifax hospitals.

Charlie's patience and good nature are endless, as are our views from every window. As an old girl in her 85th year, still fit to garden a bit, to maintain the home, to chop away the odd tree blown down across the drive in a gale – I quote, again, as I often do:

And with all the needy, oh divide I pray
This vast measure of content that is mine today.

Charles
There is a beginning and there is an end. Somehow when you have read all the foregoing you will have to face my part in this work. I was there and closely attached. I guess it goes back to 1939 when I went overseas with the Canadian Army. I was married and went to England leaving a wife behind.

We, in my regimental unit, the Royal Montreal Regiment (RMR) in company with an almost full Division, became known as the Red Patches on account of the red shoulder patches we wore that distinguished us from other Divisions, and because we were the first Division to go overseas. We were justly proud of that red patch. My wife, through the kindness of a cousin, was able to join me in England early in 1940. Marion invaded England the same day that Hitler invaded the Lowlands.

I had considerable difficulty getting a permit to meet Marion's train in London because all troops able to bear arms were put on immediate notice – all leaves were canceled to repel a possible invasion. In fact, certain Canadian troops embarked and sailed for the west coast of France to give assistance. It was not needed since France collapsed and the Canadians came back to England. As soldiers, we were all on edge, prepared to fight. After all that's what we were there for, "to face the enemy in fact."

It wasn't until 1942 in Sicily, Italy, and again in 1944 in Normandy, France, that Canadian units became actively engaged in fighting the

Germans and Italians. During the intervening years began the days I remember in England. Marion, who had joined the Women's Land Army and lived on farms, nearly all in Sussex County, was provided with a home to which I was always welcome. In the years from 1940–44 I was never more than 30 to 40 miles from her and I had bought a bicycle so transport was assured. These were interesting years and, until active war was joined in 1944, we had many leaves together and were able to see and visit many parts in the British Isles. I don't believe many other soldiers in the Canadian Army had such a pleasant time as I had.

Weekends were spent on a farm with Marion and at least twice a year we spent a week together visiting some part of the British Isles. Everywhere we went people were most hospitable and the British rationing system for food and clothing was the best system ever devised. And, according to reports, the health of the people was excellent.

There was an occasion when we were surprised at the attitude of a hotel keeper, who refused us a bed because soldiers just did not have Land Army girls to entertain them overnight. I overcame that problem by going alone and registering as a couple seeking accommodation.

And in Northern Ireland we were pleasantly surprised when our hostess at a hotel announced she could serve us with white bread, something that in England was unheard of during the war. The bread there was grey in colour and to me very pleasant tasting because it was made with grains of oats, middlings, and wheat – most nutritious. Eggs, milk, cheese, and meat were carefully rationed, but pregnant and nursing mothers were given extra allowances – school children also had an extra allowance of milk.

Marion and I shared these experiences together, whereas the wives back home in Canada were dependent on letters to know what their husbands were doing during these years. Not too many people realize that Canadians just sat and waited for four years – they were long years for soldiers to be away from their wives and families, and it was no wonder that many marriages were broken up by this long wait.

Marion received many exclamations, when in company with Canadian soldiers: they said, "Why, you're Canadian!" when they heard her voice. A Canadian married couple was the exception in England. While some could afford to bring their wives over, regulations on travel canceled any wives coming to England after May of 1940.

We saw the work of feeding the nation going on apace, every morsel of food grown locally meant there was more shipping space available for essential war supplies that were streaming across the Atlantic to England, North Africa, and later to Italy.

A regiment is a place where friendships are born. War is a catalyst that brought together Bob (an Australian), Benjie (born in Dover but having joined up in the British West Indies), Reg (a Ph.D. in physiology), Alfie, and myself. For four years we bounced around together until Reg secured a commission and disappeared to Italy. When we returned to Montreal, Alfie disappeared and we lost track of him. Benjie brought a wife and child to Canada, but he disappeared into West Africa and, when last heard of, was in a canoe with wife and child, off to manage some plantation. Bob stayed around Montreal and, when he secured his divorce, married my sister-in-law and they lived out their lives in an urban setting. It all seemed so ordinary after World War II. Benjie's wife was a very clever girl. She spoke German and French fluently and, when she joined the WAAF's, she was employed as a special radio operator misdirecting German Bomber pilots from their radio beamed targets.

I suppose that's what it is all about. We cannot all keep up a pace that brings exciting events into our lives. Had I not been severely wounded and forced to make large adjustments, I would not have done many of the things that have made my life. Marion helped me tremendously and gave me the encouragement needed. Our travels overseas to Europe and the Orient opened up windows for us and gave us a good breath of cool breezes that urged us along. Our move to Nova Scotia in 1953 was good. New friends, new places, and new ideas all came along and now, after 83 years, life still appears excellent. So this is now the end.

> Written several months before
> his death on October 15, 1993